This is a collection of essays of paramount importance written by one of the most noteworthy authorities on Marx and Hegel within the field of Western Marxism. Following Dunayevskaya's analysis of the revolutionary dialectic of Hegel's Phenomenology, Anderson has carefully crafted a concept of dialectics that moves beyond the abstract dialectics of earlier champions of dialectical reasoning such as Marcuse by taking up concrete issues such as race, class, gender and colonialism and by recognizing that Marx's dialectic, while abstractly universal in engaging capitalism in its totality, leaves sufficient room for addressing these and other concrete particularities that brush against the homogeneity so central to capitalism's need for value augmentation. Anderson is uniformly brilliant in his analysis of Marx as a multidimensional thinker who developed a multilinear pathway for revolution for societies outside of Western Europe, putting to rest the charges of determinism and Eurocentrism and patriarchal thinking that had tempted many in the left away from critical engagements with abstract universals (such as the universal struggle for liberation) during the years when postmodern theory and antifoundationalism, filled with soft tissue and pantomine theories of resistance, was in vogue. *Dialectics of Revolution* reveals a consistency of Marxist Humanist analysis that has only grown more profound in the retelling by this trailblazing scholar, especially in light of Dunayevskaya's prescient conceptualization of Blacks in the U.S. as an independent force of revolution alongside the working class. *Dialectics of Revolution* makes it clear why Anderson is among the leading lights writing on Marxism and revolution today. His work helps to account for the avidity shown among a new generation of the left for dialectical critique. As fascism has begun to rear it's ugly head once again in the theater of world politics, led this time by the United States, *Dialectics of Revolution* could not come at a more precipitous time.

—**Peter McLaren**, Distinguished Professor in Critical Studies, Chapman University.

Kevin Anderson's *Dialectics of Revolution: From Hegel, Marx and Beyond* collects four decades of Anderson's studies of Hegel, Marx, dialectics, and revolution. In this era of multiple economic, political, ecological, and health crises, radical critique and theories of revolutionary transformation are absolutely necessary, and Anderson provides much provocative material in developing critical theory and revolutionary practice for the contemporary era.

—**Douglas Kellner**, George F. Kneller Chair in the Philosophy of Education, UCLA

In this extraordinary exposition of the Hegelian dialectic, Kevin Anderson highlights the prominent debt owed to Hegel for Marx's philosophy of revolution. Through a brilliant critical analysis of some of the most important discussions on and critiques of dialectics put forth by some of the greatest minds – from Marx, Lenin, Lukács, Marcuse, and Dunayevskaya to Derrida, Foucault and other poststructuralists, Anderson demonstrates the evolution of the dialectic as a grounded philosophical concept that brings together the objective and subjective worlds and reveals contradiction as the source of all movement and, therefore, of history. This deeply intellectual, and yet highly accessible, work breathes new life into dialectical Marxism, reconciling the debates over identity politics and class struggle and positing a dialectical Marxist-humanism, in the tradition of Dunayevskaya, that recognizes that the revolutionary struggle for freedom is the struggle against class, racism, sexism, and all forms of oppression. Anderson challenges us to arm ourselves with dialectical reasoning so that we may avert the "terror" that lies within the positive and instead move toward absolute negativity and the realization of a more human world. This book is not only timely and relevant but urgently necessary.

— **Lilia Monzo**, Associate Professor, Attallah College of Educational Studies, Chapman University

Dialectics of Revolution

DIALECTICS OF REVOLUTION

Hegel, Marxism, and Its Critics Through a Lens of Race, Class, Gender, and Colonialism

Kevin B Anderson

DARAJA PRESS
OTTAWA

Published by Daraja Press
https://darajapress.com

Cover artwork: White Lines by Irene Rice Pereira, 1941
Public domain, Metropolitan Museum of Art, New York
Cover design: Kate McDonnell

Library and Archives Canada Cataloguing in Publication

Title: Dialectics of revolution : Hegel, Marxism, and its critics
through a lens of race, class,
gender, and colonialism / by Kevin B Anderson.

Names: Anderson, Kevin, 1948- author.

Description: Includes bibliographical references and index.

Identifiers: Canadiana (print) 20200294962 I Canadiana (ebook)
20200295101 I ISBN 9781988832753
(softcover) I ISBN 9781988832760 (EPUB)

Subjects: LCSH: Dialectic.

Classification: LCC B809.7 .A53 2020 I DDC 101—dc23

Contents

Acknowledgements

Since these essays were written over more than four decades, they are the product of innumerable dialogues with and influences from a large number of scholars, activists, and other intellectuals, some of them recent and others some time ago.

I owe the greatest debt to my intellectual mentor, the late Marxist and feminist philosopher Raya Dunayevskaya, who died in 1987. Over the entirety of these four decades I have also received important comments and encouragement from my partner Janet Afary, a feminist historian of Iran, and from my longtime comrade, the Marxist philosopher Peter Hudis, as well as the critical theorist Douglas Kellner and the political philosopher Bertell Ollman.

For dialogues during the 1970s and early 1980s — and sometimes beyond — I would also like to thank my two principal academic mentors at CUNY Graduate Center, Georg Uri Fischer, who chaired my dissertation on Lenin and Hegel, and Michael E. Brown, who chaired my thesis on Lukács and the young Hegel, as well as Kenley Dove for his Hegel seminar at the New School. During that period, I also engaged in dialogue with Charles Denby, Teru Kanazawa, Dennis Nurkse, Andrew Arato, Marnia Lazreg, Stanley Aronowitz, Oskar Negt, Iring Fetscher, Lawrence Krader, Danga Vileisis, Charles Herr, Angela Terrano, John Rogers, the late Narihiko Ito, Robert Stone, Nancy Fraser, William di Fazio, Lorraine Cohen, Nancy Naples, the late Jacques d'Hondt, the late Pierre Lantz, Ariane Lantz, and Sam Friedman.

I would also like to acknowledge dialogues in the later part of the 1980s and the 1990s — and sometimes beyond — with David Norman Smith,

Ted McGlone, the late Olga Domanski, the late Michael Flug, Frieda Afary, Kamran Afary, Lou Turner, Ron Kelch, Ursula Frydman, Nigel Gibson, Eugene Gogol, David Ranney, Terry Moon, Franklin Bell, the late Allen Willis, Paul Buhle, Stephen Steiger, Alan Wald, , Chris Arthur, David Joravsky, Albert Resis, the late Heinz Osterle, the late Eric Plaut, HeMartin Jay, Tom Rockmore, Patricia Altenbernd Johnson, Stephan Eric Bronner, Richard Quinney, John Rhoads, Jim Thomas, Robert Antonio, Alan Sica, David Schweickart, Thomas Sheehan, Paul Thomas, Moishe Postone, Barbara Brick, the late Joseph Buttigieg, J.P. Pittman, David Laibman, Danny Goldstick, Budd Burkhard, Rainer Funk, Hal Orbach, Samuel Kinser, Hélène Bellour, the late Donald N. Levine, and Louis Dupré.

With respect to dialogues during the last two decades, and sometimes also before that, I would like to mention Michael Löwy, Gilbert Achcar, David Black, Jim Obst, Heather Brown, Karel Ludenhoff, Richard Abernethy, Sandra Rein, Russell Rockwell, the late Eli Messinger, Andrew Kliman, Anne Jaclard, Ben Watson, Esther Leslie, John Riddell, Charles Post, Peter Marcuse, Zhang Yibing, He Ping, Wei Xiaoping, Zhang Chuanping, Xiong Min, Wu Xinwei, Meng Mugui, Bailing Li, Seongjin Jeong, Tomonaga Tairako, Kohei Saito, Isabel Garo, Pierre Beaudet, Patrick Silberstein, Didier Epsztajn, Eamonn Slater, Chandana Mathur, Dermot Dix, August Nimtz, Satnan Virdee, Andrew Nash, Joel Kovel, David McNally, the late Colin Barker, Vivek Chibber, Lucia Pradella, Hillel Ticktin, Sasha Lilley, David Alderson, Robert Spencer, Paul Reynolds, Wang Jie, Hassan Mortazavi, Lauren Langman, Andries Schutte, Paul Le Blanc, Peter Marcuse, Lynn Chancer, Joan Braune, Bill Weinberg, Jim Kaplan, Roslyn Bologh, Judy Wittner, Sebastian Budgen, Slavoj Zizek, Fredric Jameson, Nikki Keddie, Peter McLaren, Stathis Kouvelakis, Shannon Brincat, John Abromeit, Rainer Winter, Neil McLaughlin, Andrew Feenberg, Harry Dahms, Paresh Chattopadhyay, Murzban Jal, Sevgi Dogan, Guilherme Leite, Rhaysa Ruas, Marcelo Badaró, Christoph Jünke, Lars Lih, Suzi Weissman, the late Joanne Landy, Jason Schulman, Sam Farber, Barbara Epstein, Charles Reitz, Tracy Strong, Lawrence Scaff, Chris Ford, William McBride, Robert Melson, Mark Lilla, Michael Weinstein, the late Berenice Carroll, Eileen Boris, Nelson Lichtenstein, Howard Winant, Reginald Daniel, John Foran, Brian Lovato, Mark Jay, Sam Salour, Ry Clegg, Shawn Van Valkenburgh, Andrew Zimmerman, Eric Foner, John Garvey, Loren Goldner, the late Daniel Bensaid, Ottokar Luban, Terrell Carver, Marcello

Musto, Mead McCloughan, Rolf Hecker, Jürgen Rojahn, Jürgen Herres, Carl-Erich Vollgraf, Thomas Kuczynski, William Outhwaite, Sean Sayers, the late Norair Ter-Akopian, Karina Ter-Akopian, Kieran Durkin, Jonas Grahn, Thonette Myking, Lilia Monzó, Ali Kiani, Christian Shaughnessy, Rocio Hernandez, Kris Gardener, Ndindi Kitonga, Andres Mares Muro, and Kevork Sassouni.

Finally, a special thanks to Ryan Fisher for proofreading and technical editing, to Damian Delfin for proofreading and for the index, and to a very energetic and supportive editor, Firoze Manji.

◊

Daraja Press wishes to express thanks to the publishers of previously published papers that are included in this volume:

Chapter 2. Originally appeared as Kevin B. Anderson and Peter Hudis, "Dialectic" in *The Blackwell Encyclopedia of Sociology* (2020). Reproduced here with permission.

Chapter 4. Originally appeared as Kevin B. Anderson, "Lenin's Encounter with Hegel After Eighty Years: A Critical Assessment" in *Science & Society* 59:3 (1995), pp. 298-319. © 1995 Guilford Press. Reproduced here with permission from *The Guilford Press*.

Chapter 5. Originally appeared as Kevin B. Anderson, "Lenin, Bukharin and the Marxian Concepts of Dialectics and Imperialism: A Study in Contrasts," *Journal of Political and Military Sociology* 15:2 (1987), pp. 197-212. Reproduced here with permission.

Chapter 6. Originally published as Kevin B. Anderson, "On Hegel and the Rise of Social Theory: A Critical Appreciation of Herbert Marcuse's Reason and Revolution, Fifty Years Later," *Sociological Theory* 11:3 (1993), pp. 243-67. Reproduced here with permission.

Chapter 10. Originally appeared as Kevin B. Anderson, "Resistance versus Emancipation: Foucault, Marcuse, Marx, and the Present Moment," *Logos: A Journal of Modern Society & Culture* 12:1 (Winter 2013. Reproduced here with permission.

Chapter 11. Originally appeared in *Economic & Political Weekly* in 2018, "Marx at 200: Beyond Capital and Class Alone" by Kevin B. Anderson. It subsequently appeared as a pamphlet in the *Daraja Press & Monthly Review Essays* series *Thinking Freedom* entitled *Class, Gender, Race, and Colonialism: The "Intersectionality" of Marx*. Ottawa: Daraja Press, 2020]

PART I

Introduction

1

Introduction

This year, two anniversaries in the dialectical tradition have intersected, as 2020 is the 250th anniversary of the German philosopher G.W.F. Hegel's birth and the 150th anniversary of that of the Russian Marxist V.I. Lenin, the first revolutionary thinker after Marx to seriously study Hegel and to place his dialectic at the center of Marxism. This intersection of Hegel and Lenin calls attention to the fact that Karl Marx considered Hegel's "dialectic of negativity" to be inherently revolutionary, something that his immediate successors covered up, not only in their popularizations of work, but also in their own theoretical investigations. Despite the various flaws with which we might want to tax him, most importantly his building up of a single-party state after the 1917 revolution, Lenin was the first post-Marx Marxist to restore dialectics to its rightful place at the center of Marxism, writing in his *Philosophical Notebooks* that one could not fully understand Marx's *Capital* without a thorough study of Hegel's *Logic*. Afterwards, a number of Marxist thinkers followed in this pathway, from Georg Lukács to Herbert Marcuse and Raya Dunayevskaya, all of them discussed in the present volume.

The essays gathered in the present volume take up dialectics not only in an academic sense, but also as a philosophy of revolution that helps shape social activism and revolution. Here, dialectics is also presented as a key to the understanding of Marxism, and even more importantly, to its rethinking, something that each new generation of Marxists needs to do.

Doing so is even more important at points of transition and crisis. The spring 2020 Black Lives Matter Uprising in the U.S.—and its spread to a number of other countries—constitutes just such a transition point, and could, if it persists, be on a par with other epochal upheavals with global reach, like those of the revolutionary year 1968. The Black-led 2020 uprising has brought a new generation of youth of all races onto the streets, determined to eradicate the racist structures that have marked capitalist society from its inception, especially in countries like the U.S. and Brazil. In this sense, the dialectic has been at work during the stifling years of Donald Trump's rightwing populist and utterly racist presidency, as deepening leftwing opposition to the system has grown in tandem with a shift in the direction of outright fascism at the top. Outraged by the cruel murder of George Floyd by the racist police of the liberal city of Minneapolis, a new revolutionary generation has burst onto the scene with remarkable force, creativity, and courage.

This stunning turn of events has transpired during the global civilizational crisis resulting from COVID-19, both as a threat to health and to life and as the trigger for an epochal economic crisis. All of this illustrates the contradictory—and dangerous—character of progress under capitalist modernity. For just as the industrial revolution and the monopoly capitalism it spawned gave birth to World War I and then Nazism in the face of the Great Depression, so those of us living in 2020 face the possibility that the disruptions and disasters we have been facing under contemporary capitalism—ecological destruction, rightwing populism vs. democracy, global pandemic, the continuing threat of nuclear war, and the global economic crises of 2008 and 2020—have at a minimum undermined the very structure of the post-World War II global economic order, if not put the very existence of human life into question. Put another way, at no time like today has Rosa Luxemburg's century-old cry of "socialism or barbarism" rang truer. Over the past twelve years, these deep social contradictions have brought to the fore new movements for social justice and human liberation, from the environmental justice movement, to Black Lives Matter and Kurdish liberation, to the class and economically oriented Occupy Movement and the Sanders/Corbyn campaigns, to the Arab Spring of 2011, which caught a second wind in 2019, and the liberation movements in Latin America. What is clear is that the formally democratic but rapaciously exploitative neoliberal order cannot be restored, any more than can the welfare state of 1945-75. For the past twelve years, we have inhabited a kind of twilight where it is hard to discern whether night is falling or if dawn is at hand, although at this writing dawn seems the likelier possibility.

Part of why the overall direction of events is hard to discern is that the left too often lacks a vision of a humanist alternative to capitalism, or even a clear enough picture of the objective structures of domination we are facing and their dialectical opposite, the subjective or agentic forces of positive change and opposition. Grasp of the dialectic will, I argue in these essays, help us to discern such pathways. This was true of the young Marx, when he brought Hegel's dialectic down to earth in 1844, humanizing its core concept of negativity by conceptualizing the industrial proletariat as the dialectical and emancipatory force of negativity and liberation that had been brought to life by the very structures of capitalism themselves. It was true of Lenin, when during the years 1914-17 he rediscovered Hegelian dialectics and theorized those evil twins, monopoly capitalism/imperialism, as well as their dialectical opposite, the anticolonial national liberation movements, from Ireland to India. It was true during the era of fascism, when Herbert Marcuse and Georg Lukács elaborated and defended dialectical reason in the face of fascist irrationalism. It was true of Raya Dunayevskaya—and her erstwhile colleagues C.L.R. James and Grace Lee Boggs—in post-World War II America, who delved into Hegel, at first via Lenin, and also developed a theory of state-capitalism that conceptualized Blacks in the U.S. as an independent force of revolution alongside the working class. And it is true of us today, if we can meet the challenge of our time of transition, one of both dread and promise.

Because these essays were written over four decades, 1980-2020, there are some discontinuities. But I also believe that they form a whole, as I continue to hold to the overall Marxist-Humanist and dialectical perspectives I started to develop for myself in the 1970s. By that time, the hopes and dreams of my generation of revolutionaries—which had fought against racism and militarism during the 1960s, and begun to adhere to feminism as a key aspect of revolutionary theory and practice—had reached an impasse. While a large and diverse left still existed, it was growing smaller and was being put on the defensive, first with the fascist coup of 1973 in Chile, when U.S.-supported generals overthrew Allende's democratically elected socialist government, plunging the country into brutal repression and also introducing what was later called neoliberalism in economic policy.

These defeats for the left, which included Nixon's landslide re-election victory of 1972 and Mao's rapprochement with the U.S. at the very time its bombing of Vietnam reached new heights of savagery, prompted much rethinking within the more critical parts of the left. Partly as a result of this, an array of major Marxist dialectical texts were translated into English and discussed widely in the U.S. in the 1970s, among them Lukács's *History and Class Consciousness* (1971), Marx's *Grundrisse* (1973), Adorno's *Negative Dialectics* (1973), Lukács's *The Young Hegel* (1975), Karel Kosík's *Dialectics of the Concrete* (1976), as well as new translations of Marx's *Capital* (1976) and Hegel's *Phenomenology of Spirit* (1977), and new discussions of Frantz Fanon's *Wretched of the Earth* (1961), a point of reference since the 1960s, but now considered more in its dialectical aspect.

I was influenced by all of these writings, but even more so by a book written in the U.S. by the Russian-American Marxist-Humanist and feminist Raya Dunayevskaya that critically appropriated most of the above writings and went beyond many of them, *Philosophy and Revolution: From Hegel to Sartre and from Marx to Mao* (1973). I was lucky enough to begin to study its draft version in 1971, as Dunayevskaya was sharing it with her younger comrades and encouraging us to take our own plunge into dialectics. Her concept of dialectic opened toward Hegel and especially his concept of absolute negativity, but also toward the movements based on what was later to be called the intersectionality of class, race, and gender. In this sense, and in the spirit of the African liberationist dialectical thinker Frantz Fanon, her version of the Marxist-Humanist dialectic avoided both the academicized Eurocentrism and the elitist attitude toward working people prevalent among so many who took up dialectics in the 1970s. Another important feature of this form of dialectic was its deep and explicit critique not only of Stalinism, which many of the New Left had come to oppose, especially after the Russian suppression of the Prague Spring of 1968, but also of Maoism. This was especially timely because much of the New Left had been drawn to Maoism due to its having claimed to support continuous revolution, its attacks on bureaucracy, and its militant confrontations with global imperialism. But Maoism exhibited a sort of irrational subjectivism as seen in slogans like "Dare to Struggle, Dare to Win." This resulted in some huge defeats, most notably in Indonesia in 1965. This occurred some years before Mao discredited himself by siding with the U.S. against Russia in the 1970s in such a way that he ended up on the same side as South Africa in opposing most of the leading Black liberation movements of Southern Africa.

In place of this kind of subjectivism, which was divorced from any real social base or mass movement, the emancipatory Marxist-Humanist form of subjectivity asserted itself, offering not only a clear dialectical humanism, but also a critique of the transformation into opposite of both revolutionaries and revolutionary thought. This kind of thinking traced itself all the way back to Hegel's critique of the French Revolution, but was connected even more substantially to developments like the collapse of the Second International as it fell victim to reformism and prowar sentiment in 1914. Transformation into opposite also marked the rise of the era of state capitalism out of the demise of monopoly capitalism in the 1930s. In Russia, the rise of the Stalinist form of state-capitalism constituted a transformation into opposite of the liberatory aims of 1917, while Germany slid from high culture into barbarism under the Nazi form of state capitalism, and the U.S. experienced a more benign form of state capitalism under Roosevelt that nonetheless gave the world weapons of nuclear destruction. In the 1950s and 1960s, the Maoist form of state capitalism distorted and upended the very notion of revolution as it embarked upon destructive and chaotic campaigns like the Great Leap Forward of the 1950s and the Cultural Revolution of the 1960s.

In the 1980s and 1990s, I centered my work on the Marxist-Humanist dialectic, on defending and extending it through critical analyses of key writings by Lukács, Marcuse, and, above all, Lenin, whom I assessed at some length in my *Lenin, Hegel, and Western Marxism* (1995). In this period, my argument was mainly with other dialecticians, or between us and crudely materialist Marxists. The present volume includes at the beginning the introductory sketch of dialectics that forms chapter two, coauthored with my longtime comrade Peter Hudis, author of important work on Luxemburg, Fanon, and Marx. The chapter that follows on Hegel and the French Revolution explores how his critique of a revolution that transformed into its opposite could illuminate similar problems closer to our own time, from Stalinism to the results of the African liberation movements. The chapters on Lenin develop themes related to my book on Lenin and Hegel in concise form. The first of these lays out his important contributions in his 1914-15 *Philosophical Notebooks* in areas like subjectivity and the critique of vulgar materialism. The second chapter on Lenin clarifies his thought through a contrast with his fellow Bolshevik and important theorist Nikolai Bukharin, who fell into a type of scientific materialism akin to positivism and also carried out a serious but ultimately class reductionist study of imperialism that, contra Lenin, took no account of its dialectical opposition, the burgeoning national liberation movements that had begun to challenge imperialism. The chapter on Marcuse focuses on his major but somewhat neglected book, *Reason and Revolution* (1941), the first full-length study in any language of Hegel and dialectics from a Marxist standpoint. In this book, Marcuse counterposes dialectical reason to fascism, but also critiques the philosophical positions of positivism and pragmatism in light of both Hegel and the writings of the young Marx. The chapter on Lukács takes up not his famous *History and Class Consciousness* (1923), but his unjustly neglected second major book on Hegel and dialectics, *The Young Hegel* (1948), which offers an important if sometimes flawed interpretation of Hegel's critique of Romanticism and irrationalism, all of this linked to the rise of fascism. The book also contains a probing discussion of Hegel and gender, as well as a profound synopsis of the revolutionary dialectic of Hegel's Phenomenology.

As the new century approached in the wake of the collapse of the Soviet Union and its Eastern Bloc in 1989-91, numerous anti-dialectical and anti-Marxist theories came to the fore. These emerged not just from the "end of history" school of thought on the right, but also from within the intellectual left, where thinkers like the poststructuralist Michel Foucault and the postcolonialist Edward Said were attacking all forms of Marxism as well as Marx himself, under the charges of determinism, Eurocentrism, and what they saw as an antiquated form of dialectical humanism out of step with contemporary reality. Even thinkers who defended Marx in this period, like Jacques Derrida or Antonio Negri, nonetheless rejected Hegel and the dialectic. Given this context, the essays at the beginning of part three adopt a more defensive posture. The chapter on dialectical reason and its 21st century critics defends and elaborates a dialectical perspective in light of the kind of challenges mentioned above, also taking up pragmatism and evolutionary biology. The chapter on Derrida applauds his surprising and well-timed return to Marx in 1993, at the height of the drift away from Marx among radical intellectuals, while also critiquing some of his ahistorical and non-dialectical assumptions. The chapter on Foucault, Marcuse, and Marx focuses on the lack of an emancipatory vision in Foucault's concept of resistance, while finding Marcuse's dialectical alternative not fully satisfactory either, because its abstract form of negation makes it harder for dialectical analysis to fully encompass issues like race and gender. The last two chapters, on Marx, draw from my *Marx at the Margins* (2010), in which I theorize him as a multidimensional thinker whose dialectic, while abstractly universal in the positive sense of taking in the totality of global capitalism, was also concrete enough to leave plenty of room for the particularities of race, gender, and colonialism. While the chapters in the third section of the book do not always focus exclusively on the dialectic proper, they elaborate a dialectical perspective nonetheless by critiquing its critics and by showing Marx—and Hegel—to have been innocent of the charge of a totalizing form of reason that blots out the particular. For Marx, that meant attention not only to the working class, but also to the particular struggles and the lived experience of oppressed racial and ethnic minorities, of women, and of colonized peoples. The dialectical perspective, especially in the hands of Marx and the Marxist-Humanist tradition begun by Dunayevskaya, offers a necessary form of totality that grasps the dimensions of capital and class at a global level, while also striving for a concrete form of universality that immerses itself in and learns from the struggles of the working classes, but also those of people of color and of women, even if they are sometimes situated outside that working class per se.

And after having begun to do that, the dialectic subjects everything to the critique of dialectical reason, not only the racist, classist, sexist, heterosexist, and environmentally destructive system that is capitalism, but also the revolutionary freedom movements that arise to uproot it. It is my hope that the essays in this book offer insights in the direction of that kind of dialectical critique, what the young Marx called the ruthless criticism of everything existing. Of course, Marx did not do so from a stance of bare negation, of simple destruction of the given world. That would fall into sophistry. Rather, he did so in a way that also pointed toward a positive, humanist alternative to the given world, what in philosophy Hegel had termed absolute negativity, a form of negation that contains the positive within the negative.

PART II

Marxism and Hegel

2

Dialectics in brief

KEVIN B ANDERSON AND PETER HUDIS

While its roots go back to the Socratic dialogues, dialectics as social theory begins with G. W. F. Hegel, and extends—through Karl Marx—to today, and to the future.[1]

With Hegel, the dialectic takes the form of a double negation. Ideas or social forms face negativity from within. If the process deepens, the old idea or form is overthrown. However, such a first (or bare) negation remains a "formless abstraction" unless it develops some determinateness or specificity (Hegel 2010: 87). This requires going beyond "the first negation" (which is "only *abstract* negativity") to "the second negation ... which is concrete, *absolute* negativity" (p. 89). This absolute negativity creates, for example, a new idea or social form in place of the old. Then the process may resume, with negation growing again within what has been newly created. Some have erroneously described this process as one of thesis-antithesis-synthesis, an expression Hegel himself never used (Pinkard 2000).

Against such formulaic notions, Hegel's dialectic is deeply rooted in historical and social development, especially the period from the Enlightenment through the French Revolution. These form the backdrop to all of his major works. As against the earlier Socratic dialectic, conflict and dialogue

---

1.   This article originally appeared as Kevin B. Anderson and Peter Hudis, "Dialectic" in *The Blackwell Encyclopedia of Sociology* (2020). Reproduced here with permission.

DIALECTICS IN BRIEF | 13

take place between real social forces, as well as between ideas. In *The Phenomenology of Spirit* (1807), Hegel traces the development of consciousness and knowledge, from the ancient Greco-Roman world to his own time. Successive forms of consciousness are negations of previous ones.

For example, in the dialectic of the master and the slave (literally, domination and servitude [*Herrschaft und Knechtschaft*]), slaves in the Greco-Roman world acquire a more developed form of self-consciousness, as part of a struggle for recognition, than their masters. The wrenching experience of capture and enslavement unmoors human selfhood and engenders reflexivity, as "everything fixed has quaked within it" since the self has experienced "absolute negativity" (Hegel 2018a: 80). But the fact that the slave performs physical labor and achieves recognition through this process, while the master enjoys an indolent life of leisure, points in the direction of another kind of second (or absolute) negation for the enslaved consciousness: For "it is precisely in its labor, wherein it seemed to have only an *alienated mind*, that it acquires a mind of its own" (p. 81). In Hegel's narrative, the human spirit thus grows and advances through the mind of the slave, not the master, who remains at the level of an unreflective "natural consciousness" marked by "self-will" or stubbornness (p. 81). This leads in turn to a new form of consciousness, Stoicism, which Hegel portrays as a further advance. Alluding to the fact that several prominent Stoics were manumitted slaves, however, Hegel also stresses the sociohistorical limits placed upon the progress of human consciousness when he characterizes the Greco-Roman world as "a time of universal fear and bondage" (p. 83).

Hegel develops a number of other dialectical categories, including identity, difference, and contradiction. He writes that although identity between two forms also includes of necessity some sort of difference, difference also has to involve some identity, a common set of terms or a framework through which they can express that difference. This could include a common language, for example. The impasse is overcome in a third stage, that of contradiction. Expanding the notion of contradiction from the sphere of ideas to that of social life, Hegel concludes that "All things are in themselves contradictory" and "contradiction is the root of all movement and life" (Hegel 2010: 381, 382).

Hegel's negations and contradictions create ground for a radical form of subjectivity, and he enjoins us to grasp reality "not as substance but just as much as *subject*" (Hegel 2018a: 10). He sees a drive for freedom as the overarching theme of human history, although this involves contradiction, and even sometimes retrogression. As humanity strives for the universal, for an absolute liberation, internal barriers to its realization repeatedly manifest themselves. Prominent among these are abstract universals, which lack particularity or concreteness. The French Revolution, especially in its Jacobin phase, was marked by universals of "pure abstraction," which "lacked a filling and a content," thus lapsing into the "sheer horror of the negative that has nothing positive in it" (p. 608). However, Hegel's system ends not here, but with a series of absolutes in which freedom is concretized, ultimately as the idea "engenders and enjoys itself as absolute Mind" (Hegel 2007: 276).

Marx attacks the conservative side of Hegel's social and political philosophy, for example, in his 1843 critique of the anti-democratic *Philosophy of Right*. At the same time, Marx takes over the dialectic. In his "Critique of the Hegelian Dialectic" in the unpublished *Economic and Philosophic Manuscripts of 1844*, he characterizes Hegel's "outstanding achievement" as "the dialectic of negativity as the moving and creative principle" (Marx, in Fromm 1961: 176). Marx also distances himself from some aspects of Hegel's idealism: "For Hegel, human life . . . is equivalent to self-consciousness" (p. 179). In this sense, the problem with Hegel's master-slave dialectic would be his focus on the growth of self-consciousness on the part of the slave, as opposed to the quest for actual liberation from bondage, as in the great Roman slave uprisings. Thus, consciousness, albeit rooted in the experience of human labor, is privileged over the fullness of human praxis, both mental and manual. Nonetheless, many core principles of Hegel's dialectic—negation of the negation, contradiction, the concrete universal, transformation into opposite, subject-object reversal, etc.—are retained in the Marxian dialectic. Nor is idealism rejected *in toto*. A year later, in the 1845 "Theses on Feuerbach," Marx writes that many forms of materialism lack the subjective element and are too contemplative: "Hence, in contradistinction to materialism, the *active* side was set forth abstractly by idealism" (MECW 5: 3).

With Marx, the notion of contradiction migrates to the sphere of political economy, where social change is driven by class struggle, as he and Engels maintain in *The Communist Manifesto* (1848). Change also occurs when, due to social development, "the material productive forces of society come into contradiction with the existing production relationships," as he writes in the preface to *Critique of Political Economy* in 1859 (Marx, in Fromm 1961: 218). Eight years later, in Volume 1 of *Capital*, Marx confirms his debt to Hegel by writing "the Hegelian 'contradiction' . . . is the source of all dialectics" (Marx 1976: 744).

In the first chapter of *Capital*, Marx recasts the Hegelian notion of subject-object reversal [*Verkehrung*] in his discussion of commodity fetishism, wherein human relations take on "the fantastic form of a relation between things" (p. 165) because that is "what they are" in the upside-down world of capitalism (p. 166). In the closing pages of Volume 1 of *Capital*, Marx uses the Hegelian negation of the negation to frame a discussion of the possible demise of capitalism. Here, in the section on "primitive accumulation," Marx analyzes the expropriation of the English peasantry during the agricultural revolution as "the first negation of individual private property." Driven into the cities, the peasantry eventually becomes the working class. Capitalism later "begets... its own negation," however, the revolt of the working class, a class that it has called into existence. "This," Marx concludes, "is the negation of the negation" (pp. 929–30). Elsewhere, as in the 1873 preface to a new edition of *Capital*, Marx criticizes "the mystificatory side of the Hegelian dialectic," and writes, "It must be inverted, in order to discover the rational kernel within the mystical shell." Nonetheless, Marx avows himself "the pupil of that mighty thinker" (pp. 102–03). In a letter to Engels dated January 16, 1858, Marx expresses the desire to publish an essay on what was *rational* in Hegel's dialectical method, this after he reviewed Hegel's *Logic* while in the process of writing the *Grundrisse* (MECW 40: 249). He never did so.

Engels—who defines dialectics as "the science of universal inter-connection" (Engels 2012: 17)—writes, "[Marx] was the first to have brought to the fore again the forgotten dialectical method, its connection with Hegelian dialectics and its distinction from the latter, and at the same time to have applied this method in *Capital* to the facts of an empirical science, political economy" (Engels 2012: 49).

In his *Ludwig Feuerbach and the End of Classical German Philosophy* (1886), Engels develops two schemata that are embraced to this day by more orthodox currents within Marxism. First, Engels writes that Hegel's "system" was conservative, while his "dialectical method" was revolutionary, thus discouraging the deep study of Hegel. Second, he divides all of philosophy into "two great camps," idealism and materialism, with the latter the progressive and revolutionary one (MECW 26: 363, 366). It was in this spirit that Georgi Plekhanov coined the term "dialectical materialism" five years later. Engels also enunciates three "laws" of dialectics: (1) transformation of quantity into quality, (2) interpenetration of opposites, and (3) negation of the negation.

Until the publication of the *1844 Manuscripts* in German in 1932 (a Russian edition appeared in 1927), Marx's concept of dialectic and its relation to that of Hegel was obscured. Some Marxists delved directly into Hegel, however. In his 1914-15 *Notebooks* on Hegel's *Logic*, Lenin returns directly to Hegel's writings, modifying some aspects of the dominant form of dialectical materialism at the time. Having absorbed the Hegelian notion of consciousness, Lenin writes that "cognition not only reflects the objective world, but creates it" (LCW 38: 212). Lenin also expresses reservations about Engels and Plekhanov, going beyond the rigid divide between idealism and materialism by attacking not only abstract idealism but also "vulgar materialism" (LCW 38: 114). Lenin kept these reflections on the dialectic mostly private, which facilitated the very "vulgar materialism" he had critiqued. However, Lenin did on occasion refer publicly to his new grasp of the dialectic, and this is evident in his post-1915 writings on imperialism, national liberation, and the state and revolution.

In *History and Class Consciousness* (1923), Georg Lukács recovers the Hegelian dialectic for Marxism, taking as one of his cues Lenin's call to become "materialist friends of the Hegelian dialectic" (Lukács 1971: xlv). Lukács accuses Engels of confusing "the scientific experiment" with "praxis in the dialectical, philosophical sense" (p. 132). Moreover, he attacks Engels for neglecting the element of subjectivity in his three laws of dialectic: "But he does not even mention the most vital interaction, namely the dialectical relation between subject and object in the historical process." The mere recourse to "fluid" concepts does not solve this problem, Lukács holds (p. 3). He also develops a concept of concrete totality, which allows a move from the factory—"in concentrated form the whole of capitalist society" (p. 90)—to the concept of fetishism or reification. The first to point to commodity fetishism as the core of Marx's critique of capital, Lukács also extends reification from the factory to the entire human condition under capitalism: to the white-collar worker or the scientist for example. In so doing, Lukács incorporates Max Weber's theory of rationalization. Later, Lucien Goldmann (1969) discusses Lukács in relation to sociological methodology.

Frankfurt School member Herbert Marcuse's *Reason and Revolution* (1941) was the first major study of dialectics that appeared after the publication of Marx's 1844 Manuscripts. Marcuse again places negativity at the center of dialectical thought:

> Hegel's philosophy is indeed what the subsequent reaction termed it, a negative philosophy. It is originally motivated by the conviction that the given facts that appear to common sense as the positive index of truth are in reality the negation of truth, so that truth can only be established by their destruction. (Marcuse 1941: 27)

Commonsense reason also traps consciousness in the particular and the empirical, blocking it from grasping the universal, and therefore the possibilities for radical change. With dialectical reason, in contrast, "possibility belongs to the very character of reality" (p. 150). In this sense, universals such as human emancipation are actually part of social reality, whereas oppressive social forms are in an ultimate sense unreal and false. Theodor Adorno, also of the Frankfurt School, parts company with Hegel on absolute negativity, taking issue with the concept of totality as well. Adorno, who seeks to expunge the affirmative character from dialectics, goes so far as to link absolute negativity to the Holocaust, this in his *Negative Dialectics* (1966).

Dialectic also marks some of the major treatments of race and colonialism, whether in W.E.B. Du Bois's notion of "double consciousness" in *The Souls of Black Folk* (1903), or in Frantz Fanon's dialectic of colonialism and resistance in *The Wretched of the Earth* (1961). In *Black Skin, White Masks*, first published in 1952, Fanon also taxes Hegel's master-slave dialectic with failing to show that in modern racial slavery there was no "reciprocity" and that for the slave there is "not recognition but work" (2008: 195). C. L. R. James (in his *Notes on Dialectics* 1948) and especially Raya Dunayevskaya developed a concept of dialectics that eschews abstract universals, elaborating a multiple concept of subjectivity that includes not only the traditional working class, but also Blacks, women, and youth. Writing later on as a Marxist humanist, Dunayevskaya makes absolute negativity her point of departure, arguing in *Philosophy and Revolution* (1973) that Hegel's absolutes are not closures, but are imbued with absolute negativity. She holds that dialectical thought, if concretized, can impact radical social movements, helping to give them form and direction: "Philosophy and revolution will then liberate the innate talents of men and women who will become whole" (p. 292). Hegel's dialectic also allows oppositional movements to navigate periods of retrogression as well as progressive ones: "Far from expressing a sequence of never-ending progression, the Hegelian dialectic lets retrogression appear as translucent as progression" (Dunayevskaya 2002: 332).

Strong challenges to dialectics have come from scientific positivism and from French structuralism and post structuralism. Among others, post-structuralists attack the dialectic as too affirmative, counterposing a Nietzschean notion of absolute difference. These critics have also argued that Hegel's universals swallow up particularity and difference in grand totalities or narratives. Nonetheless, dialectical thought persists, especially through the traditions of Marxism and critical theory. The revival of Hegel in recent years is seen in the wealth of new translations of his major works (Hegel 2007, 2010, 2018a, 2018b). This has been accompanied by a smaller number of studies in Marxian dialectics, among them Jameson (2009) and Zizek (2012).

References and Suggested Readings

Dunayevskaya, R. (1973) *Philosophy and Revolution*. Delacorte, New York.

Dunayevskaya, R. (2002) *The Power of Negativity*. Ed. P. Hudis & K. B. Anderson, Lexington Books, Lanham, MD.

Engels, F. (2012) *Dialectics of Nature*, trans. by C. Dutt. Wellred Publications, London.

Fanon, F. (2008) *Black Skin, White Masks*, trans. by R. Philcox. Grove Press, New York.

Fromm, E. (1961) *Marx's Concept of Man*. Ungar, New York.

Goldmann, L. (1969) *The Human Sciences and Philosophy*, trans. by H. White and R. Anchor. Jonathan Cape, London.

Hegel, G. W. F. (2007) *Philosophy of Mind*, trans. by W. Wallace and A. V. Miller, revised by M. Inwood. Oxford University Press, New York.

Hegel, G. W. F. (2010) *Science of Logic*, trans. by G. di Giovanni. Cambridge University Press, Cambridge.

Hegel, G. W. F. (2018a) *Phenomenology of Spirit*, trans. by W. Wallace and A. V. Miller, revised by M. Inwood. Oxford University Press, New York.

Hegel, G. W. F. (2018b) *Phenomenology of Spirit*, trans. by T. Pinkard. Cambridge University Press, New York.

Jameson, F. (2009) *Valences of the Dialectic*. Verso, London.

Lenin, V. I. [LCW] (1972) *Philosophical Notebooks*. In: *Collected Works*, Vol. 38. Progress Publishers, Moscow.

Lukács, G. (1971) *History and Class Consciousness*, trans. by R. Livingstone. MIT Press, Cambridge, MA.

Marcuse, H. (1941) *Reason and Revolution*. Oxford University Press, New York.

Marx, K. (1976) *Capital*, Vol. 1. Penguin, New York.

Marx, K. & Engels, F. [MECW] (1975–2004) *Collected Works*, 50 vols. International Publishers, New York.

Ollman, B. (1993) *Dialectical Investigations*. Routledge, New York.

Ollman, B. and T. Smith (2008) *Dialectics for the New Century*. Palgrave Macmillan, Houndmills.

Pinkard, T. (2000) *Hegel: A Biography*. Cambridge University Press, New York.

Zizek, S. (2012). *Less Than Nothing: Hegel and the Shadow of Dialectical Materialism*. Verso, London.

[This paper originally appeared as the entry "Dialectic" in *The Blackwell Encyclopedia of Sociology* (2020)]

3

Hegel, the French revolution, and after

Our age, whether through logic or epistemology, whether through Marx or through Nietzsche, is attempting to flee Hegel.... But truly to escape Hegel... we have to determine the extent to which our anti-Hegelianism is possibly one of his tricks directed against us, at the end of which he stands, motionless, waiting for us.—Michel Foucault [1]

The reduction of the very concept of socialism to statified property is grounded in a methodology that... had developed the theory of permanent revolution without a self-developing Subject. The dualism in Trotskyism was [rooted in-KBA] the dualism in Trotsky's practice of the dialectic.... Dialectics takes its own toll of theory and theoreticians.—Raya Dunayevskaya [2]

---

1. "The Discourse on Language" (1971), appendix to his *The Archeology of Knowledge*, p. 235.

2. *Philosophy and Revolution*, pp. 129, 150.

Setting the ground:
Today's crises, the French revolution
and its philosophy,
Rousseau's concept of the 'General Will'

Because Hegel's thought is so alive today, even those like the famous French poststructuralist thinker Michel Foucault who seek to "escape" Hegel are oppressively aware that their attempt to do so may in the end be only a moment in the unfolding of the dialectic. I quote Foucault's poignant statement above not in order smugly to dismiss his thought as a mere epiphenomenon from a Hegelian Marxist standpoint. No, the problem Foucault singles out is also ours. It is not only that of poststructuralism, but also that of post-Marx Marxism. Hence, the second epigraph to this chapter, a quote from the founder of Marxist-Humanism in the U.S., Raya Dunayevskaya, part of her critique of Leon Trotsky, whom she saw as a great but flawed Marxist revolutionary and theoretician who never really delved into the dialectic. And yet, as Dunayevskaya concludes, the dialectic nonetheless took its measure of Trotsky, finding his Marxism ultimately wanting. This was in no small part because, in the end, Trotsky and his latter-day followers, who never developed a theory of state-capitalism, ended up justifying statist Communist regimes. Her point is that whether or not such post-Marx Marxists think they too have "escaped" that "idealist" Hegel, the dialectics of revolution awaits them and takes their measure. However, I don't think that Dunayevskaya would agree that the dialectic sits there motionless like the Sphinx à la Foucault. Instead, she sees the dialectic in a constant state of self-development, from Hegel to Marx to today.

Hegel critiques the greatest Revolution of his time, the French Revolution of 1789-94, in the famous chapter of the *Phenomenology* entitled "Absolute Freedom and Terror." Hegel's critique is crucial not only to the understanding of that revolution, but also to that of the whole course of twentieth century revolutions, all the more so today in the post-1989 world following the collapse of statist Communism, when the very idea of revolution is being dismissed. It is only by acknowledging that all too many revolutions have been aborted (or worse, been transformed into their opposite, into oppressive regimes that create new forms of exploitation) that the revolutionary dialectic can move forward. It is that type of awareness that makes many today in the Marxist-Humanist movement raise questions even in the midst of great victories, like the beginning of Black majority rule in South Africa after decades of struggle and sacrifice by the Black masses and their allies around the world.

As Dunayevskaya noted frequently, the issue of aborted and soured revolutions is the key problematic of our times, especially since the 1930s, when the 1917 Russian Revolution was transformed under Stalin's leadership into a state-capitalist tyranny of forced labor camps. In the concluding pages of her great work on Hegel and the dialectic, *Philosophy and Revolution*, Dunayevskaya relates this problem to Hegel's chapter on the French Revolution: "What Hegel had shown were the dangers inherent in the French revolution, which did not end in the millennium. The dialectic disclosed that the counter-revolution is *within* the revolution" (p. 287). Earlier, in a 1956 draft of what was to become Chapter 1 of her first book, *Marxism and Freedom*, a chapter that discusses Hegel and the French Revolution, she explicitly connects that discussion to the theory of state-capitalism developed in the second half of *Marxism and Freedom*: "Individual sections of the *Phenomenology* will have a special urgent meaning for each epoch. For our times the section on Absolute Freedom and Absolute Terror has imbedded in it the whole Russian development" (Raya Dunayevskaya Collection, #11850).

In the section on "Absolute Freedom and Terror," Hegel makes a critique of the Jacobin phase of the French Revolution, including the Great Terror. He also critiques its underlying philosophy, the eighteenth-century Enlightenment philosopher Jean-Jacques Rousseau's concept of the general or universal will. In his classic treatise, *On the Social Contract*, which includes on its first page the famous phrase "man is born free, and everywhere he is in chains," Rousseau conceptualizes the general will as follows: "Each of us places his person and all his power in common under the supreme direction of the general will; and as one we receive each member as an indivisible part of the whole" ([1762] 1987:17, 24). Rousseau writes further that "the general will is always right and always tends toward the public utility" but that it is to be distinguished from "the will of all" which "is merely the sum of private wills" ([1762] 1987:31). It is this rather abstract and formalistic concept of freedom as the general will that Hegel critiques under "Absolute Freedom and Terror."

Viewing Hegel's critique up close

Just before beginning the section on absolute freedom and terror, Hegel writes that with the Enlightenment notion of utility or usefulness as the criterion for truth and goodness, "heaven is transplanted to the earth below" (Phg. Baillie 598, Miller 355). What the Enlightenment brings about is that not only physical objects but also human subjects are judged by the criterion of utility. At the level of absolute freedom, human subjectivity confidently transforms not only the earth but also human society. Absolute Freedom "is conscious of its pure personality" and "the world is for it absolutely its own will, and this will is a general will" (Phg. Baillie 600, Miller 356–57). This general will uproots the old, for "negativity has permeated all its moments" (Phg. Baillie 601, Miller 357). It establishes a form of equality whereby "all social ranks or classes... are extinguished [*getilgt*]" (Phg. Baillie 601, Miller 357).[3] This type of equality eliminates social difference to the point where the sole antinomy remaining is that "between the individual and the universal consciousness" (Phg. Baillie 602, Miller 357).

With no social classes or even differences remaining, we get "a single individual will" that absorbs or attempts to absorb everything. It "lets nothing break loose to become a free object standing over against it." Because of this very restriction of the individual, the general will "cannot achieve anything positive" (Phg. Baillie 603, Miller 358), Hegel concludes. This is because the general will is too general, too abstract a concept of freedom: "there is left for it only negative action; it is merely the fury of destruction" (Phg. Baillie 604, Miller 359). Within the revolutionary society, we get two forms of consciousness, which take the form of extremes that, Hegel tells us, are "equally abstract." One of them is "a simple, inflexible, cold universality," the general will as expressed by the new rulers; the other is that of the once again alienated consciousness of the masses, the "self-willed atomism of actual self-consciousness" (Phg. Baillie 604-05, Miller 359).

---

3.   I have substituted the word "extinguished" here for Miller's "abolished" and Baillie's "effaced and annulled" and also given the German original—*getilgt*—because words such as annulled or abolished are sometimes used as translations of Hegel's famous term *aufgehoben*, which includes meanings such as abolished or annulled, but also ones such as preserved or taken to a higher level. Here, with *getilgt*, there is a simpler, cruder notion of being extinguished, without the meaning of carrying over something from the past into the new situation that one finds with the word *aufgehoben*.

Seeking to break out of this antinomy by imposing their individual wills as the universal, the new rulers resort to terror. The results are horrific: "The sole work and deed of universal freedom is therefore death, a death which has no inner significance or filling.... It is the coldest, flattest death, with no more significance than cutting off the head of a cabbage or throwing back a mouthful of water" (Phg. Baillie 605, Miller 360). This is because "what is called government is merely the victorious faction" and the various political factions, each of which claim to represent the general will, say that what the others have said or done is "a crime committed" against the general will. Next comes a law of suspects whereby "being suspected, therefore, takes the place, or has the significance and effect, of being guilty" (Phg. Baillie 605-06, Miller 360).

Out of this orgy of destruction and self-destruction, the revolutionary regime eventually collapses, and is succeeded by more moderate forms of bourgeois society, wherein social distinctions arise once again: "These individuals who have felt the fear of death, of their absolute master, again submit to negation and distinctions, arrange themselves in the various spheres, and return to an apportioned and limited task, but thereby to their substantial unity" (Phg. Baillie 607, Miller 361). It appears at first that "out of this tumult," the whole cycle might now start again: "Spirit would have to traverse anew and continually repeat this cycle of necessity" (Phg. Baillie 607, Miller 361).

But this is not to be. History and thought have moved forward, albeit hardly in a gradualist evolutionary straight line. Because of the very abstract character of the French Revolution's attempt to reach absolute freedom, spirit at this stage has laid bare the structure of negativity that underlies society and culture, something which earlier forms of alienated spirit could not do. Hegel writes that "in absolute freedom there was no reciprocal action between a consciousness that is immersed in the complexities of existence, or that sets itself specific aims and thoughts, and a valid external world, whether of reality or thought; instead, the world was absolutely in the form of consciousness as a universal will" (Phg. Baillie 608, Miller 362). But despite—or really because of—the highly abstract, dehumanized form that spirit takes here at the stage of absolute Freedom and Terror, amid the "sheer terror of the negative" (Phg. Baillie 608, Miller 362), spirit has begun to face itself in a way that other earlier forms of spirit have not done. The human spirit has achieved a new consciousness of self. It "now knows itself" as "a pure knowing or a pure will" and "it is thus the interaction of pure knowing with itself" (Phg. Baillie 609, Miller 363). This means that it has begun to overcome the contradiction between the individual will and the general will that was at the root of the reign of terror. It has done so by recognizing that the self cannot be skipped over, that self-critical self-awareness must be part of the drive to freedom in a deeper way than before. By now, "absolute freedom has . . . removed the antithesis between the universal and the individual will" (Phg. Baillie 610, Miller 363).

The human spirit or mind has achieved this new type of self-awareness and self-consciousness only because it has gone through the sheer terror and destruction of the negative during the reign of terror. The world spirit now passes from France to Germany, where in a more placid and abstractly philosophical context, thinkers such as Kant and Fichte chew on the problems created by the Enlightenment and the French Revolution. This new shape of spirit, "the moral spirit," will of course go through more negations and contradictions on the road toward absolute knowing. But that would take us beyond the topic of this essay. Let us instead backtrack a bit, and try to assess the meaning of what Hegel has done in his discussion of "Absolute Freedom and Terror."

Hegel's absolute freedom and terror in the eyes of some 20th century commentators: From Taylor to Marcuse and from Lukács to Hyppolite

Some post-Marx Marxists have interpreted Hegel's analysis of the French Revolution as that of a moderate liberal or even a conservative who recoiled before the actuality of revolution. This is belied by Hegel's own writings on the French Revolution when taken as a whole, including those long after he became a professor at the conservative University of Berlin under the Prussian monarchy. For example, in his lectures near the end of his life that were later collected as *The Philosophy of History*, he writes that "the Revolution received its first impulse from Philosophy" but that it was grounded in social issues because "the entire political system appeared one mass of injustice." Further: "This was accordingly a glorious mental dawn. All thinking beings shared in the jubilation of this epoch. Emotions of a lofty character stirred peoples' minds at that time" (1956: 446-47). The noted German Hegel scholar Joachim Ritter, who was no Marxist, sums up Hegel's overall view of revolution as follows: "In Hegel's view, the essence of modern political revolution, which differentiates it from all other forms of upheaval, uprising, rebellion, and putsch, lies not so much in the particular political form which the violence takes, but rather in the social emancipation underlying it and in the establishment of an order that according to its own principle is presupposition-less, excluding everything preexisting, historical, and traditional, like a radical new beginning that nothing should precede" ([1956] 1982:76).

A second tack taken by post-Marx Marxists is even more familiar: the dismissal of Hegel's analysis of the French Revolution as idealist and therefore unconnected to the supposedly real issues. Post-Marx Marxists continue to do so despite Marx having stated in 1844 that his own dialectic included elements of idealism as well as materialism. For example, Richard Norman writes dismissively from such a so-called "materialist" standpoint of "Hegel's confused view of the relation between history and epistemology" in the section on "Absolute Freedom and Terror." Hegel's idealism, Norman continues, "distorts the real nature of historical change," here using the word "real" in an uncritically empiricist manner. This is because of Hegel's supposed view that a mere "change in consciousness" would change history (1976:101). To be sure, Hegel ultimately sees human consciousness and spirit as more fundamental than sensuous material reality, but for a post-Marx Marxist to dismiss Hegel's analysis in the *Phenomenology* of the French Revolution and its self-destruction after Russia, after China, after Grenada, and so many others (all of them led by people claiming the mantle of Marxism) is itself a formal and abstract type of theorizing that fails to come to grips with the real issues and problems of our times. In short, Norman may think he has "escaped" Hegel, but he has not.

Others, especially liberal Hegel scholars, have argued that Hegel's analysis of the French Revolution in the *Phenomenology* is really at one with that later in the *Philosophy of Right*, where freedom can come only through a state with firmly established political institutions, not any immediate or absolute type of freedom. Charles Taylor, for example, writes that here "Hegel sees a necessity by which the aspiration to absolute freedom engenders the Terror," something Taylor also links, correctly in my view, to "the Stalinist terror." Yet Taylor also jumps to the conclusion that any concept of absolute freedom would lead to totalitarianism, something he sees lurking even behind issues posed "in our day in the demand for radical participatory democracy" (1974:186–87). Taylor implies that any attempt to achieve a direct or Paris Commune type of democracy will end inevitably in totalitarianism, and that this is Hegel's own view. This is a highly questionable reading not only of recent history, but also of Hegel's work itself. If Hegel opposes all forms of absolute freedom, as Taylor argues, how could he have ended the *Science of Logic* by speaking of having reached in the absolute idea "an absolute liberation," a form of freedom in which "therefore, no transition takes place" and where "the Idea freely releases itself in its absolute self-assurance and inner poise" (Hegel 1969: 843). Today it is all too easy to misuse Hegel to underpin a liberal rejection of all revolutionary forms of democracy. Such a misreading fails to recognize that for Hegel, if one makes a leap toward absolute freedom without having suffered through all the necessary historical stages and stages of consciousness, it will all come crashing down, as it did in 1789-94. At the same time, the human spirit keeps striving toward that absolute freedom.

Even Herbert Marcuse and Georg Lukács, the two great Marxist Hegelians of the mid-twentieth century, come up surprisingly short when they take up Hegel on the French Revolution. Marcuse's discussion of the *Phenomenology* in his otherwise great work *Reason and Revolution* is remarkably brief and superficial, and may be linked to a more general underestimation of Hegel's early masterpiece. As against nearly 50 pages on the *Logic*, Marcuse devotes a mere 20 pages to the *Phenomenology*, breaking off the discussion at Stoicism, which is only a third of the way into the text, long before the chapter on absolute freedom and terror. In a passing reference to the section on Absolute Freedom and Terror, Marcuse writes: "Hegel saw that the final result of the French Revolution was not the realization of freedom, but the establishment of a new despotism." So far, I would agree, but then he adds that for Hegel this is because "emancipating the individual necessarily results in terror and destruction as long as it is carried out by individuals against the state, and not by the state itself. The state alone can provide emancipation" (Marcuse 1941:91). Here, Marcuse sounds almost like Taylor, although he opposes Hegel and supports radical democracy, thus regarding what he perceives as Hegel's statism, even in the *Phenomenology*, as a flaw rather than a virtue.

Lukács, perhaps sensing danger if he really delved into Hegel's critique of the French Revolution while living in Russia during Stalin's Great Terror, evades the chapter on absolute freedom and terror almost entirely in his important but flawed book *The Young Hegel*. Even though Lukács devotes eighty pages of his book to the *Phenomenology*, when he gets to the young Hegel's most sustained analysis of the French Revolution in the section on absolute freedom and terror, he cops out: "Hegel's understanding of the French Revolution has now been sufficiently explored and requires no further investigations on our part." In his nearly perfunctory treatment, Lukács emphasizes only Hegel's notion that the French Revolution was an irrevocable break in world history after which, as Lukács puts it, "none of the old configurations could survive or return in their old shape." To Lukács, Hegel is once again a moderate liberal who "rejects those features of 'absolute freedom' that go beyond the destruction of lingering feudal institutions" ([1948] 1975:502). Where Marcuse leaves unmentioned any positive meaning to absolute freedom, Lukács seemingly endorses the Jacobin Terror when he places the word "tyranny" in quotation marks and, more importantly, never delves much at all into Hegel's critique of the Terror.

As against these evasions by Marcuse and Lukács, the post-World War II era saw important discussions precisely of Hegel's critique of the French Revolution. These were launched by the greatest French Hegel scholar, Jean Hyppolite, who wrote in a famous 1946 book on the *Phenomenology* that for Hegel the section on absolute freedom and terror meant that "the French Revolution failed not because its principle was false, but because it claimed to realize that principle immediately. That immediateness is an abstraction and hence an error" (Hyppolite 1946:455). I can agree only with part of this statement. The notion that a leap to freedom without passing through the various historical and dialectical stages of negation can end in disaster seems to be borne out by Hegel's text, but Hyppolite's notion that Hegel is here critiquing not Rousseau but merely the practice of Rousseau's ideas seems untenable, given Hegel's scathing critique of the very concept of the general will in this part of the *Phenomenology*. In this 1946 work, Hyppolite also seems to view some form of hierarchical social differentiation as an inevitable feature of human society, seemingly also opposing Marx's vision of a classless society. A decade later, Hyppolite returns more profoundly to these issues in another work, *Studies on Marx and Hegel*, here focusing on Hegel's analysis of the self-destructive character of the Revolution: "A total democracy emerged, but as the very opposite of what it claimed to be. It became a manifestation of the most literal totalitarianism, or anti-liberal democracy, because it completely absorbed the private individual in the citizen." However, Hyppolite concludes, "Despite its partial failure, Hegel considers the Revolution an intellectual revolution of infinite consequence" ([1955] 1969:58, 61).

Raya Dunayevskaya on absolute freedom and terror

We are now in a better position to grasp the uniqueness of Dunayevskaya's Marxist-Humanist analysis of this section of the *Phenomenology*. I have already noted that in *Philosophy and Revolution*, she concludes that Hegel's chapter on the French Revolution is crucial for a whole problematic of today, the emergence of the counter-revolution within the revolution: "What Hegel had shown were the dangers inherent in the French Revolution which did not end in the millennium. The dialectic disclosed that the counter-revolution is within the revolution" (Dunayevskaya 1989a:287). In 1960, Dunayevskaya writes in "Notes on Phenomenology" that at issue here is Hegel's notion that "by being only negative it was 'merely the rage and fury of destruction.'" She continues in this vein: "In a word, Hegel considers that if you have not faced the question of reconstruction on new beginnings, but only destruction of the old, you have, therefore, reached only 'death'" (Dunayevskaya 2002:42). She also goes into Hegel's critique of the various factions that emerged, each claiming to represent the general will. She writes further that Hegel "is criticizing all forms of abstraction, whether in thought or in fact, when fact is narrowed to mean not all reality, but only aspects of it" (Dunayevskaya 2002:43).

In reflections from 1986-87, the last years of her life, Dunayevskaya focuses on the penultimate section of the *Science of Logic* on "The Idea of the Good," where Hegel mentions "two worlds in opposition, one a realm of subjectivity in the pure regions of transparent thought, the other a realm of objectivity . . . that is an undisclosed realm of darkness." This passage, which has been so important for Marxist-Humanism,[4] is where

---

4. For many years, Dunayevskaya wrote , "Two Worlds," a monthly philosophical column inspired by this passage in the newspaper she founded, *News & Letters*, and for which I also wrote during the years 1972-2008.

Hegel also leads his readers back to the *Phenomenology* (Hegel 1969:820). Specifically, Hegel here refers us to his discussion at the end of the section on absolute freedom and terror. This is where spirit, unable to resolve the contradictions stemming from the French Revolution, seeks to escape into Kantian ethics, which Hegel dubs "Spirit Certain of Itself: Morality."

But by making a rare reference to the *Phenomenology* at this point in the *Logic*, Hegel implies that he also has in mind the whole preceding discussion of absolute freedom and terror as well, when he writes of the "unresolved contradiction between that *absolute* end and the *limitation* of this actuality that *insuperably* opposes it." Here again in the *Logic*, the Idea of the Good is only "an absolute postulate," one that cannot overcome the two separate worlds of objectivity and subjectivity. This is the idea of the good as activity, as practice, as the practical idea, as will. And it is in the very next paragraph of the *Logic* that Hegel tells us that, as great as it is, "the *practical* Idea still lacks the moment of the *theoretical* Idea" (1969:821). This brings the whole problematic closer to our own time, for this is where, as Dunayevskaya argues in her last writings, Lenin too fell down, becoming so enamored of the practical idea that the theoretical idea was lost. But was Lenin's problem also in a way the problematic of the Enlightenment, with its focus on utility, which certainly is also a practical idea? And did not the French Revolution promulgate freedom more as an "absolute postulate" in the form of Rousseau's notion of the general will, rather than a real unity of subjectivity and objectivity? I will not attempt to unscramble all of this here, but I would like to end this point by saying that there seem to be strong affinities between Hegel's critique in the *Science of Logic* of the one-sidedness of the practical idea and his critique in the *Phenomenology* of the formalistic and utilitarian concept of the general will as practiced in the French Revolution.

All of this illuminates in a new way some of Dunayevskaya's last writings on the dialectics of organization and philosophy, especially her critique of Lenin, which was published as the 1989 introduction to *Philosophy and Revolution*. There, Dunayevskaya notes the above passages from Hegel's *Logic* and concludes that Hegel's references back to the *Phenomenology* and to the need for the theoretical idea in the section on the idea of the good "did not faze Lenin because he felt that the objective, the Practical Idea" would resolve the contradiction between objectivity and subjectivity (1989b:xxxix). So too did the French revolutionaries with their notions of utility and the general will. We know the tragic outcomes in both France and Russia, where the revolutions transformed into their opposite.

I would like to conclude this essay by suggesting that Hegel's dialectic offers a sharp critique not only of the French Revolution, but also of all revolutionaries who slide over into the practical idea at the expense of really working out fully and practicing in a truly humanist manner the philosophical dialectic of liberation. In his critique of the French Revolution, Hegel pushes us, as revolutionaries, toward "looking the negative in the face" (Phg. Baillie 93, Miller 19) in order to face the counterrevolution that emerged out of the revolution in the form of the terror. Facing rather than trying to escape or dismiss Hegel on this point will help us in our theorizing not to stop at the critique of capitalism and imperialism, but to work out as well two other issues: (1) Conceptualizing new beginnings, both as the new society and as a new philosophically grounded type of organization to help us get there. (2) Being unafraid to confront and critique as Marxists the whole history of revolutions transformed into their opposites—from France to Russia to today—not as a way of saying forget revolution, but as the serious working out of all of the pitfalls that lay in wait for those who struggle for a total, humanist revolution, which will transform this racist, classist, sexist, heterosexist society.

References

Dunayevskaya, Raya. 1989a. *Philosophy and Revolution: From Hegel to Sartre, and from Marx to Mao.* New York: Columbia University Press.

_____. 1989b. "Introduction to the Morningside Edition." Pp. xxxvi-xliv in Dunayevskaya 1989a.

_____. 2002. *The Power of Negativity: Selected Writings on the Dialectic in Hegel and Marx.* Edited by Peter Hudis and Kevin B. Anderson. Lanham: Lexington Books.

Hegel, G.W.F. [1807] 1910. *Phenomenology of Mind.* Trans. by J.B. Baillie. London: Macmillan.

_____. [1807] 1977. *Phenomenology of Spirit.* Trans. by A.V. Miller. New York: Oxford University Press.

_____. 1956. *Philosophy of History.* Trans. by J. Sibree. New York: Dover.

_____. [1812-31] 1969. *Science of Logic.* Trans. by A.V. Miller. New Jersey: Humanities Press.

Hyppolite, Jean. [1946] 1974. *Genesis and Structure of Hegel's* Phenomenology of Spirit. Evanston: Northwestern University Press.

_____. [1955] 1969. *Studies on Marx and Hegel.* Trans. by John O'Neill. New York: Harper & Row.

Lukács, Georg. [1948] 1975. *The Young Hegel.* Trans. by Rodney Livingstone. London: Merlin Press.

Marcuse, Herbert. 1941. *Reason and Revolution: Hegel and the Rise of Social Theory.* New York: Oxford University Press.

Norman, Richard. 1976. *Hegel's* Phenomenology: *A Philosophical Introduction.* London: Sussex University Press.

Phg. Baillie: Hegel, G.W.F. [1807] 1910. *Phenomenology of Mind.* Trans. by J.B. Baillie. London: Macmillan.

Phg. Miller: Hegel, G.W.F. [1807] 1977. *Phenomenology of Spirit.* Trans. by A.V. Miller. New York: Oxford University Press.

Ritter, Joachim. [1956] 1982. *Hegel and the French Revolution.* Trans. by Richard Dien Winfield. Cambridge: MIT Press.

Rousseau, Jean-Jacques [1762] 1987. *On the Social Contract.* Trans. and ed. by Donald A. Cress Indianapolis: Hackett.

Taylor, Charles. 1974. *Hegel.* New York: Cambridge University Press.

[Adapted from a 1994 presentation to a Marxist-Humanist class series in Chicago.]

4

Lenin's encounter with Hegel

Lenin renewed authentic Marxism not least by a recourse to the "core" of the Hegelian dialectic ("Contradiction is the root of all movement and life") and to the selfsame Hegelian Logic.... Thus, it was precisely orthodox Marxism, restored by Lenin, which presupposed a knowledge of Hegel; as against a vulgar, traditionless, and schematic Marxism which, in isolating Marx—as if his thought emerged like a shot out of a pistol—isolated itself from Marx.
—Ernst Bloch (1962 [1949], 382–83)

He did not read or study Hegel seriously until 1914–15. Also, if one considers it objectively, one notices a great difference in tone and content between the Notebooks on the Dialectic and Materialism and Empirio-Criticism. Lenin's thought becomes supple, alive . . . in a word, dialectical. Lenin did not fully understand the dialectic until 1914, after the collapse of the International. . . . Here we see the significance of the profound reticence of the Stalinists toward the Notebooks, who for a long time put them aside in favor of Materialism and Empirio-Criticism.
—Henri Lefebvre (1959, 85)

The emphasis that Lenin put on "dialectic proper, as a philosophic science" separated him from all other post-Marx Marxists, not only up to the Russian Revolution but also after the conquest of power. ... What was most manifest of what he had gained from the 1914–15 Hegel studies was that the Hegelian dialectic needs to be studied "in and for itself." ... That Lenin kept his direct

encounter with the Hegelian dialectic—his Abstract of Hegel's Science of
Logic—*to himself, however, shows the depth of the economist mire into
which the whole Second International, and not just the German Social-
Democracy, had sunk; revolutionaries stood on the same ground!*
—Raya Dunayevskaya (1991 [1982], 116)

The outbreak of World War I in August 1914 began to undermine liberalism's modernist faith in unilinear progress toward the well-being of all.[1] Established Marxism, itself influenced philosophically by neo-Kantian and positivist evolutionary schemata, was almost as unprepared for the resurgence of violence and destruction in the heart of the world's most "advanced" and democratic capitalist societies. In what was to become the first major crisis of Marxism, the Second International split apart, as fine words about internationalism receded in the face of national chauvinism. As is well known, a small minority, among them Rosa Luxemburg, Karl Liebknecht, Leon Trotsky, and V. I. Lenin, resolutely opposed the war and called for a continuation of proletarian internationalism. One member of that minority, Lenin, went a step further. He took the opportunity of his wartime exile in Switzerland to rethink his fundamental premises by a return to what Marx (1976 [1867], 744) had referred to in *Capital* as "the Hegelian 'contradiction,' which is the source of all dialectics."

Beginning in September 1914, Lenin studied Hegel's masterwork, the *Science of Logic*. None of Lenin's contemporaries who were key leaders in the Marxist movement—neither Karl Kautsky nor Rudolf Hilferding, neither Luxemburg nor Trotsky—ever showed this type of concentration on Hegel's work, not even Lenin's erstwhile philosophical mentor Georgi Plekhanov, whose discussion of Hegel stressed the latter's social and historical works, not his core writings on the dialectic. Lenin's "Abstract of Hegel's *Science of Logic*" (1961a [1914–15]) runs some 150 pages in the English edition of his *Collected Works*. Notes from 1915 on other works by Hegel and on writings on Hegel comprise nearly 100 more pages. Lenin's *Notebooks* consist mainly of long extracts in German from Hegel, interspersed with commentary, marginalia, and his own conceptualizations of the dialectic.

---

1. This article originally appeared as Kevin B. Anderson, "Lenin's Encounter with Hegel After Eighty Years: A Critical Assessment" in *Science & Society* 59:3 (1995), pp. 298-319. © 1995 Guilford Press. Reproduced here with permission from The Guilford Press.

In addition, Lenin wrote in this period a five-page essay fragment, "On the Question of Dialectics."

The "Abstract of Hegel's *Science of Logic*" was first published in Russian in 1929, five years after Lenin's death, as *Lenin Miscellany*, Vol. 9. In 1930, the additional notes on Hegel were also published, together with a mass of other material on philosophical issues, 200 pages of which were written before 1914–15. In 1933, these two volumes were combined into a single one entitled *Philosophical Notebooks*. In these and subsequent Stalinist editions, both the title and the combining of extraneous pre-1914 material with the 1914–15 *Hegel Notebooks* served to de-emphasize the extent of Lenin's interest in Hegel from 1914 onwards. In keeping with this tradition, the six-page preface by the Institute of Marxism-Leninism in Moscow to the present English edition of the *Philosophical Notebooks* manages to devote less than half a page to discussion of Lenin's study of Hegel.

Lenin's *Hegel Notebooks* were published in German in 1932, in French in 1938, and in English and Italian in 1958. Leading Marxist theoreticians such as Henri Lefebvre (1967 [1938], 1969 [1947], 1957), Georg Lukács (1975 [1948]), Ernst Bloch (1962 [1949]), C. L. R. James (1980 [1948]), Raya Dunayevskaya (1988 [1958], 1989a [1973], 1991 [1982]), Lucio Colletti (1958), Iring Fetscher (1971), and Louis Althusser (1971) have also commented extensively on them from a variety of vantage points. Nonetheless, Lenin's notes on Hegel from 1914–15 and their impact both on his thought and on subsequent Marxist theory remain a surprisingly obscure issue. Part of this is because, as Henri Lefebvre pointed out in the passage that forms part of the epigraph to this essay, official Stalinist ideology had little room for such notions, preferring instead Lenin's crudely materialist earlier work on philosophy, *Materialism and Empirio-Criticism* (1908). For example, nothing from the 1914–15 *Hegel Notebooks* can be found in the 800-page International Publishers anthology, *Selected Works in One Volume* (Lenin 1971). But this is also true of liberal scholarship. The rival collection edited by Robert Tucker (1975), *The Lenin Anthology*, includes only four pages of this material among its 750 pages. The same is true of standard reference works. Neither Tom Bottomore's (1983) *Dictionary of Marxist Thought*, in which many of the entries are written by leading Marxist scholars, nor David Miller's more liberal-oriented (1991) *Blackwell Encyclopedia of Political Thought*, mentions Lenin's study of Hegel in either of their fairly extensive entries on Lenin. Even among the four full-length studies of Lenin's life and thought that have appeared since the 1960s, two of them (Harding 1978–81, Cliff 1975–79) do not even take up Lenin's *Hegel Notebooks*, while the other two (Liebman 1975, Service 1985) offer interesting but too brief discussions of them. Thus, reading or rereading Lenin on Hegel means also reading him against the grain of the standard interpretations of his work.

Lenin's reading of Hegel in 1914–15 is important to us today for at least four reasons. First, it constitutes a serious, interesting, and original reading of Hegel in its own right by a major Marxist theorist. Second, it offers us important insight into the methodological foundations of Lenin's better-known post-1914 writings on imperialism, the state, national liberation, and revolution. Third, it forms part of the pathway that led leading "Western" Marxists such as Georg Lukács to develop from the 1920s onward what has often been termed Hegelian Marxism. Fourth, Lenin's work on Hegel, despite some serious flaws, offers an example for today of how, if it is to be a living body of ideas rather than a stale dogmatism, Marxism needs at every crisis point to re-examine its premises. In this essay (for a more extensive discussion see Anderson 1995), I address mainly the first of these points, while also touching on the last one.

What Lenin achieved from his study of Hegel

To grasp Lenin's achievement in the *Hegel Notebooks*, it is important to view them against his crude early work, *Materialism and Empirio-Criticism*. The existential Marxist Maurice Merleau-Ponty (1973 [1955], 59–60) once termed this work "pre-Kantian" as he asked pointedly how from such a standpoint "one could introduce a Marxist dialectic"? While a few commentators (Althusser 1971, Ruben 1977) have attempted to salvage this work for contemporary Marxism, their arguments are for the most part unconvincing, especially since they tend to downplay even Marx's debt to Hegel. In Lenin's 1908 work, much of it a critique of the positivistic conceptions of Ernst Mach, he spends over 300 pages arguing such concepts as the material existence of the objective world independent of human consciousness. Not content to charge his various opponents with idealism or solipsism, he evidently feels the necessity to show their "reactionary" character by attributing a necessary link to mysticism or the conservative religious views of the British philosopher George Berkeley, by the use of parallel quotations. Seldom if ever is Marx cited as a source—but there are plenty of quotes on materialism from Feuerbach, Plekhanov, and Engels. Lenin (1962 [1908], 182) repeatedly ties his opponents, and idealism generally, to mysticism and religion: "Philosophical idealism is nothing but a disguised and embellished ghost story." The extreme crudity of Lenin's materialism is seen in his well-known statement that theory is nothing more than a direct reflection of objective reality: "The recognition of theory as a copy, as an approximate copy of objective reality, is materialism" (Lenin 1962 [1908], 265). He writes further (1962 [1908], 267) that "the materialist regards sensation, perception, idea, and the mind of man generally, as an image of objective reality." This is what is often termed Lenin's photocopy or reflection theory of knowledge. Any other view means falling into mysticism and spiritualism, Lenin maintains.

Six years later, in the 1914–15 "Abstract of Hegel's *Science of Logic*," Lenin moves away from such crudities, and toward a notion of Marxism as the unity of idealism and materialism, a notion already present in Marx's 1844 *Economic and Philosophical Manuscripts*, a text that was not yet published in Lenin's lifetime. One example of this is found in Lenin's notes on Hegel's early chapter in the *Science of Logic* on Being-for-Self, where he concludes that the "ideal" and the "real" are not absolute opposites, any more than are "immediacy" and "mediation." This is no small point, for it constitutes a major advance from the notion developed by Engels and Plekhanov, and followed by the whole Second International, including Lenin himself before 1914, of dividing philosophical perspectives rigidly into "two camps," those of idealism and materialism. Let us examine this point more closely as it is developed in Lenin's *Hegel Notebooks*. First, he takes down the following passage from Hegel's text, from the middle of the chapter on Being-for-Self: "The *ideality* of Being-for-Self as a totality thus passes over [*schlägt um*], in the first place, to *reality*, and that too in its most fixed, abstract form, as the *one*" (Hegel 1969 [1812–31], 164, trans. altered slightly). Then Lenin makes the following statement, an apparent response to the single sentence quoted above:

> The idea of the transformation of the ideal into the real is *profound!* Very important for history. But also in the personal life of man it is evident that there is much truth in this. Against vulgar materialism. NB. The difference of the ideal from the material is also

not unconditional, not boundless [*überschwenglich*]. (Lenin 1961a [1914–15], 114)

While the above remark by Lenin is hardly a thorough exposition of Hegel's category of Being-for-Self, it is a key statement of what Lenin is developing for himself out of his reading of Hegel's text. Here, having barely begun his study of Hegel's text, Lenin has started to identify himself fairly openly with Hegel's idealism. This is very different from his pre-1914 view. Then he had, to be sure—as had Engels and Plekhanov—defended Hegel's "objective idealism" against Kantianism. Now it is not only a question of Hegel as merely the greatest idealist philosopher, but also one of using Hegel's idealism to critique narrow and crude forms of Marxist materialism. Most important in this is Lenin's recovery, in his appellation "vulgar materialism," of Marx's critique of one-sided, non-dialectical, and contemplative forms of materialism, as seen for example in the first *Thesis on Feuerbach*.

Somewhat later in his notes on the *Science of Logic*, by now having reached the Doctrine of Essence, the second part of Hegel's book, Lenin summarizes and comments on the key Hegelian categories Identity, Difference, and Contradiction and, in doing so, also appropriates for himself Hegel's concept of self-movement. In this discussion, Lenin summarizes and appears to agree with Hegel's critique of the Aristotelian laws of identity and non-contradiction, whereby if A = A, it cannot at the same time be not-A. In his notes Lenin (1961a [1914–15], 134–35) then comments: "Therefore Hegel elucidates the one-sidedness, the incorrectness, of the 'law of Identity' (A = A)." For Hegel, Identity leads not to harmony, but to Difference. Once he gets into the key and often-discussed section on Contradiction, Lenin (1961a [1914–15], 138), writes: "This is acute and correct. Every concrete thing, every concrete something, stands in multifarious and often contradictory relations to everything else, ergo it is itself and some other." Lenin now makes Hegel's "law of Contradiction" and his concept of "self-movement [*Selbstbewegung*]" or, more generally, his "dialectic," not only the key to an understanding of Hegel but also of Marxism. First, he takes down five full paragraphs from Hegel's brief section on the "Law of Contradiction." The extract from Hegel includes the following material:

But it is one of the fundamental prejudices of logic as hitherto understood and of ordinary thinking, that Contradiction is not so characteristically essential and immanent a determination as Identity; but in fact, if it were a question of grading the two determinations and they had to be kept separate, then Contradiction would have to be taken as the profounder determination and more characteristic of Essence. For as against Contradiction, Identity is merely the determination of the simple immediate, of dead Being; but Contradiction is the root of all movement and vitality; it is only in so far as something has Contradiction within it that it moves, has an urge and activity. . . . Further, it is not to be taken merely as an abnormality which only occurs here and there, but is rather the negative as determined in the sphere of Essence, the principle of all self-movement [*Selbstbewegung*], which consists solely in an exhibition of it. (Hegel 1969 [1812–31], 439–40)

Here we are some distance from crude materialism. The key has become "self-movement" and not merely "movement." And this self-movement arises from within the subject matter. Thus, it is not a steady "flow" or the product of external force, but of the inner contradictions of the subject matter that constitutes the heart of dialectical development and change. Putting it in terms of social theory, the "internal contradictions" of a given society are the key to grasping changes within that society, changes that develop as a process of self-development and self-movement.

Lenin (1961a [1914–15], 141) becomes very enthusiastic over having discovered this, not in Marx, but directly in Hegel:

Movement and "self-movement" (this *NB!* arbitrary (independent) spontaneous, *internally-necessary* movement), "change," "movement and life," "the principle of every self-movement," "impulse" (*Trieb*) to "movement" and "activity"—opposite of "dead being."—Who would believe that this is the core of "Hegelianism," of abstract and abstruse (difficult, absurd?) Hegelianism??

Thus, movement and self-movement have their basis in the internal contradictions of things and social phenomena. In his view of this movement as at the same time spontaneous and internally necessary, Lenin is rejecting the crudely deterministic models of the Marxism of the Second International, while at the same time identifying with Hegel's notion of an historically and socially grounded concept of subjectivity. This concept of self-movement through contradiction, not Identity or "dead Being," is for Lenin the core of Hegel's *Science of Logic*, something which he is evidently surprised to discover. Here is how Lenin (1961a [1914–15], 143) sums up what he has taken from Hegel's concept of Contradiction:

> (1) Ordinary perception grasps the difference and the contradiction, but not *the transition* from the one to the other, *but this is the most important.* (2) Intelligent reflection and understanding. Reflection grasps the contradiction, *expresses* it, brings things into relation to one another, allows the "concept to show through the contradiction," but does not express the concept of things and their relation. (3) Thinking reason (mind) [*denkende Vernunft*] sharpens the blunt difference of variety, the mere manifold of imagination, to the *essential* difference, into *Opposition*. Only when the contradictions reach the peak do the manifold entities become active (*regsam*) and lively in relation to one another,—they acquire that negativity which is the *inner pulsation of self-movement and vitality.*

What is especially new here is the relationship Lenin is drawing between what would intuitively appear to be total opposites: on one hand spontaneous self-movement, and on the other "thinking reason" [*denkende Vernunft*]. Contradiction occurs not only between inanimate forces, but also and most importantly, in the lives and interactions of human beings, who possess thinking reason.

But it is in his study of the concluding part of Hegel's *Science of Logic*, the "Doctrine of the Notion [Concept]," where Lenin goes furthest, beginning with his discussion early in that section of the chapter on the Syllogism. Here Lenin develops in his notes what he calls "Two aphorisms." He directs them against the established Marxist philosophy that he had been brought up on, and against Plekhanov especially. He entitles them, "Regarding the question of the criticism of contemporary Kantianism, Machism, etc.":

> Plekhanov criticizes Kantianism (and agnosticism in general) more from the vulgar materialistic than the dialectical materialistic point of view, *insofar* as he merely rejects their views from the out-

side, but does not correct them (as Hegel corrected Kant), deepening, generalizing, broadening them, showing the *connections* and *transitions* of each and every notion. 2. Marxists criticized (at the beginning of the twentieth century) the Kantians and Humists more in a Feuerbachian (and Büchnerian), than a Hegelian, manner. (Lenin 1961a [1914–15], 179)

There are several major issues here. First, there is the application of the term "vulgar materialist" to the chief philosopher of Russian Marxism, Plekhanov. Second, there is the issue of becoming "Hegelian." Never before has Lenin suggested that Marxists would need to carry out a "Hegelian" analysis. Up to now, he has pointed more to the need to study Hegel as a way of really understanding Marx, etc. Here, he implies that on certain philosophical issues such as the critique of Kantianism, an analysis in "a Hegelian manner" is called for. Thus, I would argue, Lenin has become the first Hegelian Marxist of the 20th century. Third, there are strong indications here of a self-critique of his earlier views. While many Marxists had written against Kantianism, only in Russian Marxism did Machism become a major issue. Lenin and Plekhanov were the two major figures to critique Mach within Russian Marxism. Thus, Lenin's reference to "criticism of contemporary Kantianism, Machism, etc.," which he places "at the beginning of the 20th century," very likely refers not only to Plekhanov's work, but also to his own *Materialism and Empirio-Criticism*.

Still in Hegel's chapter on the Syllogism, Lenin writes another aphorism, perhaps the most quoted one of all from the *Hegel Notebooks*. It reads: "Aphorism: It is impossible fully to grasp Marx's *Capital*, and especially its first chapter, if you have not studied through and understood the whole of Hegel's *Logic*. Consequently, none of the Marxists for the past 1/2 century have understood Marx!!" (Lenin 1961a [1914–15], 180). This is the most dramatically explicit statement by Lenin anywhere on the centrality of Hegel to Marxism. Let us examine its implications in detail. First, he calls for Marxists to study "the whole of Hegel's *Logic*." Lenin, who was brought up on Engels and Plekhanov and their discussions of materialist dialectics, now calls for others to follow him in studying the whole of the *Science of Logic*. Earlier, Engels had written in his best-known philosophical book, *Ludwig Feuerbach and the End of Classical German Philosophy*, that Marxists needed to adopt materialistically Hegel's "method," but to reject his "system." Lenin does not mention that type of division between system and method here, and his call for the study of *the whole* of the *Science of Logic* could easily be read as a move beyond Engels' simplistic division. Secondly, where the previous aphorism suggested the need to go to Hegel in order to critique what Lenin regards as rivals to Marxism, such as Kantianism and Machism, here the emphasis is quite different. Marxists need to study Hegel directly in order to understand the most important theoretical work in all of Marxism, *Capital*.

This is true for the whole of that work, but "especially its first chapter." This emphasis on the first chapter is a very innovative one for Marxism in 1914. Although he never explicitly mentions the section on the fetishism of commodities from chapter one of *Capital* in his Abstract, something which Lukács was the first to stress in *History and Class Consciousness* (1971 [1923]), we can see that the dialectic rather than economics is beginning to emerge for Lenin as the center of *Capital* and thus perhaps even the whole of Marxism.[2]

The third point here for Lenin is once again his break with his own philosophic past, especially *Materialism and Empirio-Criticism*. Here I would argue that, as in the two previous aphorisms, Lenin would seem to include himself amongst the Marxists who, by not having "studied through and understood the *whole* of Hegel's *Logic*," created a situation where "none of the Marxists for the past 1/2 century have understood Marx." I interpret this as a very grave charge by Lenin, not only against other theorists, but also against himself. Once again, I argue this in part on the basis that both this aphorism and the one explicitly criticizing Plekhanov are preceded by the phrase "criticism of contemporary Kantianism, Machism, etc." Who else besides Lenin and Plekhanov were so preoccupied with these issues?

Somewhat later in his notes on the *Science of Logic*, as he enters that work's penultimate chapter, "The Idea of Cognition," Lenin continues a procedure developed in earlier sections of his *Notebooks*, that of placing

---

2.   While Lenin's statement is by no means as explicit or as far-reaching as was Lukács's (1971 [1923], 170) remark that in *Capital* "the chapter dealing with the fetish character of the commodity contains within itself the whole of historical materialism," it should also be pointed out that by 1923 Lukács had not read Lenin's *Hegel Notebooks*, which had not yet been published. Still, it would appear that Lenin anticipated by several years Lukács' rediscovery of the integral relationship of Marxism to Hegel. However, Lukács explicitly and publicly criticized Engels, something Lenin never did. For an intricate but ultimately unsuccessful attempt at a virtual "deconstruction" of Lenin's aphorism after which we are told that Lenin did not need to read Hegel after all, *see* Althusser (1971).

long extracts from Hegel on the left side of the page, and his own "translation" on the right-hand side. His own statement at this point is one of his most far-reaching: "Man's cognition not only reflects the objective world, but creates it" (Lenin 1961a [1914–15], 212). He has traveled a very long distance from the crude reflection theory of *Materialism and Empirio-Criticism* if cognition "creates" rather than merely "reflects" the world. By cognition here Lenin surely means not only philosophical or scientific cognition as developed so far by Hegel in the Idea of Cognition, but also the type of cognition embodied in revolutionary theory, since that is after all his focus, his aim in reading Hegel. To be sure, this Cognition reflects and describes the world, which to Lenin would mean the material and historical world. In addition, however, as Lenin now holds, Cognition "creates" the world. In many respects, this aphorism is the high point of the entire *Hegel Notebooks* in terms of Lenin's rethinking and reorganization of his pre-1914 philosophical categories.[3] But, from now on, he turns back somewhat toward traditional Marxist materialism: in the concluding pages of his "Abstract of Hegel's *Science of Logic*," Lenin becomes more and more concerned with the issues of practice and materialism, although he does continue to refer to subjectivity.

The most substantial part of Lenin's *Hegel Notebooks* besides the 1914–15 "Abstract of Hegel's *Science of Logic*" is the nearly sixty pages of notes he wrote in 1915 on Hegel's three-volume *History of Philosophy*. Lenin's notes only cover about the first half of this massive work, and are notable more for his general statements on dialectics than for his commentary on Hegel's text on Greek philosophy. At one crucial point in these notes, Lenin (1961b [1915], 276) seems to argue for some type of unity of idealism and materialism, and definitely for the merits of an "intelligent idealism": "Intelligent idealism is nearer to intelligent materialism than is stupid materialism. Dialectical idealism instead of intelligent; metaphysical, undeveloped, dead, vulgar, static, instead of stupid." While the second sentence above is very obscure, and illustrates some of the difficulties in analyzing a text that was obviously not intended for publication, the first sentence is a remarkably forceful statement on the unity of certain types of idealism with materialism. Assuming a similarity between what he here calls "stupid materialism" and his earlier developed category, "vul-

---

3.   This aphorism led to some rather tortuous attempts by Soviet philosophers to argue that Lenin is here merely summarizing (but disagreeing) with Hegel (Kedrov 1970).

gar materialism," the above can be read as a very sharp critique of the Marxism of the Second International. More importantly, it represents a reaching back toward the perspective of Marx's 1844 *Economic and Philosophical Manuscripts*, a text unknown to Lenin, but one in which Marx (1968 [1844], 577), as is well known, pointed to the unity of idealism and materialism, terming his standpoint one of a "thoroughgoing Naturalism or Humanism which differentiates itself from Idealism as well as Materialism and is at the same time their unifying truth."

In another statement on the following page of his notes, Lenin goes on to make explicit to himself that it is Hegelian dialectics (intelligent idealism) as against the Plekhanov-type philosophical materialism (stupid materialism) that he is seeing as the dividing line. No longer is it a question of accepting Plekhanov's philosophy—as in 1908—while opposing his political conclusions. Here Lenin (1961b [1915], 277) makes his most explicit attack anywhere on what he views as Plekhanov's failure to grapple with Hegelian dialectics in a serious way: "Work out: Plekhanov wrote probably nearly 1000 pages (Beltov against Bogdanov against Kantians basic questions, etc. etc. on philosophy (dialectic). There is in them *nil* about the Larger Logic, its thoughts (*i.e.*, dialectic *proper*, as a philosophic science) nil!!" These statements show the extent to which Lenin was breaking with the foundation of his early philosophic concepts, the concepts of both mainstream Bolshevism and Menshevism: Plekhanovite philosophical materialism. The above is a sharp critique of established Marxism and a pointing back toward Marx's own 1844 *Economic and Philosophical Manuscripts*. It is also important to note, however, that Lenin never made public these attacks on Plekhanov and vulgar materialism, not even in his writings on Hegel and dialectics after 1917.

The closest Lenin comes to making his 1914–15 *Hegel Notebooks* public is his 1922 article "On the Significance of Militant Materialism," written for *Pod Znamenem Marksizma* (Under the Banner of Marxism), a major new theoretical journal. This article soon appeared in German as well, in 1925, although Karl Korsch was already aware of it even earlier, making a passage from it the epigraph to his *Marxism and Philosophy* (1923). In this 1922 article, Lenin (1965b [1922], 233) eases his readers into the subject of Hegel by declaring that although the materialism of natural science was surely to be welcomed in the struggle against "clerical obscurantism," on the other hand "it must be realized that no natural science and no materialism can hold its own in the struggles against the onslaught of bourgeois ideas and the restoration of the bourgeois world outlook unless it stands on a solid philosophical ground." Therefore, one must be a "consistent," "modern," and "Marxist" materialist, "a dialectical materialist," Lenin continues. Then comes his explicit advocacy of the direct study of Hegelian dialectics, linked directly to his post-1914 concept of new revolutionary subjects outside the working class, in the anti-colonial national liberation struggles in Asia:

> In order to attain this aim, the contributors to *Pod Znamenem Marksizma* must arrange for the systematic study of Hegelian dialectics from a materialist standpoint, i.e., the dialectics which Marx applied practically in his *Capital* and in his historical and political works, and applied so successfully that now every day of the awakening to life and struggle of the new classes in the East (Japan, India, and China)—i.e., the hundreds of millions of human beings who form the greater part of the world population and whose historical passivity and historical torpor have hitherto conditioned the stagnation and decay of many advanced European countries—every day of the awakening to life of new peoples and new classes serves as a fresh confirmation of Marxism. (Lenin 1965b [1922], 233)

Sensing perhaps that his readers would be skeptical not only on ideological grounds but also because of the difficulty of understanding Hegel, Lenin (1965b [1922], 233–34) adds:

> Of course, this study, this interpretation, this propaganda of Hegelian dialectics is extremely difficult, and the first experiments in this direction will undoubtedly be accompanied by errors. But only he who never does anything never makes mistakes. Taking as our basis Marx's method of applying materialistically conceived Hegelian dialectics, we can and should elaborate this dialectics from all aspects, print in the journal excerpts from Hegel's principal works, interpret them materialistically and comment on them with the help of examples of dialectics in the sphere of economic and political relations, which recent history, especially modem imperialist war and revolution, provides in unusual abundance. In

my opinion, the editors and contributors of *Pod Znamenem Mark-sizma* should be a kind of "Society of Materialist Friends of Hegelian Dialectics." . . . Unless it sets itself such a task and systematically fulfills it, materialism cannot be militant materialism.

This essay's most striking feature is its open call for intensive study not of dialectics in general, but specifically of Hegelian dialectics, and for the publication of Hegel's writings in Soviet Russia's leading Marxist journal. It is Lenin's fullest public indication of what he had developed in his *Hegel Notebooks*. It was presented, however, under the category of "militant materialism," rather than what he had pointed to in the *Hegel Notebooks*, the unity of idealism and materialism, a concept which re-connected to the young Marx.

The limits of Lenin's reading of Hegel

One type of limitation of Lenin's Hegel studies is an external one related to his failure to publish them or to refer publicly to the most profound and daring concepts he had developed there. In his frequent public statements on dialectics after 1914, there is sometimes a strange combination of, on the one hand, implicit references to the new vantage point of the *Hegel Notebooks* and, on the other hand, praise of what is termed "vulgar materialism" in those same *Notebooks* as a valuable source for Marxist theory. Dunayevskaya (1989a [1973]) has termed this problem Lenin's "philosophic ambivalence." A good example of it is found in the much-praised (*see, e.g.*, Marcuse 1941) section on dialectics in Lenin's 1921 pamphlet "Once Again on the Trade Unions." Lenin (1965a [1921], 90) begins this discussion on dialectics by touting Bukharin for "his theoretical ability and keen interest in getting at the theoretical roots of every question." A few lines later, however, he attacks Bukharin's statement that "neither the political nor the economic factor can be ignored." Lenin (1965a [1921], 91) adds, raising the issue of totality:

> The gist of his theoretical mistake in this case is substitution of eclecticism for the dialectical interplay of politics and economics (which we find in Marxism). His theoretical attitude is: "on the one hand, and on the other," "the one and the other." That is eclec-

ticism. Dialectics requires an all-round consideration of relationships in their concrete development but not a patchwork of bits and pieces.

Lenin (1965a [1921], 94) also brings in Hegel directly, giving the following definition of dialectical logic, in which he rounds out the concept of dialectics as totality alluded to above:

> Dialectical logic demands that we should go further. Firstly, if we are to have a true knowledge of an object we must look at and examine all its facets, its connections and "mediations." That is something we cannot ever hope to achieve completely, but the rule of comprehensiveness is a safeguard against mistakes and rigidity. Secondly, dialectical logic requires that an object should be taken in development, in change, in "self-movement" (as Hegel sometimes puts it). This is not immediately obvious in respect of such an object as a tumbler, but it, too, is in flux, and this holds especially true for its purpose, use and *connection* with the surrounding world. Thirdly, a full "definition" of an object must include the whole of human experience, both as a criterion of truth and a practical indicator of its connection with human wants. Fourthly, dialectical logic holds that "truth is always concrete ..."

Especially noteworthy here is the explicit mention of Hegelian dialectics, and the brief elaboration of some of the key categories from the *Hegel Notebooks*: interconnection, contradiction, and self-movement, among others.

The way Lenin does so, however, also raises the question of his ambivalence toward his new philosophical explorations of Hegelian dialectics. In the above-cited discussion of dialectical logic, he suddenly reverts to bringing in Plekhanov, who was (as we have seen) nearly dismissed as a vulgar materialist in the unpublished *Notebooks*. This is seen when Lenin's fourth point on dialectical logic is quoted in full:

> Fourthly, dialectical logic holds that "truth is always concrete, never abstract," as the late Plekhanov liked to say after Hegel. (Let me add in parenthesis for the benefit of young Party members that you *cannot* hope to become a *real*, intelligent Communist without making a study—and I mean *study*—of all of Plekhanov's philosophical

writings, because nothing better has been written on Marxism anywhere in the world.) *Ibid.*

Lenin's attached footnote continues his praise of Plekhanov:

> By the way, it would be a good thing, first, if the current edition of Plekhanov's works contained a special volume or volumes of all his philosophical articles, with detailed indexes, etc., to be included in a series of standard textbooks on communism; secondly, I think the workers' state must demand that professors of philosophy should have a knowledge of Plekhanov's exposition of Marxist philosophy and ability to impart it to their students. *Ibid.*

Thus, the discussion of dialectics in Lenin's pamphlet, as interesting and innovative as it was, nonetheless avoids mentioning any of the critiques of Plekhanov, which occur numerous times in the *Hegel Notebooks*, whether around the issue of vulgar materialism or on Plekhanov's never having made a systematic study of Hegel's *Science of Logic*. Was this done deliberately to soften Lenin's otherwise "Hegelian" argument for his Bolshevik audience? Few of them, if any, had also become involved in the direct study of Hegel. Mainly they held Plekhanovite-type views of Marxism as materialism, as had Lenin himself before 1914. Or was Lenin himself ambivalent in his own mind about his new work around dialectics?

Whether it was more a matter of his own reluctance to add yet another controversy for his fellow Bolsheviks to grapple with, or whether he was too occupied with concrete political questions—such as the national question, the bureaucratization of the new Soviet state, not to mention civil war, economic reconstruction, and the attempt to extend the Russian revolution internationally to Europe and Asia—Lenin did for one reason or another fail to finish or publish his study of dialectics. He also left a trail of somewhat ambivalent statements behind on dialectics. While the main thrust of his public statements on dialectics was toward Hegelian Marxism, as seen in the Trade Union Debate, he was also capable of referring in glowing terms to Plekhanov. This is a step backward from his characterization of Plekhanov in the *Hegel Notebooks* as a "vulgar materialist" who had never made a serious study of Hegel's *Science of Logic*, a characterization Lenin never made public at any time after writing it in those 1914–15 *Notebooks*.

In 1920, Lenin also allowed the reprinting without changes of his *Materialism and Empirio-Criticism*. In a very brief one-paragraph preface to the new edition, Lenin (1962 [1908], 21) expressed the hope that the book would "prove useful as an aid to acquaintance with the philosophy of Marxism, dialectical materialism." Whether intended or not, its reissue with a new preface that did not mention his *Hegel Notebooks* muddied the waters considerably as to what was Lenin's post-1914 concept of dialectic. It is a prime example of Lenin's philosophical ambivalence.

A second limitation of Lenin's 1914–15 Hegel studies is an internal one, found in his one-sided and truncated interpretations even in the *Notebooks* of several key Hegelian concepts. One important example is Lenin's reading of Hegel's discussion of the relationship between theory and practice in the penultimate chapter of the *Science of Logic*, "The Idea of Cognition," and especially the last section of that chapter, "The Idea of the Good." Here, once again, Dunayevskaya (1989a [1973], xxix) has pointed to the crucial issue, writing that Lenin became so enamored of Hegel's reference here to the Practical Idea, that "[n]othing, in fact, led Lenin back to the Idea of Theory and away from dependence on the Practical Idea," resulting in a one-sided reading of a crucial Hegelian text. Lukács (1975 [1948], 350), however, offers a sharply divergent interpretation of Hegel's and Lenin's discussion here of theory and practice. He praises Lenin for seeing in Hegel's text "the concrete superiority of the practical over the theoretical Idea," but here Lukács's discussion is surprisingly superficial. Keeping these interpretations by Dunayevskaya and Lukács in mind, let us turn to Lenin's discussion.

In this part of the *Hegel Notebooks*, Lenin (1961a [1914–15], 213) tends to read Hegel as follows: "Practice is higher than (theoretical) knowledge, for it has not only the dignity of universality, but also of immediate actuality." At one point, he takes down the following passage from Hegel (1969 [1812–31], 818) in full:

> In the Theoretical Idea the subjective Notion, as the universal that lacks any determination of its own, stands opposed to the objective world from which it takes to itself a determinate content and filling. But in the Practical Idea it is as actual that it confronts the actual; but the certainty of itself which the subject possesses in

being determined in and for itself is a certainty of its own actuality and of the non-actuality of the world . . .

Lenin seems to read the above as a move beyond a merely Theoretical Idea. The above passage is also an extremely idealistic statement, especially in the last part on the "non-actuality of the world," which suggests that the Practical Idea can negate the actual world. Lenin comments: "i.e., that the world does not satisfy man and man decides to change it by his activity" (1961a [1914–15], 213). To Lenin, practice stands opposed to the world of actuality, but not merely quantitatively or materialistically: practice embodied in a live human subject that is certain of "its own actuality" to the point where it "negates" the existing social world. For Lenin here, the context is obviously social revolution; however, the key to revolution is not only objective forces, but also the development of a self-conscious subjectivity aware of its own actuality.

In the same part of Hegel's text, however, Lenin also fails to take down clear and blunt passages such as the following one, a few pages later, passages that strongly qualify the primacy of the Practical Idea: " . . . the Practical Idea still lacks the moment of the Theoretical Idea" (Hegel 1969 [1812–31], 821). Lenin skips over most of this passage and several similar ones that either critique the limitations of the Practical Idea or stress the importance of the Theoretical Idea. While he takes down passages where Hegel critiques the limits of the Theoretical Idea, he never takes down any of Hegel's strong critiques of the Practical Idea. Lenin (1961a [1914–15], 217) makes the following commentary on Hegel's discussion of the Idea of the Good as a whole:

> The "syllogism of action." For Hegel *action*, practice, is the *logical conclusion* of the figure of logic. And this is true! Of course, not in the sense that the figure of logic has by its Otherness in the practice of man (= absolute idealism), but vice versa: the practice of man, repeated billions of times, fastens itself in the consciousness of man by the figures of logic.

Apparently, he is so excited by his discovery that the philosopher of mediation and of abstracted human thought is, in his own way, also a philosopher of action, that Lenin misses the multi-faceted nature of Hegel's presentation.

Some notes toward an assessment of Lenin's contribution to Marxism

How does all of the above relate to a more general assessment of Lenin? Here, I would like to offer some necessarily brief comments (for more elaboration *see* Anderson 1995), which will take the form more of theses or propositions than of theoretical arguments.

Lenin's yearning to solve philosophical problems at the level of practice, noted above, is not an obscure point, but a crucial one that has plagued twentieth century Marxism as a whole. I would suggest that, too often, Marxists have acted as if practice alone could settle theoretical and political questions, or that it alone could bring about a new, liberated society. This is not good enough, especially not today, as Marxism has entered one of its deepest crises ever. The recourse to practice cannot answer the question of why the collapse of Communism in Europe during the years 1989–91 has derailed not only Stalinist groups and parties, but also why since 1989 even strands of Marxism that had separated themselves from Stalinism have also been placed on the defensive. Nor can the recourse to practice answer the claims of a whole range of rival philosophies to Marxism, from pragmatism to poststructuralism, each of them arguing that Marxism is a totalizing discourse that blocks us from perceiving pluralism and difference. To the extent that it attempts to answer core philosophical issues via practice, including by the building of a vanguard party to lead—an elitist and undialectical notion to which Lenin clung even after 1914—Lenin's Marxism cannot help us very much to confront today's crisis of Marxism, or to find a way out.

There are two levels, however, at which Lenin's Marxism may be vital to us today. First, there is the level of the dialectic proper. As Lukács (1971 [1923], 1–2) suggested, writing after the collapse of established Marxism in his time, it is not "the uncritical acceptance of the results of Marx's investigations" but "the revolutionary dialectic" that is the core of Marxism. As much as capitalism and imperialism have changed since Lenin's day, if Lukács is correct, Lenin's work on the dialectic in the *Hegel Notebooks* could be the most important and enduring part of his Marxism. Its importance could very well continue even as other aspects of his Marxism are being called into question.

At a second level, however, Lenin's theoretical work as a whole during the years 1914–17 can serve as an example for today and the future. In order to confront the crisis of Marxism in 1914, as we have seen, he sought a solution not in practice alone—although he did work mightily during the years 1914 and after to reconstruct a revolutionary international and to prepare for the coming revolution in Russia—but also in the rethinking and reworking of the most fundamental issues in his theorizing. As we have seen, he began with philosophy, in the *Hegel Notebooks*. It should also be noted that then, unlike so many other Hegelian Marxists, Lenin moved from philosophy to political and economic theory, the results of which are seen in works such as *Imperialism* (1916) and *State and Revolution* (1917). In so doing, he developed new conceptualizations of capital and the state to fit early twentieth century conditions. At the same time, he also developed a newer, broader view of the forces of negativity and contradiction within and outside the system.

Thus, in Lenin's conceptualization, paired with imperialism is its dialectical opposite, the anti-colonial national liberation movements of what is today termed the Third World. And paired with the more centralized and bureaucratic capitalist state is the demand from below for direct democracy in the form of soviets or councils. Despite its flaws, Lenin's rethinking of Marxism during the years 1914–17 is an example of the dialectic in action.[4] For those today who want to continue in the tradition of Marx, it suggests that the taking into account of new phenomena needs to be combined with the reconceptualization of the dialectic itself by going creatively to its source: Hegel.

References

Althusser, Louis. 1971. *Lenin and Philosophy and Other Essays*. Trans. Ben Brewster. London: New Left Books.

---

4. I am leaving aside the issue of how Lenin concretized his new dialectical concepts once the Bolsheviks came to power. Beginning in the spring of 1918, there was much backtracking and even betrayal, whether on soviet democracy (Farber 1990) or on national liberation (Carrère d'Encausse 1987), all of this rooted in Lenin's failure even in 1914–17 to rethink the dialectics of organization and philosophy in a way that could overcome the elitist and undialectical form of the vanguard party to lead (Dunayevskaya 1989b). That doctrine of the vanguard party to lead increasingly undermined the more liberatory content of the Russian Revolution. Stalin and his cohorts of course built on these and other contradictions in Lenin's thought, twisting them into something they termed "Marxism-Leninism," promulgated as the ruling ideology of their totalitarian state-capitalist regime.

Anderson, Kevin. 1995. *Lenin, Hegel, and Western Marxism: A Critical Study*. Urbana: University of Illinois Press.

Bloch, Ernst. 1962 (1949). *Subjekt-Objekt: Erläuterungen zu Hegel*. Frankfurt: Suhrkamp Verlag.

Bottomore, Tom, ed. 1983. *A Dictionary of Marxist Thought*. Cambridge: Harvard University Press.

Carrère d'Encausse, Hélène. 1987. *Le grand Défi: Bolsheviks et nations (1917-1930)*. Paris: Éditions Flammarion.

Cliff, Tony. 1978–81. *Lenin*. 4 Vols. London: Pluto Press.

Colletti, Lucio. 1958. "Il marxismo e Hegel." In Lenin, *Quaderni filosofici*. Milan: Feltrinelli Editore, pp. ix-clxviii.

Dunayevskaya, Raya. 1988 (1958). *Marxism and Freedom: From 1776 until Today*. New York: Columbia University Press.

_____. 1989a (1973). *Philosophy and Revolution: From Hegel to Sartre, and from Marx to Mao*. New York: Columbia University Press.

_____. 1989b. *The Philosophic Moment of Marxist-Humanism*. Chicago: News and Letters.

_____. 1991 (1982). *Rosa Luxemburg, Women's Liberation, and Marx's Philosophy of Revolution*. Urbana: University of Illinois Press.

Farber, Samuel. 1990. *Before Stalinism: The Rise and Fall of Soviet Democracy*. New York: Verso.

Fetscher, Iring. 1971. *Marx and Marxism*. Trans. John Hargreaves. New York: Herder and Herder.

Harding, Neil. 1978-81. *Lenin's Political Thought*. 2 Vols. New York: St. Martin's Press.

Hegel, G. W. F. 1969 (1812–31). *Science of Logic*. Trans. A. V. Miller. London: Allen & Unwin.

James, C. L. R. 1980 (1948). *Notes on Dialectics: Hegel-Marx-Lenin*. Westport: Lawrence Hill.

Kedrov, B.M. 1970. "On the Distinctive Characteristics of Lenin's *Philosophical Notebooks*." *Soviet Studies in Philosophy* 9:1 (Summer), 28–44.

Lefebvre, Henri. 1957. *La Pensée de Lenine*. Paris: Bordas.

_____. 1959. *La Somme et le reste*. Paris: La Nef.

_____. 1967 (1938). Introduction to Lenine, *Cahiers sur la Dialectique de Hegel*. Paris: Éditions Gallimard, 7–135.

_____. 1969 (1947). *Logique formelle, logique dialectique*. Paris: Éditions Anthropos.

Lenin, V. I. 1961a (1914–15). "Abstract of Hegel's *Science of Logic*." Trans. Clemens Dutt. Pp. 85–238 in *Collected Works*, Vol. 38. Moscow: Progress Publishers.

_____. 1961b (1915). "Abstract of Hegel's Lectures on the *History of Philosophy*." Trans. Clemens Dutt. Pp. 245–304 in *Collected Works*, Vol. 38. Moscow: Progress Publishers.

_____. 1962 (1908). *Materialism and Empirio-Criticism*. Trans. Abraham Fineberg. Pp. 17–361 in *Collected Works*, Vol. 14. Moscow: Progress Publishers.

_____. 1965a (1921). "Once Again on the Trade Unions." Pp. 70–107 in *Collected Works*, Vol. 32. Moscow: Progress Publishers.

_____.1965b. (1922). "On the Significance of Militant Materialism." Pp. 227–36 in, *Collected Works*, Vol. 33. Moscow: Progress Publishers.

_____. 1971. *Selected Works in One Volume*. New York: International Publishers.

Liebman, Marcel. 1975 (1973). *Leninism under Lenin*. Trans. Brian Pearce. London: Merlin Press.

Lukács, Georg. 1971 (1923). *History and Class Consciousness*. Trans. Rodney Livingstone. Cambridge: MIT Press.

_____.1975 (1948). *The Young Hegel*. Trans. Rodney Livingstone. London: Merlin Press.

Marcuse, Herbert. 1941. *Reason and Revolution: Hegel and the Rise of Social Theory*. New York: Oxford University Press.

Marx, Karl. 1968 [1844]. "Kritik der Hegelschen Dialektik und Philosophie überhaupt." Pp. 568–88 in Marx and Engels. *Werke. Ergänzungsband. Erster Teil*. Berlin: Dietz Verlag.

_____. 1976 (1867). *Capital*, Vol. I. Trans. Ben Fowkes. London: Penguin Books.

Merleau-Ponty, Maurice. 1973 (1955). *Adventures of the Dialectic*. Trans. Joseph Bien. Evanston: Northwestern University Press.

Miller, David, ed. 1991. *The Blackwell Encyclopedia of Political Thought*. Cambridge, MA: Basil Blackwell.

Ruben, David-Hillel. 1977. *Marxism and Materialism*. Atlantic Highlands: Humanities Press.

Service, Robert. 1985. *Lenin: A Political Life*. 3 Vols. Bloomington: Indiana University Press.

Tucker, Robert C., ed. 1975. *The Lenin Anthology*. New York: Norton.

5

Lenin, Bukharin, dialectics, and imperialism

The concept of Marxist dialectics and the theory of imperialism are two major topics of discussion in Marxism and critical sociology.[1] On both topics, the Russian Marxists V. I. Lenin and Nikolai Bukharin stand out as serious and important theoreticians. Especially on the theory of imperialism, the dominant tendency has been to stress the similarities between Lenin and Bukharin (Kiernan 1974, Brewer 1980, Mommsen 1980).

At the same time, much scholarship has tended to stress Bukharin's originality and creativity as a thinker and to see him as a precursor of Eurocommunism, while downplaying Lenin's theoretical originality (Cohen 1980, 1985; Haynes 1985; Medvedev 1980). Two massive studies of Lenin (Cliff 1975–79, Harding 1978–81) have downplayed the issue of dialectics, while stressing that Bukharin's theoretical writings were the more original ones. These studies stress that Bukharin's 1915–16 writings on imperialism and the state each preceded Lenin's writings on those subjects. But once the issue of dialectics is made more central to the discussion of Lenin and Bukharin as theorists, sharper differences begin to emerge, and Lenin's writings no longer seem to be following the lead of those by Bukharin. In fact, while Bukharin was finishing his 1915 study of

---

1.   This article originally appeared as Kevin B. Anderson, "Lenin, Bukharin and the Marxian Concepts of Dialectics and Imperialism: A Study in Contrasts," *Journal of Political and Military Sociology* 15:2 (1987), pp. 197–212. Reproduced here with permission.

imperialism, Lenin was still working on his study of Hegel's dialectic, a topic that Bukharin never delved into in any depth.

This essay assumes both Lenin and Bukharin to have been major and original Marxist theoreticians and key leaders of the revolution, in order to engage in a critical discussion of their theoretical importance today.

Lenin on dialectics

Ever since Marx's death, the nature of the Marxian dialectic and its relationship to the Hegelian dialectic has been debated. Both Friedrich Engels and official Russian commentators have stressed the materialist and scientific character of Marx's dialectic, where changing economic structures shape human history and society in a more or less automatic fashion. This view also holds that Marx broke sharply with Hegelian philosophy in the 1840s, after which he stood Hegel on his head, transforming Hegel's idealist dialectic into dialectical materialism.

Western Marxists such as Georg Lukács and Karl Korsch, the Frankfurt School, and the Marxist humanists have argued for a continuing strong affinity between the Marxian and the Hegelian concepts of dialectics. They view the Marxian dialectic more as a unity of materialism and idealism, where human consciousness and the individual shape history as much as they are shaped by it. These writers tend to view dialectical materialism as a vulgarization of Marxism by his heirs.

Lenin's concept of Marxian dialectics remains a controversial issue, given the ambivalent legacy he left and the more general arguments around Marxism since Lenin's death in 1924. On the one hand, his 1914–15 *Philosophical Notebooks* (Lenin 1961, Vol. 38, hereinafter Lenin CW 38), which he never published, show a rich and creative probing into Hegelian idealism as a major source of the Marxian dialectic. On the other hand, Lenin's earlier writings on dialectics—such as the 1908 book *Materialism and Empirio-Criticism* (Lenin CW 14), which he never publicly repudiated—argue for a crude reflection theory where the idea is determined by the material in a more or less mechanistic manner. This issue has been debated since Lenin's death.

Some writers who are quite critical of Lenin have downplayed the notion of a shift toward a fuller concept of dialectic in the *Philosophical Notebooks*. George Lichtheim (1965), Richard De George (1966), and especially Leszek Kolakowski (1978) do not see even the *Notebooks* as a terribly serious or original contribution to Marxist thought; Kolakowski, for example, writes that "these ideas are presented in brief and general terms and are therefore not suited to over-precise analysis" (463). Kolakowski concludes his discussion of Lenin's philosophical thought by referring to what he considers to be "Lenin's indolent and superficial approach and his contempt for all problems that could not be put to direct use in the struggle for power" (466).

Other writers, such as Louis Althusser (1971), David-Hillel Ruben (1977), and Helena Sheehan (1985), as well as official Russian commentators, tend to downplay any shift in the *Philosophical Notebooks* from the earlier Lenin because they admire the positivistic and anti-Hegelian Marxism of the early Lenin. Sheehan writes, for example, that in the *Philosophical Notebooks* Lenin "still held to a realist theory of knowledge" and that "commentators who see some kind of radical 'epistemological break' here are quite wrong, whether their preference is for the later Lenin . . . or for the earlier Lenin" (140). According to the Russian academician B. M. Kedrov, those passages in Lenin's *Notebooks* that seem to reflect a new appreciation for the element of idealism in Marxism, such as "consciousness not only reflects the objective world, but creates it" (Lenin CW 38: 212), in Kedrov's view merely represent "a paraphrase" of Hegel. Kedrov strongly denies that the 1914–15 writings "are in fundamental contravention of *Materialism and Empirio-Criticism*," writing that "Lenin categorically rejects and acidly ridicules the slightest slip by Hegel in the direction of ascribing to an idea, to a thought, to consciousness the ability to create the world" (Kedrov 1970: 42). The French Communist philosopher Althusser (1971) likewise attacks the idea of a continuity between Lenin's concept of dialectic and Hegelian idealism. The problem with such views, however, is they seem to be contradicted many times in the more than 200 pages of Lenin's 1914-15 notes on Hegel.

Contrary to the above interpretations, a large group of writers, including Herbert Marcuse (1955), David Joravsky (1961), Henri Lefebvre (1967), Michael Löwy (1973), Lucien Goldmann (1976), and especially Raya Dunayevskaya (1973, 1982a, 1982b), have argued that Lenin's *Philosophical Notebooks* are a significant contribution to dialectical theory, representing a break in Lenin's thought and placing him closer to Hegelian and humanistic Marxism than is usually supposed. The French sociologist Goldmann saw Lenin as the originator of the Hegelianized Marxism that became popular beginning in the 1920s. Goldmann writes that "Hegelian categories are all recovered in Marxism . . . first by Lenin in the *Philosophical Notebooks*, secondly by Lukács in *History and Class Consciousness* (1923), and . . . somewhat later [by] Gramsci" (112–13). To Goldmann, Lenin's *Philosophical Notebooks* evidence a break with Lenin's earlier views where "Lenin at the time he wrote *Materialism and Empirio-Criticism*" saw Marxism as "just as positivistic as academic science" (113). The discussion below builds upon these latter interpretations of Lenin, especially that of Dunayevskaya.

Dunayevskaya (1982a, 1982b) has argued that V. I. Lenin's most original and creative theoretical contributions to Marxism rest not on his famous theory of the vanguard party to lead but rather on three other areas of his theoretical work: (1) his contribution to dialectical philosophy in his 1914–15 *Philosophical Notebooks* on Hegel; (2) his theory of imperialism and its dialectical opposite, the national liberation movements; and (3) his theory of the state and revolution, including his concept of "proletarian democracy."

In August 1914 and immediately thereafter, in response to the outbreak of World War I and the breakup of the Second International, Lenin moved in two seemingly contradictory directions: (1) he spent long weeks in the library in Bern, Switzerland, engaged in daily study of Hegel's *Science of Logic*, writing hundreds of pages of notes on that and other works by Hegel; and, as is more widely known, (2) he moved toward a stance of "revolutionary defeatism" as the policy Marxists should in his view have adopted toward the governments of the various belligerent countries, and called for the establishment of a new international. In so doing, Lenin partially broke with the concept of Marxism as a "vulgar materialism" that characterized the Second International, including his own earlier views. Let us turn directly to those *Philosophical Notebooks* of 1914–15.

Toward the end of his Hegel studies, Lenin wrote two "aphorisms" against the established Marxist philosophy of the time:

1. Plekhanov criticises Kantianism . . . more from a vulgar-materialistic standpoint than from a dialectical-materialistic standpoint, *insofar as* he merely *rejects* their views [from the threshold], but does not *correct* them (as Hegel corrected Kant) . . .

2. Marxists criticised (at the beginning of the twentieth century) the

Kantians and Humists more in the manner of Feuerbach (and Büchner) than of Hegel. (Lenin CW 38: 179)

In opposing both Georgi Plekhanov and Ludwig Feuerbach, whose views Lenin had supported in his 1908 book on Marxist philosophy, Lenin is also criticizing himself.

Lenin goes on to write another "aphorism"—this time on *Capital*—again implicitly criticizing his own earlier work:

> It is impossible completely to understand Marx's *Capital*, and especially its first chapter, without having thoroughly studied and understood the *whole* of Hegel's *Logic*. Consequently, half a century later none of the Marxists understood Marx!! (Lenin CW 38: 180)

This meant a new unity of materialism with idealism, as seen in Lenin's seemingly idealistic statement a bit further on in the *Philosophical Notebooks*: "consciousness not only reflects the objective world, but creates it" (212).

While Lenin's *Philosophical Notebooks* have become known, his continued preoccupation with Hegelian dialectics right through the revolution and until his death is less known. He attempted unsuccessfully to make "some corrections to the section on dialectics" (Lenin CW 36: 317) in his famous 1914 essay *Karl Marx*, submitted as an article for a Russian encyclopedia before he had gotten very far in his Hegel studies.

Lenin also referred increasingly to his opponents' failure to grasp "dialectics" in his post-1914 published critiques of Plekhanov as well as fellow revolutionary Marxist Rosa Luxemburg, and even in his own 1922 "Will," where he wrote his famous critique of Stalin, calling for Stalin to be "removed" as party secretary. Less known was the milder critique of Trotsky as well as Bukharin in that same "Will." In criticizing Bukharin, Lenin emphasized dialectics:

> Bukharin is not only the most valuable and biggest theoretician of the party, but also may legitimately be considered the favorite of the whole party; but his theoretical views can only with the very greatest doubt be regarded as fully Marxian, for there is something

scholastic in him. (He has never learned, and I think never fully understood, the dialectic.)[2]

References to dialectics also occur in Lenin's contribution to the 1920 Trade-Union Debate. There, on the one hand, Trotsky and Bukharin were accused of thinking nondialectically because they proposed subordinating the trade unions to the state, while the Workers' Opposition (Alexandra Kollontai and A. G. Shliapnikov) had wanted, in Lenin's view, to subordinate the state to the unions, thus ignoring the peasantry.

In 1922, when Lenin addressed the new philosophical journal *Under the Banner of Marxism*, he proposed connecting the concept of Hegelian subjectivity to the type of creative thought that, he argued, young Marxist intellectuals would need to grasp theoretically the new revolutionary subjects emerging, especially in the anti-colonial revolutions:

> In order to attain this aim, the contributors to [*Under the Banner of Marxism*] must arrange for the systematic study of Hegelian dialectics from a materialist standpoint, i.e., the dialectics which Marx applied practically in his *Capital* and in his historical and political works, and applied so successfully that now every day of the awakening to life and struggle of the new classes in the East (Japan, India, and China) . . . every day of the awakening to life of new peoples and new classes serves as a fresh confirmation of Marxism. (Lenin CW 33: 233)

Both of these questions—Hegelian dialectics and national liberation movements—were major points of difference between Lenin and Bukharin.

At the same time, the philosophical differences over dialectics were left somewhat ambiguous by Lenin, who in the above speech also referred repeatedly to the more mechanistic Marxist concept of "militant materialism." Since he never published his *Philosophical Notebooks*, Lenin left an ambivalent legacy on dialectics, shifting back and forth in public between more Hegelian concepts and the traditional "scientific" and "materialist"

---

2.   I am using the version of Lenin's Will as cited by Trotsky's former secretary Raya Dunayevskaya (1982b: 118–19), which is the version published by Trotsky in the 1930s. For a slightly different rendering—in which Bukharin is not "the" but only "a most valuable and major theorist"—*see* the official Russian version, first published under Khrushchev (Lenin CW 36: 595).

vocabulary of postMarx Marxism, which he had inherited from Engels and Plekhanov. It is the latter type of Marxism that Bukharin never appeared to question.

Bukharin on dialectics

According to David Joravsky, Bukharin, in a 1923 article in *Pravda* (which he then edited) attacked the journal *Under the Banner of Marxism*. The journal had been running negative reviews on Bukharin's book *Historical Materialism: A System of Sociology*. Joravsky writes that, in his 1923 counter-attack in *Pravda*, "Bukharin announced his intention of having nothing more to do with *Under the Banner of Marxism*, which was the chief journal of Soviet Marxist philosophy" (1961: 58).

Historical Materialism was considered a major official text of Russian Marxism until the 1930s, and even afterwards many of its concepts were retained in official Russian Marxism, albeit not Bukharin's authorship. The book has also been considered a serious work by at least two major non-Marxist American sociologists, Pitirim Sorokin and Seymour Martin Lipset, themselves (like Bukharin) fairly uncritical admirers of technological progress. In a 1922 review, Sorokin called *Historical Materialism* "far more literate, interesting and scientific" than other Bolshevik works (cited by Cohen 1980: 114).

Even greater praise was bestowed on this work by Lipset, who wrote in a new preface to Robert Michels's classic *Political Parties* that Bukharin's

> (*Historical Materialism*) deserves more attention than it now receives. It represents the one sophisticated effort by a major Marxist to come to terms with the emerging body of sociological theory and research. Unfortunately, since Bukharin was murdered by Stalin in 1936 as a "Fascist beast and traitor," the Communist movement lost all interest in his books. Though the American edition of this book was reprinted as late as 1934, socialists and others have been uninterested in a volume which had been a basic text of world Communism. (Lipset 1962: 27)

Lipset then quotes Bukharin's view in *Historical Materialism* that the emergence of a new ruling class in Soviet Russia

... will be retarded by two opposing tendencies, first by the *growth of the productive forces*, second by the abolition of the *educational monopoly*. The increasing reproduction of technologists and of organizers in general, out of the working class itself, will undermine this possible new class alignment. (26–27)

Lipset uses the above passage from Bukharin to bolster his own view that Michels saw "only the restrictive side of bureaucracy" (Lipset 1962: 27).

On the other hand, unorthodox Marxist thinkers have tended to evaluate *Historical Materialism* far more negatively. Georg Lukács published a fairly critical review of the book in 1925, writing that "instead of making a historical-materialist critique of the natural sciences and their methods ... [Bukharin] extends these methods to the study of society without hesitation, uncritically, unhistorically and undialectically" (1973: 59–60). If Lukács is correct, the affinity between Bukharin and mainstream U.S. sociology of the 1950s is not so surprising, and it should perhaps have credited Bukharin as one of its founders (at least with respect to his major work of system theory, *Historical Materialism*).

A few years later, Antonio Gramsci wrote angrily in his *Prison Notebooks* both on *Historical Materialism* and on Bukharin's 1931 speech to a scientific conference in London:

> It would appear from the contribution presented at the London Congress on the History of Science that he continues to maintain that the philosophy of praxis has always been split into two: a doctrine of history and politics, and a philosophy. . . . But if the question is framed in this way, one can no longer understand the importance and significance of the dialectic, which is relegated from its position as a doctrine of knowledge and the very marrow of historiography and the science of politics, to the level of a subspecies of formal logic and elementary scholastics. (Gramsci 1971: 434–35)

Further, Gramsci writes:

> The philosophy implicit in [*Historical Materialism*] could be called a positivistic Aristotelianism, an adaptation of formal logic to the methods of physical and natural science. The historical dialectic is

replaced by the law of causality and the search for regularity, normality and uniformity. (437)

The extremely sharp philosophical critique of Bukharin occupies over one hundred pages of the *Prison Notebooks*.

Bukharin's June 1931 speech entitled "Theory and Practice from the Standpoint of Dialectical Materialism" at the Second International Congress of the History of Science and Technology in London continued and deepened what many have termed his fetishization of science and technology. In London, he argues:

> But the plan of Socialist construction is not only a plan of economy: the process of the *rationalisation of life*, beginning with the suppression of irrationality in the economic sphere, wins away from it one position after another: the principle of planning invades the sphere of "mental production," the sphere of science, the sphere of *theory*. (Bukharin 1931: 20)

Everything is moving onward and upward, not only in science, but even in agriculture!

> One can feel with one's hands how the development of Socialist agriculture pushes forward the development of genetics, biology generally, and so on. . . . Great practice requires great theory. The building of science in the U.S.S.R. is proceeding as the conscious construction of the scientific "superstructures": the plan of scientific works is determined in the first instance by the technical and economic plan, the perspectives of technical and economic development (Bukharin 1931: 21)

In this speech, the great theoretician Bukharin seemed to give at least a partial theoretical defense of Stalin's policy of rapid industrialization, something which his group had opposed in the 1920s.[3]

Historical Materialism was written years before Bukharin became first

---

3. This major 22-page speech is passed over in a single sentence in Cohen's massive study of Bukharin (Cohen 1980: 352). Cohen does not even include it in his bibliography, even though the speech was published in English in London in 1931 as part of the speeches by the Soviet delegation to the International Congress on the History of Science and Technology. Sheehan (1985), on the other hand, takes it up at some length, but offers a far more laudatory view of its contribution to Marxist theory than did Gramsci (1971).

the theoretician for Stalin's faction, then Stalin's Right Opposition, and later Stalin's victim in the purges of the 1930s. As discussed above, Lenin called Bukharin "the most valuable and biggest theoretician" of the Communist Party. Bukharin, in *Historical Materialism*—in his section on "dialectic materialism"—calls himself a "determinist," writing:

> In our consideration of the question of the human will, the question whether it is free, or determined by certain causes, like everything else in the world, we arrived at the conclusion that we must adopt the point of view of determinism. (Bukharin 1925: 53)

And here is Bukharin on Hegel and idealism:

> But we have seen above that idealism involves an admission of the independence of ideas from the material, and of the dependence of these ideas on divine and mysterious springs. It is therefore obvious that the idealist point of view involves a downright mysticism, or other tomfoolery, in the social sciences, and consequently leads to a destruction of these *sciences*, to their substitution by *faith* in the acts of God or in some other such conception. ... Hegel, the greatest philosopher of idealism, defined the history of the world as a "rational, necessary evolution (*Gang*) of the world spirit." (Bukharin 1925: 59)

As Richard Day, the editor of Bukharin's writings on the state, puts it in his introduction: "In the *Philosophical Notebooks* Lenin had come much closer to appreciating the humanistic aspect of Marxism with the observation that 'man's consciousness not only reflects the objective world but creates it'" (Day in Bukharin 1982: xiv). In fact, it would be hard to find a more divergent view of Marxist dialectics to that of Lenin's *Philosophical Notebooks* than that elaborated in Bukharin's *Historical Materialism*.

As we have seen, Bukharin's concept of dialectic stresses science, determinism, and materialism. Lenin's, at least after 1914, moves away from this view and toward a non-deterministic, multilinear conception which saw Hegel's dialectical idealism as the ground for a fully dialectical Marxist materialism.

While few today would claim Bukharin's *Historical Materialism* to be a creative and original work offering much for contemporary Marxism, is it possible to separate Bukharin's mechanistic and vulgarized concept of dialectic from his Marxist economics, where he made so many original contributions? Let us now turn to Lenin's and Bukharin's respective writings on imperialism and national liberation.

Lenin on imperialism and national liberation

Marxist writers such as Lenin and Bukharin viewed imperialism as a specific product of the capitalist epoch. They argued that the final partition of the globe by the colonial powers in the late nineteenth century was different in both form and substance from precapitalist imperialism, and even from the early colonialism of merchant capitalism. They saw the modern form of imperialism as a part of what they considered to be the monopoly stage of world capitalism. Before Lenin and Bukharin wrote on imperialism in 1915–16, it had been a major subject of debate for over a decade among leading German Marxists such as Rosa Luxemburg, Rudolf Hilferding, and Karl Kautsky.

Harding (1978-81) and many other writers have stressed the affinity between Lenin's 1916 study of imperialism and the one by Bukharin a year earlier. To be sure, the two Russian Bolshevik theorists of imperialism were closer to each other's views than to those of any of the German interpretations mentioned above. Nevertheless, I argue below there were important and usually overlooked differences between Bukharin and Lenin on imperialism. These differences emerge more clearly if one discusses the two Bolshevik theorists' analyses of national liberation movements alongside their study of imperialism proper.

In 1914-17, Lenin wrote *Imperialism: The Highest Stage of Capitalism*. He also filled up 768 pages of what are now termed *Notebooks on Imperialism* (Lenin CW 39), and wrote several hundred pages of articles on national self-determination and the war. In taking this material as a whole, I am following Lenin's own suggestion in the 1917 preface to the Russian edition of *Imperialism*.

Dunayevskaya (1967) has argued there is a profound difference between Lenin's study of imperialism and that of Bukharin:

> Because Lenin had also introduced Bukharin's work, and took no issue with it, the impression created when the two disagreed

sharply on the question of national self-determination during the same period, was that the point at issue was "only political." In truth, the methodology of the two works shows they are poles apart. Thus, as opposed to Bukharin's concept of capitalist growth in a straight line, or via a quantitative ratio, Lenin's own work holds on tightly to the dialectical principle, "transformation into opposite." (15)

Dunayevskaya specifies the key point:

> Lenin held that, just when capitalism had reached this high stage of "'organization," monopoly (which extended itself into imperialism), is the time to see new, national revolutionary forces that would act as "bacilli" for proletarian revolutions as well. (15–16)

That Lenin wrote an introduction to Bukharin's book on imperialism has been claimed to mean that he agreed with that work. This claim is then used by writers such as Cohen and Harding to show that, since Bukharin's book was written ahead of Lenin's, Bukharin led the way and Lenin followed. In fact, Lenin did at least once sharply criticize that work. This was done in a major speech on the question of self-determination of nations at the 1919 Party Congress. There, Lenin and Bukharin once again disagreed sharply. Lenin stated, regarding Bukharin's view of imperialism:

> Comrade Bukharin's concreteness is a bookish description of finance capitalism. In reality we have heterogenous phenomena to deal with. . . . Nowhere in the world has monopoly capitalism existed in a whole series of branches without free competition, nor will it exist. . . . To maintain that there is such a thing as integral imperialism without the old capitalism is merely making the wish father to the thought. . . . And if we had an integral imperialism before us, which had entirely altered capitalism, our task would have been a hundred thousand times easier. It would have resulted in a system in which everything would be subordinated to finance capital alone. (Lenin CW 29: 168)

This critique of Bukharin's economics was followed immediately in Lenin's speech by an even sharper critique of Bukharin on national self-determination, as we shall see in a moment. But first, let us look at Lenin's *Imperialism*.

Lenin's *Imperialism* never refers explicitly to "dialectics." Therefore, the question of its relationship to Lenin's *Philosophical Notebooks* lies not in specific references to dialectics but in the form of Lenin's study. Lenin begins with a discussion of the growth of monopoly during the heyday of imperialism. To Lenin, this is not a smooth or evolutionary transition, but a sometimes violent transformation. He writes that "[c]ompetition becomes transformed into monopoly" (Lenin CW 22: 205), and stresses the forceful, even violent, character of this transformation. For Lenin, violent competition between monopolies, whole industries, and nation states increases as production becomes centralized into fewer and fewer hands.

The key to everything for Lenin is *transition*, the development of monopoly and imperialism, not from "outside" earlier capitalism but from within, from the dialectical process Hegel called "transformation into opposite." As Lenin puts it:

> In other words, the old capitalism, the capitalism of free competition with its indispensable regulator, the Stock Exchange, is passing away. A new capitalism has come to take its place, bearing obvious features of something transient, a mixture of free competition and monopoly. (Lenin CW 22: 219)

Far from peace between nation states being more likely under imperialism and monopoly, Lenin argues that the reverse is true, because the expanding empires, having virtually absorbed all the non-industrialized world, now have nowhere to turn but upon each other. Evidently World War I is the climax of such a conflict, in Lenin's view.

In the central chapter "Imperialism, as a Special Stage of Capitalism," Lenin sums up, emphasizing the heterogeneity of processes involved in the emergence of imperialism:

> Imperialism emerged as the development and direct continuation of the fundamental characteristics of capitalism in general. But capitalism only became capitalist imperialism at a definite and very high stage of development, when certain of its fundamental characteristics began to change into their *opposites*, when the features of the epoch of transition from capitalism to a higher social and

economic system had taken shape and revealed themselves in all spheres. . . . [M]onopoly is the exact opposite of free competition, but we have seen the latter being transformed into monopoly before our eyes, creating large-scale industry and forcing out small industry. ... (Lenin CW 22: 265, emphasis added)

The above brief passage is a crucial one, containing elements of a uniquely "Leninist" view. We can see its apparent close relationship to Lenin's *Philosophical Notebooks*, and especially the category he singled out there from Hegel: transformation into opposite. As Lenin had written to those *Notebooks*:

> *Dialectics* is the teaching which shows how *Opposites* can be and how they happen to be (how they become) *identical*,—under what conditions they are identical, becoming transformed into one another,—why the human mind should grasp these opposites not as dead, rigid, but as living, conditional, mobile, becoming transformed into one another. En lisant Hegel [In reading Hegel] . . . (Lenin CW 38: 109)

That Hegelian dialectic was in fact part of the ground of the whole study of imperialism. It is not merely a question of Lenin's use of apparently Hegelian language from his *Philosophical Notebooks* in his book on *Imperialism*.

Lenin's relation to Hegel is seen as well in the overall shape of his argument, where he employs Hegelian categories such as negation or "transformation into opposite" to discuss how imperialism and monopoly arose dialectically out of an earlier stage of capitalism. Imperialism and monopoly do not arise *ab novo*, nor do they arise gradually; for Lenin, they arise as a simultaneous preservation, destruction, and transcendence of the old capitalism (in Hegel's German original, the concept is *Aufhebung*).

In this sense, monopoly and imperialism arise dialectically from competitive, pre-imperialist capitalism. As in the Hegelian syllogism that Lenin wrote on in his *Philosophical Notebooks*, monopoly involves the destruction of competitive capitalism, the apparent overcoming of some of its contradictions between individual capitalist entities inside a particular national economy. Yet the overcoming of one set of contradictions only sets the stage for another: the competition between entities within a single capitalist economy has now been displaced outward. Competition in the monopoly stage certainly includes a struggle between large firms in either the same or different industries in a given national economy. But it also takes the form in Lenin's schema of competition for empire and world markets between monopoly capitalist nation states, leading ultimately toward world war once the non-capitalist lands have been fully occupied. The war is fought in order to redivide the world economy among the imperialist powers.

But there was, for Lenin, an even bigger contradiction inside capitalism in the new era of imperialism. Even more crucial to Lenin's concept of the dialectics of revolution in the era of imperialism than the transformation of capitalism into monopoly and of part of the working class into an "aristocracy of labor" was the at-first-little-noticed shift in his concept of the self-determination of nations. Earlier, it had been a "principle" for a Bolshevik leader in an old empire ruling over Finland, Poland, the Ukraine, and Central and East Asian peoples.

For Lenin, after 1914 it became a question of the dialectics of world revolution. The movements for national liberation were to Lenin nothing less than the "dialectical opposite" of the new capitalist stage marked by monopoly and imperialism. True, in Lenin's view, part of the Western proletariat had been "bribed" by the "crumbs" from imperialism, especially in Britain, and capitalism thus emerged all the stronger after 1900 (at least temporarily). But it was equally true that the new stage contained its own "opposite": both the revolt from the "lower and deeper" layer of the working class inside the imperialist countries and the still newer revolutionary subject: the national liberation movements.

In 1916, Lenin made explicit reference to "dialectics" in one of his first formulations of the new concept of national liberation, here arguing against the point of view of Rosa Luxemburg, whose antiwar manifesto known as the *Junius Pamphlet* had held that nationalism was reactionary in the era of imperialism. Lenin contends:

> The fallacy of this argument is obvious. That all dividing lines, both in nature and society, are conventional and dynamic, and that *every* phenomenon might, under certain conditions, be transformed into its opposite, is, of course, a basic proposition of Marxist dialectics. A national war *might* be transformed into an

imperialist war *and vice versa*. . . . Only a sophist can disregard the difference between an imperialist and a national war on the grounds that one *might* develop into the other. (Lenin CW 22: 309)

Once again, we see Lenin's explicit use of the terminology "transform[ation] into its opposite," which he developed and elaborated in his *Philosophical Notebooks*, here as the grounding for his point of view on national liberation. Also to be noted is his use of the word dialectics without a qualifying adjective such as "materialist," a usage somewhat unusual for the Marxism of his period. A bit further on in his argument with Luxemburg, Lenin again takes up the issue of dialectics, arguing that in taking her position against nationalism, Luxemburg "applies Marxist dialectics only half way" (Lenin CW 22: 316). Nor was Lenin dismissing Luxemburg's brilliant and groundbreaking Marxist critique of imperialist war in the *Junius Pamphlet*; rather, he was writing a sympathetic critique in which he was beginning to develop his own new position on national liberation.

In another 1916 article Lenin develops his concept of dialectics and national liberation further:

> The dialectics of history are such that small nations, powerless as an *independent* factor in the struggle against imperialism, play a part as one of the ferments, one of the bacilli, which help the *real* anti-imperialist force, the socialist proletariat, to make its appearance on the scene. (Lenin CW 22: 357)

In this case, the reference was to the Irish uprising of Easter 1916, which Lenin saw as a new type of contradiction developing inside one of the warring powers, Britain. It was a tremendous innovation for the Marxism of 1916 to place such national movements alongside the proletariat as revolutionary subjects, and this view was in sharp contrast to other commentators on Easter 1916, such as Karl Radek and Leon Trotsky. Radek and Trotsky shared many of Lenin's views, but not his analysis of Ireland.[4]

At this point, Lenin sharply polemicized against what he termed Bukharin's "imperialist economism." In the process, he also deepened his own view of national liberation:

---

4. For the texts of Lenin, Radek, and Trotsky on Easter 1916 side by side, see Riddell (1984: 372–79).

While the proletariat of the advanced countries is overthrowing the bourgeoisie and repelling its attempts at counter-revolution, the undeveloped and oppressed nations do not just wait, do not cease to exist, do not disappear. . . . [T]here can be no doubt that they will all the more readily take advantage of the *great crisis* of civil war in the advanced countries to rise in revolt. (Lenin CW 23: 60)

The clash with Bukharin on national liberation continued after 1917, especially at the 1919 Party congress. There, as discussed above, Lenin criticized Bukharin's concept of imperialism, but the real fireworks came on the national question:

"I want to recognise only the right of the working classes to self-determination," says Comrade Bukharin. That is to say, you want to recognise something that has not been achieved in a single country except Russia. That is ridiculous. . . . When Comrade Bukharin said, "We can recognize this right in some cases," I even wrote down that he had included in the list the Hottentots, the Bushmen and the Indians. Hearing this enumeration, I thought, how is it that Comrade Bukharin has forgotten a small tribe, the Bashkirs? There are no Bushmen in Russia, nor have I heard that the Hottentots have laid claim to an autonomous republic, but we have Bashkirs, Kirghiz and a number of other peoples, and to these we cannot deny recognition. We cannot deny it to a single one of the peoples living within the boundaries of the former Russian Empire. (Lenin CW 29: 171–72)

In his even sharper exchange with Bukharin's ally Pyatakov, Lenin stated:

Many over-enthusiastic comrades here went as far as to talk about a world Economic Council, and about subordinating all the national parties to the Central Committee of the Russian Communist Party. . . . These are the kind of objections which induce me to say, "*Scratch some Communists and you will find Great-Russian chauvinists.*" (Lenin CW 29: 187–94, emphasis added)

Such were some of Lenin's continuing disagreements with Bukharin.

Bukharin on imperialism and national liberation

Bukharin's 1915 book *Imperialism and World Economy* preceded Lenin's book on imperialism by a year, and, it has been argued, Lenin "borrowed freely from it" (Cohen 1980). Even if there were not the type of sharp differences on imperialism as on dialectics or the national question, the two concepts of imperialism were not necessarily as similar as often suggested. Bukharin spends the first half of his book meticulously tracing the development of monopoly capitalism on a world scale, but concludes that although capitalism was still organized around the nation state, "one must not overestimate the significance of international organizations" (Bukharin 1973: 60). He also includes an incisive critique of those who view capitalist imperialism as essentially similar to previous empires.

The last section of his book explores the effect of what he terms "state capitalist imperialism" during World War I on the working class of Europe, marred by an ethnocentric reference to "savages":

> Imperialism has turned in its true face to the working class of Europe. Hitherto its barbarous, destructive, wasteful activities were almost entirely confined to the savages; now it thrusts itself upon Europe with all the horrifying power of a bloodthirsty elemental power let loose. . . . The war severs the last chain that binds the workers to the masters, their slavish submission to the imperialist state. The last limitation of the proletariat's philosophy is being overcome: its clinging to the narrowness of the national slate, its patriotism. (167)

This is certainly a detailed economic study of imperialism by a writer with revolutionary convictions, but does it have a truly dialectical form?

To Bukharin, imperialism was a product of "extensive and intensive growth of world economy" (1967: 28). Yet once it had evolved, seemingly without contradiction, it suddenly became a new "state capitalist imperialism," totally different from the old capitalism. As we have seen in Lenin's 1919 critique, Bukharin's "integral imperialism" was not a "unity of opposites"—to adopt Lenin's terminology from the *Philosophical Notebooks*—between competitive and monopolistic features of capitalism. Rather, it was an "abstract universal" of "state capitalist imperialism," without much of a concept of contradictions emerging within this new stage. In 1919, Lenin accused Bukharin of constructing an "integral imperialism without the old capitalism" (Lenin CW 29: 168).

But the much bigger lack of differentiation within Bukharin's concept of imperialism was in his failure to connect it to national liberation. As Bukharin wrote in 1915 in a statement also signed by Pyatakov and Bosh:

> The imperialist epoch is an epoch of the absorption of small states by the large state units and of a constant reshuffling of the political map of the world toward a more uniform type of state … It is therefore impossible to struggle against the enslavement of nations otherwise than by struggling against imperialism *ergo*— . . . by struggling against finance capital, *ergo* against *capitalism* in general. (Gankin and Fisher 1940: 219)

This "abstract universal" then leads Bukharin and his colleagues to their conclusion:

> The slogan of "self determination of nations" is first of all *utopian* (it cannot be realized *within the limits* of capitalism) and *harmful* as a slogan which *disseminates illusions.* In this respect it does not differ at all from the slogans of the courts of arbitration, of disarmament, etc, which presuppose the possibility of so called "peaceful capitalism." (Gankin and Fisher 1940: 219)

It is not that they did not regard colonial revolts as well-intentioned, but that they saw them as "illusory," as vestiges of pre-capitalist formations on their way out. In that sense, capitalist imperialism was perhaps even "progressive" in that it cleared the way for a world socialist system including the colonies. In such a political-economic framework, nationalism could only be reactionary and the task of socialism was to promote the "abstract universal" of internationalism, even to oppressed nationalities and nations.

As even Cohen, Bukharin's sympathetic biographer, concludes:

> Bukharin's failure to see anti-imperialist nationalism as a revolutionary force was the most glaring defect in his original treatment of imperialism; he did not anticipate the historic development of

the postwar period—the groundswell of national liberation movements. (Cohen 1980: 36)

But Cohen adds that "Bukharin's argument in *Imperialism and World Economy* was not incompatible" with a different view of national liberation movements, as shown by the fact that Bukharin "was later able to take them into account" (1980: 35).

But is it true that Bukharin was able to change his view after 1917 to accord with that of Lenin and the objective situation that revealed national movements in Russia and the world? Lenin did not apparently think so, as shown by his attack on Bukharin once again at the 1919 Congress. At that time, Lenin asked publicly that his 1916–17 articles against Bukharin's group, on "imperialist economism," be published. They were not published, at least not until 1929 when Stalin did so in order to use them for narrowly factional reasons against Bukharin.

Looking at Bukharin's post-1917 writings, it is hard to find more than occasional, almost obligatory mention of the national question, such as in *The ABC of Communism*, an explication of the Communist Party's revised 1919 program, co-authored with Evgeny Preobrazhensky. In their rather superficial view, in the section on "Communism and the Problem of Nationality":

> If we are to eradicate the mistrust felt by the workers of oppressed nations for the workers of oppressor nations . . . [t]he [party] must be ready to grant complete national self-determination . . . (Bukharin and Preobrazhensky 1967: 197)

While there is plenty of mention of various western European nationalities, there is no substantial reference to Asia, Africa, or Latin America. Nowhere are the oppressed and colonized nations and nationalities discussed as capable of national revolt alongside the European working class, thus adding something to the world revolution, as we have seen that Lenin argued.

Lenin, Bukharin and the dialectic today

The differences over national liberation between Lenin and Bukharin were part of a major public debate, unlike their differences over imperialism and dialectics, which were not broached publicly except in occasional (almost cryptic) statements by Lenin. But these differences over dialectics and imperialism demonstrate that the dispute over national liberation was apparently rooted in major theoretical and philosophical issues.

Taking their different concepts of dialectic as ground, the more one digs into Lenin's and Bukharin's writings on imperialism and the national question the more divergent their theoretical work appears. Not until the 1950s and the rise of a whole new Third World would the themes raised by Lenin be taken up again and developed. This is what makes these writings by Lenin especially relevant for our period. In taking the position that national liberation was a decisive dialectical opposite of imperialism, Lenin stood alone among major Marxist theorists of his time.

Today, since the publication of Marx's 1844 *Essays* and his *Grundrisse*—as well as the transcription of his *Ethnological Notebooks*—the multilinear and Hegelian character of Marx's Marxism is better known than it was in Lenin's and Bukharin's time (Dunayevskaya 1982c), although Bukharin did, after their first-ever publication in Russian in 1927, presumably have access to Marx's 1844 *Essays.*

Today, national revolutions span the globe, from South Africa to Central America, in opposition to various forms of imperialism and local ruling classes, and disclosing within those revolutions a still newer revolutionary subject—women's liberation (Dunayevskaya 1985). Lenin moved toward anticipating at least some of those trends, in part on the basis of his 1914–15 study of Hegel. Bukharin's theorizing seemed, on the other hand, to anticipate both Russian party ideology and mainstream American sociology of the 1950s, each of them making a fetish out of science and technology.

Still, Lenin's legacy is quite ambivalent in several ways: (1) In failing to publish his studies on dialectics, mechanical materialism was more easily able to continue as official Marxism after his death. (2) In failing to break with his own concept of the vanguard party, Lenin played no small part in the eventual outcome of events in Russia in the 1930s. I have attempted here to unravel some of the differences between Lenin and Bukharin who, along with Trotsky, were the major theorists of Bolshevism, in order better to grasp some of the diversity within post-Marx Marxism and to shed light on some contemporary problems within Marxian and critical sociology.

References

Althusser, Louis. 1971. *Lenin and Philosophy and Other Essays*. Translated by Ben Brewster. London: New Left Books.

Brewer, Anthony. 1980. *Marxist Theories of Imperialism: A Critical Survey*. Boston: Routledge & Kegan Paul.

Bukharin, Nikolai. 1925. *Historical Materialism: A System of Sociology*. New York: International Publishers. https://bit.ly/2ATIaep.

———. 1931. "Theory and Practice from the Standpoint of Dialectical Materialism." In *Science at the Cross Roads*, edited by N I Bukharin, 1–23. London: Kniga (England) Ltd. https://bit.ly/2zWZJtu.

———. 1973. *Imperialism and World Economy*. [1929]. New York: Monthly Review Press.

———. 1982. *Selected Writings on the State and the Transition to Socialism*. Edited and translated by Richard B Day. Armonk, New York: M E Sharpe.

——— and Evgeny Preobrazhensky. 1967. *The ABC of Communism*. [1922]. Ann Arbor: University of Michigan Press.

Cliff, Tony. 1975-79. *Lenin (Four Volumes)*. London: Pluto Press.

Cohen, Stephen F. 1980. *Bukharin and the Bolshevik Revolution: A Political Biography, 1888-1938*. New York: Oxford University Press.

———. 1985. "Bukharin, the NEP and the Idea of an Alternative to Stalinism." In *Rethinking the Soviet Experience: Politics & History Since 1917*, 71–92. New York: Oxford University Press.

Dunayevskaya, Raya. 1967. *State-Capitalism and Marx's Humanism or Philosophy and Revolution*. Detroit: News & Letters. https://bit.ly/3bNBdZ3.

———. 1973. "Hegelian Leninism." In *Towards a New Marxism*, edited by Bart Grahl and Paul Piccone, 159–75. St. Louis: Telos Press.

———. 1982a. *Marxism and Freedom: From 1776 until Today*. [1958]. Atlantic Highlands, NJ: Humanities Press.

———. 1982b. *Philosophy and Revolution: From Hegel to Sartre, and from Marx to Mao*. [1973]. 2nd ed. Atlantic Highlands, NJ: Humanities Press.

———. 1982c. *Rosa Luxemburg, Women's Liberation, and Marx's Philosophy of Revolution*. Atlantic Highlands, NJ: Humanities Press.

———. 1985. *Women's Liberation and the Dialectics of Revolution: Reaching for the Future*. Atlantic Highlands, NJ: Humanities Press.

Gankin, Olga Hess, and H. H. Fisher. 1940. *The Bolsheviks and the World*

War: The Origin of the Third International. Stanford: Stanford University Press. https://bit.ly/3e6fJrN.

George, Richard de. 1966. *Patterns of Soviet Thought: The Origins and Development of Dialectical and Historical Materialism*. Ann Arbor: University of Michigan Press.

Goldmann, Lucien. 1976. *Cultural Creation in Modern Society*. Edited by William Mayrl. Translated by Bart Grahl. St. Louis: Telos Press. https://bit.ly/2WsOl12.

Gramsci, Antonio. 1971. *Selections from the Prison Notebooks*. Edited and translated by Quintin Hoare and Geoffrey Nowell Smith. New York: International Publishers. https://bit.ly/3e8L25q.

Harding, Neil. n.d. *Lenin's Political Thought [Two Volumes]*. 1978-81. New York: St. Martin's.

Haynes, Michael. 1985. *Nikolai Bukharin and the Transition from Capitalism to Socialism*. New York: Holmes & Meier.

Joravsky, David. 1961. *Soviet Marxism and Natural Science, 1917-1932*. New York: Columbia University Press.

Kedrov, B. M. 1970. "On the Distinctive Characteristics of Lenin's Philosophical Notebooks." *Soviet Studies in Philosophy* 9 (1): 28–44.

Kiernan, Victor G. 1974. "The Marxist Theory of Imperialism and Its Historical Formation." In *Marxism and Imperialism*, 1–68. London: Edward Arnold.

Kolakowski, Leszek. 1978. *Main Currents of Marxism, Vol. 2: The Golden Age*. Oxford: Oxford University Press.

Lefebvre, Henri and Norberto Guterman. 1967. "Introduction." In *Cahiers Sur La Dialectique de Hegel*. Paris: Éditions Gallimard.

Lenin, V I. 1961. *Collected Works*. Vol. 1–45. Moscow: Progress Publishers. https://bit.ly/3e8bko7.

Lichtheim, George. 1965. *Marxism: An Historical and Critical Study*. New York: Praeger Publishers.

Lipset, Seymour Martin. 1962. "Introduction." In *Political Parties*, 15–39. New York: Crowell-Collier.

Löwy, Michael. 1973. *Dialectique et Révolution: Essais de Sociologie et d'histoire du Marxisme*. Paris: Éditions Anthropos.

Lukács, Georg. 1971. *History and Class Consciousness: Studies in Marxist Dialectics*. Orig. 1923.Translated by Rodney Livingstone. Cambridge, MA: The MIT Press.

————. 1973. "Technology and Social Relations." In *Marxism and Human Liberation*, 49–60. New York: Delta.

Marcuse, Herbert. 1955. *Reason and Revolution: Hegel and the Rise of Social Theory*. 2nd ed. London: Routledge & Kegan Paul.

Medvedev, Roy A. 1980. *Nikolai Bukharin: The Last Years*. Translated by A. D. P. Briggs. New York: W W Norton & Company.

Mommsen, Wolfgang J. 1980. *Theories of Imperialism*. New York: Random House.

Riddell, John, ed. 1984. *Lenin's Struggle for a Revolutionary International*. New York: Monad Press.

Ruben, David-Hillel. 1977. *Marxism and Materialism: A Study in Marxist Theory of Knowledge*. Atlantic Highlands, NJ: Humanities Press.

Sheehan, Helena. 1985. *Marxism and the Philosophy of Science: A Critical History*. Atlantic Highlands, NJ: Humanities Press.

[First appeared in 1987 in *Journal of Political & Military Sociology* 15:2. I thank Janet Afary, Stephen Eric Bronner, the late Raya Dunayevskaya, the late George Fischer, Douglas Kellner, for helpful comments and criticisms.]

6

Marcuse, Hegel, and critical theory

Hegel and Hegelianism have lurked in the background of sociological theory from the very beginning of the sociological enterprise.[1] In *Capital*, Vol. I, Marx wrote in praise of "the Hegelian 'contradiction,' which is the source of all dialectic" ([1867-75] 1976, p. 744), while in a later postface to the same text he argued: "My dialectical method is, in its foundations, not only different from the Hegelian, but exactly opposite to it" ([1867-75] 1976, p. 102). The next generation of Marxist theorists, who were the contemporaries of Weber and Durkheim, tended to favor the second type of statement over the first, in part because they had not read the *1844 Manuscripts*, which were published only in 1927 (in Russian) and then in 1932 (in German). As the French sociologist Lucien Goldmann (1976, p. 112–13) writes, the Marxist attitude toward Hegel did not begin to change until after World War I:

> Hegelian categories are all recovered in Marxism; and it is no accident that they were reactualized in Europe around, say, the years 1917–23: first by Lenin in the *Philosophic Notebooks*, secondly by Lukács in *History and Class Consciousness*, and thirdly, I believe,

---

1.   Originally published as Kevin B. Anderson, "On Hegel and the Rise of Social Theory: A Critical Appreciation of Herbert Marcuse's Reason and Revolution, Fifty Years Later," *Sociological Theory* 11:3 (1993), pp. 243-67. Reproduced here with permission.

somewhat later in Gramsci's concretely philosophical analyses. Furthermore, it is not accidental that in the interim, with Mehring, Plekhanov, Kautsky, Bernstein, and even Lenin at the time he wrote *Materialism and Empirio-Criticism*, Marxism was just as positivistic as academic science.

Thus, Marx's debt to Hegel was muted nearly to the point of invisibility by the leading Marxist theorists of the turn of the century.

During this period the non-Marxist founders of sociology were also rather hostile to Hegel, and seemed to regard any lingering influence of Hegelianism as essentially pernicious to sociological theory. This was certainly true of Durkheim. In the years immediately preceding the publication of Durkheim's *Suicide*, Georges Noël's major study of Hegel, which included a sharp attack on positivism, was published in the *Revue de métaphysique et de morale*, a journal devoted both to philosophy and sociology, and in which Durkheim also published articles. Noël's *La Logique de Hegel* was subsequently issued as a book in 1897 by the prestigious Paris publishing house of Félix Alcan, which also published *Suicide* that same year (Noël 1897, Durkheim [1897] 1951). While Durkheim never published a critique of Hegel, it is likely that his statement in the preface to *Suicide* that "real laws are discoverable which demonstrate the possibility of science better than any dialectical argument" ([1897] 1951, p. 37) is directed at least in part against the type of Hegelianism represented by Noël. To Durkheim, Hegelianism contained an outdated, pre-scientific theory of society. While it is certainly evident today that positivism was to overshadow Hegelianism in French social thought for many years afterwards, in 1897 Durkheim could have had no way of knowing that the pernicious shadow of Hegel was soon to be banished to the sidelines.

Weber seems to have regarded Hegel with greater respect, but evidently more as a rival than a co-thinker. Donald N. Levine (1985, p. 150) writes of "Weber's silent homage to and acute consciousness of Hegel as his major intellectual antagonist," referring to an unpublished 1909 letter where Weber wrote: "Two ways of treating things stand open: Hegel's or *ours*" (cited in Bruun 1972, p. 39). It was during this same period that Dilthey's influential book *Jugendgeschichte Hegels* ([1905] 1959) helped to begin a Hegel revival in Central Europe. For example, three decades later,

Dilthey's work was referred to frequently in Marcuse's first book on Hegel (Marcuse [1932a] 1987).

In the U.S., at least since the 1960s, it has become commonplace to refer to Hegelian Marxism and to regard the Hegel-Marx relationship as a key point of debate in social theory. Such was not the case in 1941 when Marcuse's *Reason and Revolution: Hegel and the Rise of Social Theory* was first published. Below I propose to assess the importance and subsequent influence of Marcuse's pathbreaking book.

The Originality of *Reason and Revolution*

Reason and Revolution holds the important distinction of being the first Hegelian Marxist book to appear in English. In addition, it was the first systematic published analysis of Hegel's major works from a Marxist standpoint in any language, preceding those by Georg Lukács ([1948] 1975) and Ernst Bloch ([1949] 1962) by several years. To this day *Reason and Revolution* stands as one of the major Marxist treatments of Hegel. It views Marx's work as grounded in Hegel's concept of dialectic. Theoretically, Marx's work is presented as a critique not only of capitalism, but also, at least implicitly, as the foundation for a critique of Stalinist Communism. Not only does Marcuse's book contain a critical analysis of Hegel's major works such as the *Phenomenology of Mind*, the *Science of Logic*, the *Philosophy of History*, and the *Philosophy of Right*, but it also includes the first serious treatment in English of Marx's *Economic and Philosophical Manuscripts of 1844*. This Hegelian-Marxian heritage is counterposed to what Marcuse considered to be the essentially conservative world-view of positivism, which teaches people "to view and study the phenomena of their world as neutral objects governed by universally valid laws" (1941, p. 326).

In the preface to the original edition, Marcuse (1941, p. vii) argues that "the rise of Fascism calls for a reinterpretation of Hegel's philosophy." One major theme of his work, he writes, is that it "will demonstrate that Hegel's basic concepts are hostile to the tendencies that have led into Fascist theory and practice" (1941, p. vii). A second major theme is Hegel's link to Marx. Marcuse writes that he "tried to go beyond mere restatement" in his "survey of the structure of Hegel's system," in order to connect it "particularly with the Marxian theory" (1941, p. vii). A third theme, he continues, is the critique of positivism, a theory "which undertook to subordinate reason to the authority of established fact." Positivism counterposes itself to the negative and critical character of Hegel's dialectical concept of Reason, where Hegel's "critical and rational standards, and especially his dialectics, had to come into conflict with the prevailing social reality" (1941, p. vii).

Marcuse locates Hegel's thought as part of the heritage of the Enlightenment concept of reason and the French Revolution: "Reason presupposes freedom, the power to act in accordance with knowledge of the truth, the power to shape reality in line with its potentialities" (1941, p. 9). By drawing "history into philosophy," Hegel culminates the journey of German idealism, but at the same time this historical dimension ultimately "shatters the idealistic framework" (1941, p. 16) of that tradition. Hegel's critique of empiricism is not entirely new, but is part of the origin of German idealism, which Marcuse writes, "rescued philosophy from the attack of British empiricism" (1941, p. 16). Kant began the counterattack on empiricism, but to Hegel the "skeptical element of Kant's philosophy" in the end "vitiat[es] ... his attempt to rescue reason from the empiricist onslaught" (1941, p. 23). Where philosophers "from Hume to the present-day logical positivists" have made recourse to "the ultimate authority of the fact," for Hegel, "the facts in themselves possess no authority" (1941, p. 27), until they are subjected to the critique of dialectical Reason.

Before taking up Hegel's first major work, the *Phenomenology of Mind*, Marcuse surveys some of his largely unpublished earlier writings, in the first discussion of them to appear in English. He singles out the radicalism of Hegel's early writings on industrialism and labor, where the attack on alienation and exploitation is scathing. For Marcuse "the tone and pathos of the descriptions point strikingly to Marx's *Capital*" when Hegel writes: "The faculties of the individual are infinitely restricted, and the consciousness of the factory worker is degraded to the lowest level of dullness" (1941, p. 79). At the same time, writes Marcuse, the very manuscript which developed this critique of capitalism breaks off, as if Hegel "was terrified by what his analysis of the commodity-producing society disclosed" (1941, p. 79). He writes that for Hegel the "wild animal" that is capitalist society and its class contradictions "must be curbed, and such a process requires the organization of a strong state"(1941, p. 79). Marcuse develops this argument further when he takes up the *Philosophy of Right*.

In his discussion of Hegel's *Phenomenology*, Marcuse notes Hegel's sharp critique of the results of Enlightenment reason in the French Revolution: "Hegel saw that the result of the French Revolution was not the realization of freedom, but the establishment of a new despotism" (1941, p. 91). The central theme of the *Phenomenology*, as it moves from sense awareness through Reason to Absolute Knowledge, is that the "world in reality is not as it appears, but as it is comprehended by philosophy" (1941, p. 93). Further, for Hegel: "Knowledge begins when philosophy destroys the experience of daily life." The latter is only "the starting point of the search for truth" (1941, p. 103), which is ultimately based on a critique of commonsense notions of reality. Thus, Marcuse identifies strongly with the specifically Hegelian critique of commonsense experience, a position for which he has been sharply criticized as a mystical idealist by more orthodox Marxist theorists such as Lucio Colletti, as we shall see later.

Marcuse's interpretation of Hegel contains a radical concept of the Subject. "The first three sections of the *Phenomenology* are a critique of positivism and, even more, of 'reification,'" he writes (1941, p. 112). This is because "common sense and traditional scientific thought" are not subject-centered: "there is, in the last analysis, no truth that does not *essentially concern* the living subject" (1941, p. 113). Marcuse links all of this to Marx's thought when he discusses Hegel's concept of labor in light of Marx's treatment of the *Phenomenology* in his "Critique of the Hegelian Dialectic" in the *1844 Manuscripts*. There, writes Marcuse, Marx "caught the critical impact of Hegel's analysis" (1941, p. 115):

> The greatness of that work he saw in the fact that Hegel conceived the "self-creation" of man (that is, the creation of a reasonable social order through man's own free action) as the process of "reification" and its "negation," in short, that he grasped the "nature of labor" and saw man to be "the result of his labor."

Eventually, however, Hegel's idealism seems to overtake both history and subjectivity. Marcuse writes that at the end of the *Phenomenology*, in the chapter on Absolute Knowledge, "pure thought again seems to swallow up living freedom" (1941, p. 120). However, Marcuse questions "whether this solution was Hegel's last word" (1941, p. 120).

Marcuse's treatment of Hegel's *Science of Logic* in *Reason and Revolution* is particularly original and probing. There is an interesting discussion of the famous beginning section of the *Science of Logic* on Being, Nothing and Becoming, the section that, contended Lukács in *History and Class Consciousness* ([1923] 1971, p. 170), "contained the whole of his philosophy." This section of the *Science of Logic* was important also to Jean-Paul Sartre, whose *Being and Nothingness* appeared two years after *Reason and Revolution*. Marcuse argues that the "togetherness of being and nothing" in Hegel's chapter allows him to demonstrate "the negative and contradictory nature of reality" (1941, p. 130), and to thus develop a critical stance toward the social world.

As against contemporary religious interpretations "that the world was a finite one because it was a created world and that its negativity referred to its sinfulness" (1941, p. 136), Hegel's interpretation of the problem of infinity and finitude is critical and revolutionary. Where conservative religious thought counterposes a human, finite world to a religious, infinite one, Marcuse writes that for Hegel "[t]here are not two worlds, the finite and the infinite," but "only one world, in which finite things attain their self-determination through perishing" (1941, p. 139). Marcuse links this notion to Marx:

> Marx later laid down the historical law that a social system can set free its productive forces only by perishing and passing into another form of social organization. Hegel saw this law of history operative in all being. (1941, p. 137)

Thus, for Marcuse, Hegel's concept of infinity is rooted in the world of being, where when "a finite thing perishes" it actually develops "its true potentialities" (1941, p. 137) by moving to a higher stage through a process of negation of what has existed before. Further, this dialectical concept underlies one of the central elements of Marx's economic theory.

Especially in his discussion of the *Science of Logic*, Marcuse focuses on Hegel's concept of the "negation of the negation." For Marcuse, negativity and the negation of the negation are the core of the dialectic for both Hegel and Marx (Bernstein 1988). Marcuse writes (1941, p. 26) that "Hegel's philosophy is indeed what the subsequent reaction termed it, a negative philosophy." He holds further (1941, p. 27) that this is because to Hegel the "facts that appear to common sense" as the truth "are in reality the negation of truth" and that "truth can only be established by their destruction."

Robert Pippin (1988, p. 82) has discussed this emphasis on negativity in *Reason and Revolution*:

> Most clearly, what Marcuse wants to preserve and defend in Hegel is the central place given in his system to "negativity," the "power" of thought and action to reject and transform any putative "positive" reality, and the impossibility of understanding any such reality except in relation to this possibility. Accordingly, in *Reason and Revolution*, he again rejects in Hegel all those aspects of his thought that tend to suppress or overcome this negating potential . . .

Pippin implies further that this is due at least in part to the influence of Heidegger, as seen in Marcuse's first book on Hegel ([1932a] 1987), even though Heidegger, with whom Marcuse had by then broken because of Heidegger's ties to Nazism, is not mentioned in the text of *Reason and Revolution*. The only work by Heidegger to which Marcuse refers even in the bibliography is a 1933 work on the German university, which Marcuse (1941, p. 428) lists pointedly under the heading "Philosophy under Fascism and National Socialism." Thus, if there is a Heideggerian influence, it is subterranean and implicit.

But I would argue that probably more important with regard to the concept of negativity in *Reason and Revolution* is what Marcuse *does* refer to explicitly there, the "Critique of the Hegelian Dialectic" from Marx's *1844 Manuscripts*, a text which Marcuse apparently read only after he had completed his earlier "Heideggerian" Hegel book ([1932a] 1987, see also Kellner 1984). Marcuse wrote a lengthy article on the *1844 Manuscripts* immediately after they appeared for the first time in German in 1932. There, in the conclusion, he quotes the following passage from the young Marx's Hegel critique:

> The outstanding achievement of Hegel's *Phenomenology* and of its final result, *the dialectic of negativity as the moving and creative principle*—is thus that Hegel conceives the self-creation of the human being [*des Menschen*] as a process . . . (Marx [1844] 1968, p. 574, emphasis added)

In his essay on the young Marx, Marcuse ([1932b] 1973, p. 46) already points to the above as illustrating "the positive meaning of negation."

A decade later, in *Reason and Revolution* (1941, p. 282), Marcuse takes up this passage again, but now he spells out more explicitly the centrality to Marx of Hegel's concept of negativity, arguing that here, in this text, lie "the origins of the Marxian dialectic." He writes further: "For Marx, as for Hegel, the dialectic takes note of the fact that the negation inherent in reality is 'the moving and creative principle.' The dialectic is the 'dialectic of negativity.'" Negativity is important to Marx in part because: "Economic realities exhibit their own inherent negativity." Marcuse's stress on Hegel's concept of negativity is new and original. It is, of course, at variance with the interpretations of more conservative Hegel scholars, who tend instead to stress categories such as reconciliation and mediation. But it also differs from the emphasis on the category of totality in Lukács's *History and Class Consciousness*, written before Marx's 1844 discussion on Hegel's concept of negativity as "the moving and creative principle" had been published in any language. Even after the 1844 *Manuscripts* were published, however, official Soviet Marxists were generally hostile to any emphasis on the concept of negation, seeing it as a trace of idealistic Hegelianism. In the 1950s for example, the Soviet ideologist V. A. Karpushin (cited in Dunayevskaya [1958] 1988, p. 62) tried to banish the issue of negativity from Marxism, arguing in a discussion of the *Manuscripts* that Marx opposed the notion of "some kind of negativity which allegedly inherently clings to things, as Hegel put it."

Where Marcuse's discussion of Hegel's *Phenomenology* concentrates mainly on the early chapters of that work, in his discussion of the *Science of Logic* he follows Hegel's text from the Doctrine of Being to the Doctrine of Essence, the middle book of the *Science of Logic*. Marcuse discusses what he terms "Hegel's concept of real possibility" (1941, p. 151). He writes that in Hegel's concept of essence, the "possible and the real are in a dialectical relation" (1941, p. 150). This leads Marcuse, as a Marxist, to write that for Hegel "a new [social] system is really possible if the conditions for it are present in the old" (1941, p. 152).

Marcuse's discussion of the third and final book of Hegel's *Science of Logic*, the Doctrine of the Notion or concept, is briefer, but notable for its rather unusual focus on "a rough interpretation of its closing paragraphs" (1941, p. 161). He devotes seven pages to these closing paragraphs, writing that "Hegel's chapter on the Absolute Idea gives us a final comprehensive demonstration of dialectic method," and that even the Absolute Idea "is *dialectical* thought and thus contains its negation; it is not a harmonious and stable form but a process of unification of opposites" (1941, p. 165).

At the same time, however, he writes that in its closing paragraphs "Hegel's Logic resumes the metaphysical tradition of Western philosophy, a tradition that it had abandoned in so many of its aspects" (1941, p. 166). This is because "the basic concepts of idealism reflect a social separation of the intellectual sphere from the sphere of material production," present in a situation where "a 'leisure class' . . . became the guardian of the idea by virtue of the fact that it was not compelled to work for the material reproduction of society" (1941, p. 163). Marcuse holds that although Hegel attempts to go beyond this traditional type of idealism, he is ultimately unsuccessful. For Marcuse then, Hegel's Absolute Idea moves out of history and negativity and toward a purely ontological position. He also points to what he considers to be the theological aspects of the Absolute Idea, as "the Christian tradition, in which Hegel's philosophy was deeply rooted, asserts its right" (1941, p. 167), quoting a passage where Hegel asserts that his concept of logic "shows forth God as he is in his eternal essence" (1941, p. 167). But the passage Marcuse cites is not from the conclusion, but rather the introduction to the *Science of Logic*. Very few direct references to God or religion can be found in the Absolute Idea chapter of the *Science of Logic*, as an earlier Marxist reader, Lenin ([1914–15] 1961, p. 234) noted:

> It is noteworthy that the whole chapter on the "Absolute Idea" scarcely says a word about God . . . it contains almost nothing that is specifically *idealism*, but has for its main subject the *dialectical method*.

In a somewhat similar vein, but not moving as far as Lenin in rejecting religious roots for Hegel's Absolute Idea, Marcuse nonetheless sees Hegel's Absolute Idea seeking "to prove its freedom by freely releasing itself into otherness, that is, nature" (1941, p. 167). In this sense, he seems to view the conclusion of the *Science of Logic* as less of a closure than the end of the *Phenomenology*.

In the text of Hegel's *Science of Logic*, it is true that in the last paragraph Hegel writes that the Idea engages in a process where it "freely releases itself" in a "relationship to nature" (Hegel [1831] 1969, p. 843). To Marcuse, this shows the "rationalistic tendencies" (1941, p. 167) in Hegel's philosophy, even where he sees, at least to some degree, a move to theology as well. By freely releasing itself into Nature, Hegel has made a transition to the world of material reality, which takes us eventually to human praxis and history. Nature is for Hegel the transition to history, writes Marcuse, where the "identity of subject and object" is "attained" (1941, p. 168). This allows Marcuse to move from the discussion of the Absolute Idea at the end of the *Science of Logic* to Hegel's political philosophy. What he has skipped over is the way in which Hegel in the closing paragraph of the *Science of Logic* points not only to Nature but also to Spirit (Mind), writing that the Notion "completes its self-liberation in the science of Spirit (Mind)" (Hegel [1831] 1969, p. 844). I read Hegel here as outlining the whole of his philosophical system, which in the form of the *Encyclopedia of the Philosophical Sciences* would include three books: the *Shorter Logic* (a more popularized version of the *Science of Logic*), the *Philosophy of Nature*, and the *Philosophy of Mind* (Spirit). Thus, there is a transition from Logic to Nature and then to Mind (Spirit). Marcuse does not take up the latter two parts of Hegel's *Encyclopedia*.

Four decades earlier, Noël addressed the question of the place of the Logic in Hegel's overall philosophy somewhat differently. In a remark that seems to offer a critique before the fact of Marcuse's position, Noël (1897, p. 129), whose work is listed in Marcuse's bibliography, writes: "To treat Nature in itself, abstracted from Spirit (Mind), is that not an implicit return to the most naive realism?" While Lenin ([1914-15] 1961, p. 321) sharply attacked Noël as "an idealist and a shallow one" for this particular passage, to this reader, Marcuse's avoidance of Hegel's category of Spirit (Mind) in the Absolute Idea chapter of the *Science of Logic* does seem to rob social theory of a key Hegelian category, one which indeed helps us to critique naive realism.

This is important because, as we shall see below, critics of Marcuse such as Paul Tillich, Karl Löwith, Karel Kosík, and Raya Dunayevskaya have pointed out in different ways that Marcuse, in seeking to portray the transition from Hegel to Marx as one from philosophy to social theory, fails to discuss some of the most idealistic texts in Hegel's work, such as his treatment of Mind, religion, and aesthetics. Marcuse's overlooking of the more idealistic transition from Logic to Mind is an example of the type of procedure in *Reason and Revolution* that these critics of Marcuse have singled out.

Resuming a step-by-step discussion of Marcuse's text, we see that he *does* move from Hegel's *Science of Logic* to a discussion of his political philosophy. In this subsequent discussion, Marcuse sharply criticizes Hegel's political philosophy and his philosophy of history, and he sees Hegel's concept of negation of the negation rather than Hegel's specific writings on history and politics as the key link to Marx. According to Marcuse, Hegel's appointment to the leading chair in German philosophy at the University of Berlin in 1817 marked "the end of his philosophical development" at the very time when he became "the philosophical dictator of Germany" as "the so-called official philosopher of the Prussian state" (1941, p. 169). It was in this period that Hegel composed his *Philosophy of Right*, a work that expresses "the underlying identity of social and economic relations" of "middle-class society" (1941, p. 172). Thus, Hegel wanted a powerful bureaucracy to create a stronger foundation for the new social order "than the interests of relatively small proprietors can provide" (1941, p. 176). However, writes Marcuse, Hegel's determined opposition to the anti-government German youth movement of J.F. Fries has to be seen in the context of that movement's anti-Semitism and concern with "the Teutonic race alone" (1941, p. 179), a movement Marcuse regards as a precursor of fascism. At the same time, Hegel's state was to be "one governed by the standards of critical reason and by universally valid laws" and was thus "a weapon against reaction" (1941, p. 180).

However, in the working out of the analysis of social relations, Hegel's philosophy of the state "loses its critical content and comes to serve as a metaphysical justification of private property" (1941, p. 189). To Marcuse, this is because the "authoritarian trend that appears in Hegel's political philosophy is made necessary by the antagonistic structure of civil society" (1941, p. 202), a society divided into classes. In Hegel's schema, three institutions—the police, the corporations, and the state itself—are to help alleviate and reconcile class conflict. This is hardly a radical or even a democratic philosophy, but rather one bound to the authoritarian and underdeveloped conditions of Germany in the 1820s. Marcuse writes that this is because for Hegel "philosophy cannot jump ahead of history" (1941, p. 215). Marcuse also criticizes Hegel's cynicism on war and conquest between states as "oppressive" and a form of "authoritarianism" (1941, p. 221).

This chapter on the *Philosophy of Right* is a crucially important one for Marcuse's attempt to portray Hegel's philosophy as critical and revolutionary, and it was the target of many of the attacks on the book ever since, attacks that have accused Marcuse of being too uncritical in his appropriation of Hegel. But as we have seen, Marcuse is scathingly critical of Hegel at many points in this chapter. MacGregor (1984) has attempted to portray Hegel's *Philosophy of Right* as an essentially leftist work that has a strong affinity to Marx's thought, but MacGregor's statist reading of Marx, which relies on that of Althusser, is sharply divergent from Marcuse's subject-centered one.

Before coming to Marx, Marcuse includes a briefer but no less critical discussion of Hegel's *Philosophy of History*. Once he gets to Marx, Marcuse writes that "[t]he critical tendencies of the Hegelian philosophy . . . were taken over by, and continued in, the Marxian social theory" (1941, p. 252). For Marcuse, this does not mean, however, that Marx's early writings are primarily philosophical. Rather, "[t]hey express the negation of philosophy, though they still do so in philosophical language" (1941, p. 258). It is in this sense, he writes, that the transition from Hegel to Marx is one from philosophy to social theory.

In his treatment of Marx's *1844 Manuscripts*, Marcuse focuses his attention on Marx's discussion of alienation. Many sociological accounts of Marx's concept of alienation (Ollman 1971, Schwalbe 1986) have focused on an elaboration of Marx's four forms of alienated labor: (1) workers are alienated from the products of their labor; (2) the work process itself lacks creativity; (3) workers are alienated from themselves as well as from other human beings; (4) workers are alienated from their species being and from nature. This schematic elaboration, valuable as it may be in certain contexts, nonetheless serves to fix Marx's concept of alienated labor as a sociological description rooted in an economic relationship.

Marcuse focuses more on the underlying dialectical framework of Marx's argument, and on the link between the essay "Alienated Labor" and the more general statements in the same *Manuscripts*, as is seen especially in Marx's most fundamental concluding essay, "Critique of the Hegelian Dialectic." In his earlier 1932 analysis of those same essays, Marcuse stresses that all of Marx's economic categories are also philosophical ones.

He notes the statement in the essay "Alienated Labor" that private property is not the basis of alienated labor, but rather its result. While calling this statement a seemingly "idealistic distortion" of economic facts, Marcuse ([1932b] 1973, p. 12) concludes that it shows instead Marx's sociological depth. The whole issue is an important one because capitalism's central feature then becomes not a property relationship but a social one. The move from private to collective property relations alone, as for example under statist Communism, does not therefore remove the problem of alienated labor, and may even intensify it. Now, in *Reason and Revolution*, Marcuse writes, "Marx views the abolition of private property entirely as a means for the abolition of alienated labor, and not as an end in itself" (1941, p. 282).

Further, in an implicit but very sharp critique of Stalin's Russia, Marcuse concludes on the basis of the writings of the young Marx that state ownership of the economy, if "not utilized for the development and gratification of the free individual . . . will amount simply to a new form for subjugating individuals to a hypostatized universality" (1941, p. 283). Marcuse roots his concept of the liberated individual in passages from Marx's 1844 text such as the following: "One must above all avoid setting 'the society' up again as an abstraction opposed to the individual. The individual *is* the social entity" (1941, p. 283). Such an emphasis on Marx's notion of the "free individual" was extremely rare in 1941. This does not mean, however, a complete repudiation of the results of the 1917 Russian Revolution. Citing the writings of the reformist social democrat Eduard Bernstein, Marcuse holds that: "The schools of Marxism that abandoned the revolutionary foundations of the Marxian theory were the same that outspokenly repudiated the Hegelian aspects of the Marxian theory, especially the dialectic" (1941, p. 398). On the other hand, he writes, in an apparent reference to Lenin's 1914–15 Hegel Notebooks, that "Lenin insisted on dialectical method to such an extent that he considered it the hallmark of revolutionary Marxism" (1941, p. 401).

As Jay (1973, p. 76) has argued, Marcuse in 1941 places "the ontological significance of labor" at the center of his concept of dialectical Reason, something that his Frankfurt School colleagues Max Horkheimer and Theodor Adorno "were less sure about." This is seen in how Marcuse develops Marx's concept of a revolutionary working class:

The revolution requires the maturity of many forces, but the greatest among them is the subjective force, namely, the revolutionary class itself. The realization of freedom and reason requires the free rationality of those who achieve it. (Marcuse 1941, p. 319)

In this sense, the working class is to be armed intellectually with the concept of dialectical Reason developed by Hegel and Marx. Marcuse's discussion of Marx concludes on a more sanguine note, however, stressing the persistence of radical theory even in the face of a blocked objective situation: "Theory will preserve the truth even if revolutionary practice deviates from its proper path. Practice follows the truth, not vice versa" (1941, p. 322). In this passage, which concludes his discussion of Marx, Marcuse's stance is substantially similar to that of his Frankfurt School colleagues.

To Marcuse, positivism represents a theoretical counter-revolution against the heritage of Hegel and Marx. He writes (1941, p. 340) that Comte's attempt to found "an independent science of *sociology*" is at the price of "renouncing the transcendent point of view of the philosophical critique," especially the negative and critical stance toward the world found in German philosophy. Comte viewed himself as focusing on "useful knowledge," i.e., knowledge useful to ruling elites, "instead of negation and destruction" (1941, p. 341). Furthermore:

Rarely in the past has any philosophy urged itself forward with so strong and so overt a recommendation that it be utilized for the maintenance of prevailing authority and for the protection of vested interest from any and all revolutionary onset. (1941, p. 345)

The problem is not that positivism "excluded reform and change" but rather that change was to take place as "part of the machinery of the given order" (1941, p. 348). Throughout, Marcuse sharply contrasts Comte's "positive philosophy" to the "negative philosophy" not only of Marx but also of Hegel. He also discusses some conservative German positivists, but he does not connect this critique to contemporary positivists or pragmatists, or to the work of other major figures such as Durkheim. He does critique pragmatism in some of his writings in German for the Frankfurt School's own *Zeitschrift für Sozialforschung* (Kellner 1984), but does not do so in English during this period. This reticence may have had something to do with the precarious position of an exile scholar in the U.S.

Marcuse also defends Hegel against charges, still common even today in the English-speaking world, that Hegel's thought is somehow the forerunner of fascism and totalitarianism. Marcuse argues that, far from embracing Hegel, Nazi ideologists regarded him as one of their chief enemies. The book closes with a quote from Carl Schmitt, whom Marcuse terms "the one serious political theorist of National Socialism." Schmitt wrote that on the day of Hitler's ascent to power, "Hegel, so to speak, died" (1941, p. 419). This is important today in light of the renewed discussion of Schmitt's political theory.

The book's stinging attack on positivism along with its ringing defense of Hegel as a revolutionary thinker subjected it to some sharp attacks, especially from more empiricist minded American Marxists and socialists, who considered pragmatism and even positivism as having more in common with Marx's thought than Hegel. These attacks have persisted to today; at the same time, the book has attained classic status as a major work of Hegelian Marxism.

Reviews and critiques in the 1940s

When *Reason and Revolution* was first published, the sharpest attack on it came from the pragmatist Sidney Hook, then still a member of the Marxist left, who went to the trouble of writing two negative reviews. Hook was as outraged by Marcuse's defense of Hegel as critical and revolutionary as he was by Marcuse's attack on positivism as essentially conservative. In a review for *The New Republic*, Hook (1941a, p. 91) reproaches Marcuse for not dealing with the ways in which Hegelian logic is opposed to "scientific method," i. e. positivism. In his defense of positivism against what he terms "the idealist principle" underlying Marcuse's approach, Hook writes that "positivism seeks to discover by scientific, not dialectical methods what the facts are" and advocates "testing our ideals and principles by available facts." He objects especially to Marcuse's notion that positivism is essentially conservative: "positivists can be and have been revolutionists just as dialecticians can be and have been reformists, and even stand-patters." Hook also maintains that Hegel's *Philosophy of Right* does provide "a connection between Hegel and National Socialism" (1941a, p. 91). Hook's more academic review for *The Living Age* concentrates almost entirely on Hegel's *Philosophy of Right*, a work that Marcuse discussed only briefly. In this review, Hook attacks Hegel's "absolute idealism" as essentially "conservative," and defends empiricism "as a philosophical attitude" that is "essentially public and critical" (1941b, p. 595). In neither of these reviews does Hook even mention the writings of the young Marx, or Marcuse's discussion of the Hegel-Marx relationship. Hook's reviews are more an occasion for attacking Hegel than a serious grappling with any of Marcuse's arguments. From another quarter of the American left, a less vitriolic but somewhat similar discussion was published in the Communist Party-oriented theoretical journal, *Science & Society*. There, the Marxist philosopher Vernon J. McGill (1942, p. 161) pointed to the "author's interesting argument to demonstrate the Hegelian component in Marx's philosophy," but here too, positivism was defended as scientific and therefore revolutionary, while Marcuse's pathbreaking discussion of the young Marx was ignored. In a similar vein to that of Hook and McGill, Erich Franzen's critique in the *American Sociological Review* attacked Marcuse for failing to critique Hegel's basic concepts, and also suggested that, contra Marcuse, there was a possible link between Hegel and fascism. Franzen concludes that Husserl and Simmel offer better alternatives for sociological theory than Marcuse's "dubious expedient" of a "revivification of Hegel" (Franzen 1942, p. 128).

On the other hand, Marcuse's book fared quite a bit better in the pages of the *American Journal of Sociology*, where the political theorist George Sabine's more balanced and respectful review linked *Reason and Revolution* to Dilthey's 1905 *Jugendgeschichte Hegels*, calling Marcuse's book "much the best account of Hegel in English." He also identified strongly with Marcuse's refutation of the notion of a link between Hegel and fascism, writing that "Hegel's philosophy was fundamentally rationalist, while the philosophy of national socialism is fundamentally irrationalist" (Sabine 1942, p. 259). However, even Sabine expressed strong disagreement with Marcuse's attack on positivism.

In retrospect, the most curious feature of these and other early reviews by American scholars was that not a single one of them even mentioned the lengthy discussion of Marx's *1844 Manuscripts* in *Reason and Revolution*, even though Marcuse here introduced for the first time to the American intellectual public key issues such as Marx's discussion of alienation. That topic did not begin to receive attention in the U.S. until the late 1950s, after the *Manuscripts*, including the essay "Alienated Labor," were finally published in English, and after the new popularity of European philosophies such as existentialism had helped to undermine the hegemony of empiricism and positivism even among left wing intellectuals.

Among German emigré scholars, Karl Löwith, whose own important book, *From Hegel to Nietzsche*, also appeared in 1941, and the theologian Paul Tillich each wrote interesting critiques of *Reason and Revolution* soon after it appeared. Tillich, writing in the Frankfurt School's journal *Studies in Philosophy and Social Science*, formerly the *Zeitschrift für Sozialforschung*, singles out Marcuse's emphasis on the "negative" character of Hegel's thought as the link between Hegel and Marx. He sees Marcuse as part of a group of younger German philosophers "whose philosophical education occurred in the period of war and revolution," something which drew them to Hegel and Marx (1941, p. 476). Despite his overall praise for the book as a pioneering study of Hegel from the point of view of Critical Theory, Tillich criticizes Marcuse for not taking up Hegel's writings on religion or aesthetics. While mainly defending the need for a religious perspective, there is a bit more to Tillich's argument, which is in some ways similar to critiques of Marcuse made in the 1960s by the Marxist Humanists Kosík and Dunayevskaya. Tillich is apparently referring to the general issue of Hegel's Absolutes and their relationship to religion and, at the same time, to Marcuse's stress on Hegel as a political and social thinker. He writes: "Even a critical social theory cannot avoid an 'ultimate' in which its criticism is rooted because reason itself is rooted therein. Otherwise criticism itself becomes positivistic and contingent" (1941, p. 478).

A somewhat similar critique was made by Löwith, who knew Marcuse from the days they both studied under Heidegger in the 1920s. Löwith writes that the "book gives in its first part an excellent analysis of Hegel's philosophy" (1942a, p. 561), but he also takes *Reason and Revolution* to task for downplaying the religious and non-revolutionary parts of Hegel's work. Löwith writes further, taking issue with Marcuse's stress on categories such as negativity, that Hegel is primarily a philosopher of "progressive mediation and reconciliation," and criticizes what he terms Marcuse's one-sided stress on "criticism of the given state of affairs" (1942a, p. 562) in his treatment of Hegel's philosophy as a critique of fascism. This review was published together with Marcuse's response and Löwith's rejoinder (1942b). In his response, Marcuse (1942, p. 565) writes that Löwith's statement about Hegel on "progressive mediation and reconciliation" shows that "he apparently confuses Hegel's dialectic with a shallow philosophy of progress." As to his alleged politicization of Hegel's thought, Marcuse replies that "although Löwith is a good student of the development from Hegel to Marx," he unfortunately "deems it incompatible with the dignity of philosophy to take sides in the great historical struggles of our time" (1942, p. 564).

Marcuse's 1954 epilogue and 1960 preface

Although many writers in the Critical Theory tradition have tended to downplay the importance of *Reason and Revolution*, even in Marcuse's own work, one indication of its central importance to Marcuse himself is the fact that it is the only one of his works for which he added new material, not once, but twice, in 1954 and again in 1960. The new material that Marcuse adds to *Reason and Revolution* in the 1954 and 1960 editions also illustrates the evolution of his thought on Hegel, Marx, and dialectics. Marcuse wrote an epilogue for the 1954 edition that begins on a far more resigned and pessimistic note than does the 1941 text:

> The defeat of Fascism and National Socialism has not arrested the trend toward totalitarianism. Freedom is on the retreat—in the realm of thought as well as in that of society. Neither the Hegelian nor the Marxian idea of Reason have come closer to realization. (Marcuse 1954, p. 433)

This is because "late industrial civilization" has been able to transform the conditions and mental outlook of the working class, enabling it to "absorb its negativity" (1954, p. 437). This is true not only in the West, but also in the East, where "the Soviet state grew into a highly rationalized and industrialized society" (1954, p. 439) as well. Where in 1941 dialectical Reason seemed to have a chance to appear as the revolutionary philosophy guiding working class action toward a practically possible transcendence of alienation, for Marcuse in 1954 such aspirations are utopian: "The idea of a different form of Reason and Freedom, envisioned by dialectical idealism as well as materialism, appears again as Utopia" (1954, p. 439). But he concludes that, even in a utopian form, dialectical concepts such as Reason and Freedom remain a distant possibility, which is why the established forces in society propagandize so endlessly against the very idea of liberation.

Marcuse's more important preface to the 1960 edition, "A Note on Dialectic," develops further some of the concepts in the 1954 preface, but here the focus is more on the dialectic proper than on social and economic developments after 1945. Marcuse speaks of the "power of negative thinking" as seen in Hegel and Marx as being "in danger of being obliterated" (1960, p. vii). Dialectical Reason is "alien to the whole established universe of discourse and action" (1960, p. vii). Although Hegel's dialectic of negativity critiques the existing world on the basis of a "principle of freedom," such freedom "is relegated to the realm of pure thought, to the Absolute Idea" (1960, p. ix). For Hegel, according to Marcuse, this impasse leads dialectical thought "to become historical analysis." But how to do that in 1960, he asks, when the power of negative thought is virtually obliterated? Negativity, having been virtually abolished in philosophy and social theory due to the domination of positivist and empiricist thought, can be found elsewhere: in "poetic language" and "avant-garde literature" (1960, p. x). They help move us toward what he terms "the Great Refusal" (1960, p. x) of industrial and technocratic society, a point Marcuse illustrates by quoting from Mallarmé, Valéry, and other French poets.

This leads Marcuse to move away from Hegel's concept of dialectical Reason, the concept that formed one of the central threads in *Reason and Revolution*:

> I believe it is the idea of Reason itself which is the undialectical element in Hegel's philosophy. This idea of Reason comprehends everything and ultimately absolves everything, because it has its place and function in the whole . . . It may even be justifiable, logically as well as historically, to define Reason in terms which include slavery, the Inquisition, child labor, concentration camps, gas chambers, and nuclear preparedness. (1960, p. xii)

Reason is therefore "a part rather than . . . the whole."

Marx's critical appropriation of Hegel, according to Marcuse, stemmed from "a recognition that the established forms of life were reaching the stage of their historical negation" (1960, p. xiii). Unfortunately, however:

> Those social groups which dialectical theory identified as the forces

of negation are either defeated or reconciled with the established system. Before the power of the given facts, the power of negative thinking stands condemned. (1960, p. xiv)

Hegel's concept of totality is true and yet at the same time *not* true, because "no method can claim a monopoly of cognition" (1960, p. xiv). Therefore, there are two poles around which we can think a dialectical negation of the existing society: "'The whole is the truth,' and the whole is false" (1960, p. xiv).

While the language is abstract, the central thrust seems to be twofold: (1) The workers are no longer a revolutionary class, as Marx had concluded, thus calling much of his concept of dialectic into question. (2) The Hegelian concept of the unfoldment of freedom as dialectical Reason was increasingly blocked as well, due to the pervasiveness of technological rationality in modern society. Since in Marcuse's view Western Reason had been used to create mass destruction and genocide, it too needs to be questioned. The critique of society to be found in avant-garde art might ultimately be more dialectical than Hegel's concept of dialectical Reason. Marcuse thus questions Hegel's totalizing notion of Reason, which he by now sees as leading back toward instrumental reason, and he points to less totalizing forms of thought. Thus, to continue to be critical in a technocratic society, dialectical Reason needs to move outside the Hegelian-Marxian tradition, while holding onto many of its achievements.

A view of this problem that may have a relationship to Marcuse's 1960 position, but which was at variance with the 1941 text of *Reason and Revolution*, was developed in the early 1960s by second generation critical theorist Oskar Negt in West Germany. His study of Hegel and Comte points not only to differences, as did Marcuse in 1941, but also to affinities between Comte and Hegel in their respective theories of society. In a preface to this work, Negt's teachers Horkheimer and Adorno write that his book shows "the latent positivism implicit in the Hegelian construction of social reality, something which one would not expect because of Hegel's own hostility to positivism" (Negt [1963] 1974, p. 8). Negt himself ([1963] 1974, p. 133) links Hegel's concept of "objective spirit" to Durkheim's concept of a "collective consciousness."

By the 1960s, when Marcuse became well known internationally, sharp critiques of his work appeared from a variety of perspectives. Most of these discussions centered on his later works such as *One-Dimensional Man* (1964), but there were also new critical discussions of *Reason and Revolution*. Below I concentrate on four representative discussions since 1960: those by the anti-Hegelian Italian philosopher Lucio Colletti, the American critical theorist Douglas Kellner, the Czech Marxist Humanist philosopher Karel Kosík, and the Russian-American Marxist Humanist and Hegel scholar Raya Dunayevskaya.

Critical discussions since 1960: Colletti and Kellner

Colletti ([1968] 1972, [1969] 1973] published two major critiques of Marcuse as part of a general attack on Hegelian Marxism, which had gained wide popularity in Italy by the late 1960s. Colletti's work was quickly translated into English in the 1970s and, along with that of Althusser, became part of the critique of Hegelian Marxism and Critical Theory in the English-speaking world. In an article entitled "From Hegel to Marcuse," Colletti takes up some similar themes to those of Hook in 1941. He wants to criticize both Hegel and Marcuse from the point of view of "science" ([1968] 1972, p. 131). In sharp contrast to Marcuse's view, which I discussed above, Colletti ([1968] 1972, p. 112) attacks Hegel's concept of infinity as an essentially mystical and religious "annihilation of the world" of facts and things. According to Colletti, Marcuse takes up this Hegelian notion of annihilation and "negativity" in a one-sided sense and creates out of it a philosophy of generalized revolt against human existence. Colletti ([1968] 1972, p. 130) links this "revolt" to what he regards as Hegel's "old spiritualist contempt for the finite and the terrestrial world." In so doing, Colletti ignores Marcuse's strong arguments in *Reason and Revolution* to the effect that Hegel's philosophy is more historically based than that of other German idealists, and thus closer to Marx.

Colletti scathingly attacks Marcuse's "idealistic reaction against science" in his critique of positivism ([1968] 1972, p. 131). Marcuse's attack on capitalism is therefore not Marxist, but "an indiscriminate attack on science and technology" ([1968] 1972, p. 135). Colletti attempts to link this attack on science and positivism to Sartre's existentialist concept of "nausea" toward the material world in order to argue that Marcuse is not a Marxist thinker, but "descends from Heidegger" ([1968] 1972, p. 131).

A fundamental problem in Colletti's discussion is that he constructs his

"Marxist" view of Hegel without ever seriously discussing Marx's crucially important "Critique of the Hegelian Dialectic" in the 1844 *Manuscripts*. It is in this essay that, as Marcuse notes in *Reason and Revolution*, Marx singles out the concept of negativity as the creative and revolutionary element in Hegel's dialectic. Colletti avoids discussion of this key essay by Marx not only in his critique of Marcuse, but even in a lengthy fifty-page introduction to an edition of Marx's early writings published in association with the *New Left Review*. There, in his discussion of the 1844 *Manuscripts*, he takes up only the concept of alienation (Colletti 1975). Also, where Marcuse honestly confronts and comes to grip with those parts of Hegel's writings, such as the *Philosophy of Right*, which create difficulty for his view of Hegel as an essentially revolutionary thinker, Colletti does not seriously engage arguments contrary to his own. Thus, his polemic against Marcuse misfires. Colletti's own anti-Hegelianism eventually led to a break with Marxism as well in the 1970s (Jay 1984, McGlone 1985).

Kellner's book on Marcuse, the most thorough theoretical study to date, expresses greater affinity for his later work than for *Reason and Revolution*. He writes (1984, p. 133) that in *Reason and Revolution*, "the thrust of Marcuse's interpretation is to valorize the radical components in Hegel," giving us "a powerful critique of empiricism and positivism." He views these critiques as having anticipated Marcuse's later critiques of empiricism and positivism in works such as *One-Dimensional Man*. Kellner argues that although Marcuse never directly answered Hook's polemics against *Reason and Revolution*, much of his later work was taken up with a critique of positions similar to Hook's. In emphasizing the critique of positivism, Kellner stresses the similarities between Marcuse's book and those of the other critical theorists such as Adorno and Horkheimer. On the one hand, this procedure has the merit of effectively showing the link to Marcuse's later work, such as *One-Dimensional Man*, and to that of Adorno and Horkheimer. On the other hand, Marcuse's Hegelian Marxism, which had a somewhat different orientation than Adorno's and Horkheimer's to both the dialectic and to politics, already visible in 1941, is missed. The latter helps us to anticipate one aspect of Marcuse in the 1960s as well: his public return to a variant of the left revolutionary politics that his Frankfurt School colleagues Adorno and Horkheimer gave up after the early 1940s.

Kellner makes three major criticisms of *Reason and Revolution*. First, he sees problems with Marcuse's overall perspective on Hegel. He complains (1984, p. 144) that "Marcuse's appropriation of Hegel's ontology and epistemology is too uncritical" and that he "never really criticizes Hegel's philosophy as such." To Kellner (1984, p. 144), it is "precisely Hegel's philosophical positions" that are at the root of the authoritarian flaws in those works of Hegel which Marcuse criticizes sharply, such as the *Philosophy of Right*. Kellner criticizes in particular Hegel's "thoroughgoing panrationalism and his concept of the Absolute" (1984, p. 144). The latter "contains mystifying overtones of finality, completeness and perfection" and leads us to the notion that "reason was realized in the Prussian state" (1984, p. 145). He accuses Marcuse of having evaded these issues.

Second, on the relation of Hegel to Marx, Kellner writes that Marcuse "pictures Marx as emerging fully developed from Hegel," while "a more balanced interpretation would have indicated the influences on Marxism of French socialism and British political economy" (1984, p. 419). Thus, writes Kellner, Marcuse's Marxism is too uncritically Hegelian, and does not bring in enough political economy. Kellner does not take up Marcuse's lengthy treatment of Marx on alienation, in which he discusses how Marx critically appropriated Hegel's dialectic as he "focused his theory on the labor process" (1941, p. 272).

Third, Kellner (1984, p. 143) writes that, as against his "later questioning of the proletariat," Marcuse's Marxism in *Reason and Revolution* "is remarkably 'orthodox'" in its treatment of the working class as (in Marx's terms) the living negation of capitalism. To Kellner, this aspect of Marcuse's work shows *Reason and Revolution* to be almost an aberration when seen alongside his earlier and later writings:

> There is a "rationalist" turn in his thought during this period where he affirms the heritage of critical rationalism and distances himself from Heidegger, existentialism, *Lebensphilosophie* and phenomenology. Later Marcuse would respond to Adorno and Horkheimer's critique of technology and instrumental reason, and in *Eros and Civilization* and other later works would reformulate the concept of reason and reconstruct critical theory. (Kellner 1984, p. 128–29)

While agreeing with Kellner that the Hegelian Marxism of *Reason and Revolution* is altered considerably after the 1940s, I would argue that it also expresses the dialectical core of Marcuse's left radical vision, something which—although it appeared in a different form by the 1960s—was at the same time a partial return to the left revolutionary vision of Germany in the 1920s, as seen in the writings of Lukács and Korsch.

Kellner does not fully draw the threads of his various critiques together. If Marcuse's Marxism is both too Hegelian and too orthodox, how do these two flaws fit together? But the main problem in Kellner's critique is that he focuses too little on what Marcuse was doing with Hegel in 1941, tending to let the critique of instrumental reason and of positivism overshadow the other major themes in Marcuse's book.

In 1991, in the introduction to a new edition of Marcuse's *One-Dimensional Man*, Kellner discusses for the first time some recently discovered manuscripts on theories of social change, composed by Marcuse and fellow critical theorist Franz Neumann during the period right after publication of Marcuse's *Reason and Revolution* and Neumann's *Behemoth*, the latter book a study of the social structure of Nazi Germany. Kellner writes that these manuscripts show "the typically Marcusean tendency, shared by the Frankfurt School, to integrate philosophy, social theory and politics" (Kellner in Marcuse [1964] 1991, p. xxi). He argues that *Reason and Revolution* was connected to a broader project within critical theory, one opposed to the solely "philosophical-cultural analysis of the trends of Western civilization being developed by Horkheimer and Adorno" (Kellner in Marcuse [1964] 1991, p. xxii). Thus, despite the seemingly abstract and philosophical character of *Reason and Revolution*, it apparently served as the theoretical foundation for a more empirical study of social change.

Further critical discussions: Kosík and Dunayevskaya

Beginning in the 1960s, Marxist Humanists have challenged *Reason and Revolution* on still different grounds. In his widely discussed book *The Dialectics of the Concrete*, the Czech Marxist Humanist Karel Kosík suggests that even Marcuse is guilty of "abolishing philosophy" within Marxism when he moves from Hegel to a consideration of Marxism as the "dialectical theory of society" ([1963] 1976, p. 104). Kosík is referring to Marcuse's view of the shift from Hegel to Marx as one from philosophy to social theory. He hits out sharply against any attempt to "abolish" philosophy within Marxism, even when this means moving from philosophy to a critical social theory. If philosophy is so abolished, writes Kosík, Marx's theory "is transformed into its very opposite" and "praxis ceases to be the sphere of humanizing man." If we move one-sidedly into social theory, a certain "openness" is lost and "turns into a closedness." We reach a point where "socialness is a cave" in which the human being is "walled" ([1963] 1976, p. 106). Kosík seems to point to a continual cross-fertilization between philosophy and social theory.

At a time when postmodernists have attacked the writings of Hegel and Marx as oppressive "great narratives" that radical thought should leave behind (Lyotard 1989) and a second-generation critical theorist Habermas (1990, p. 15) distanced himself from what he considered the "romantic socialism" of the young Marx, Marcuse's *Reason and Revolution* might seem far from current concerns in its emphasis on Hegel's concept of dialectical Reason as a revolutionary and critical concept and on Marx's theory of alienation. Yet these are precisely some of the threads that the Russian-American Marxist Humanist Raya Dunayevskaya picks up from Marcuse's work, carrying them into current theoretical problematics, but all the while engaging Marcuse's work very critically. Her interest in Marcuse's *Reason and Revolution* began in the 1940s, but she continued to write about it up to her death in 1987.

In 1979, at the time of Marcuse's death, Dunayevskaya (1979, p. 10–11) wrote of the enthusiasm with which she and her colleagues greeted *Reason and Revolution* when it first appeared:

> In that seminal work, Marcuse established the Humanism of Marxism and re-established the revolutionary dialectic of Hegel-Marx, for the first time for the American public. It is impossible to forget the indebtedness we felt for Marcuse when that breath of fresh air and vision of a truly classless society was published . . .

Similar to Marcuse, Dunayevskaya, also following Marx's 1844 "Critique of the Hegelian Dialectic," was drawn to Hegel's concept of negativity. Ollman (1992, p. 26–27) argues that "for Raya Dunayevskaya, it was the 'negation of the negation'" that was the "pivotal" dialectical category. She was, in the 1940s, part of the "Johnson-Forest Tendency" within American Trotskyism under the pseudonym "Freddie Forest," together with the Afro-Caribbean theorist C.L.R. James (aka J.R. Johnson) and the Chinese-American philosopher Grace Lee Boggs. In an unpublished letter,

Dunayevskaya ([1966] 1981f, p. 13936]) writes that at the end of 1941 she "read a new book, *Reason and Revolution* by Herbert Marcuse. The first part on Hegel meant nothing to me then, but the second part which dealt with Marx's Early Essays opened a new world to me."

Scattered through the published and unpublished writings of Dunayevskaya, who became a friend of Marcuse in the 1950s, are a number of interesting discussions of *Reason and Revolution*. In her *Marxism and Freedom* ([1958] 1988, p. 349), a book to which Marcuse contributed a critical preface, she describes *Reason and Revolution* as "a truly pioneering and profound work" to which "I would like to acknowledge my debt." Dunayevskaya (1980, [1973] 1989a; see also Anderson 1986) attempts critically to appropriate Hegel's Absolutes, the very category that even other Hegelian Marxists have tended to avoid or dismiss (Lukács [1947] 1975, Bloch ([1949] 1962). To Dunayevskaya, Hegel's Absolutes were not a closed totality, but rather a source of "absolute negativity," out of which could be constructed a radical concept of dialectics that would expand the traditional Marxist concept of the labor movement to include new social movements of Blacks, women, and youth. By the 1980s she was increasingly connecting these issues to a subject-centered feminist theory (Dunayevskaya [1982] 1991; see also Rich 1986, Afary 1989, Johnson 1989).

As part of his extensive correspondence with Dunayevskaya in the 1950s (Dunayevskaya and Marcuse 1989, p. 4), Marcuse expresses some doubt about this procedure:

> I admire your way of concretizing the most abstract philosophical notions. However, I still cannot get along with the direct translation of idealistic philosophy into politics: I think you somehow minimize the "negation" which the application of the Hegelian dialectic to political phenomena presupposes.

Dunayevskaya responds:

> You seem to think that I . . . minimize the "negation" which the application of the Hegelian dialectic to political phenomena presupposes. But surely Hegel's Absolute Idea has nothing in common with Schelling's conception of the Absolute as the synthesis or identity in which all differences are absorbed by the "One." (Dunayevskaya and Marcuse 1989, p. 4)

Their correspondence illustrates some of the key differences between Dunayevskaya and Marcuse on Hegelian dialectics as well as on automation and the labor process (Anderson 1989a, 1989b, 1990; Kellner 1984, 1989a, 1989b).

At a later point in their correspondence, Marcuse writes in 1960: "The very concept of the Absolute Idea is altogether tied to and justifies the separation of material and intellectual productivity at the pre-technological stage" (Dunayevskaya and Marcuse 1989, p. 12). This statement is a further development of an aspect of his discussion of the Absolute Idea in *Reason and Revolution* where, as we saw earlier, he writes (1941, p. 163) that it reflected "the social separation of the intellectual sphere from the sphere of material production." This theme later became central to the chapter on pre-technological thought in Marcuse's *One-Dimensional Man* ([1964] 1991). There, without mentioning his correspondence with Dunayevskaya, Marcuse treats pre-technological thought, from Plato to Hegel, as critical and dialectical Reason, which is counterposed to the dominant positivist, "one-dimensional," and technological thought. In her *Philosophy and Revolution*, Dunayevskaya ([1973] 1989, p. 44), without directly naming Marcuse, seems to respond to his argument when she writes: "it would be a complete misreading of Hegel's philosophy were we to think . . . that his Absolute is a mere reflection of the separation between philosopher and the world of material production."

Dunayevskaya makes two types of critiques of *Reason and Revolution*: (1) She contrasts the 1941 text to the preface Marcuse added in 1960, "A Note on Dialectic," attacking the latter as an abandonment of the type of revolutionary dialectic Marcuse held to in the 1940s. (2) She criticizes Marcuse's treatment of the Absolute Idea in Hegel's *Science of Logic* (even in the original 1941 text) arguing that he stops short of a fully Hegelian Marxism by not seriously taking up Hegel's Absolutes. She also critiques a few other aspects of his discussion of Hegelian idealism, even though she is in broad agreement with the central thrust of much of the 1941 text. The first critique is made publicly on several occasions, but often very briefly and cryptically, and can be best understood by looking as well at some of her unpublished writings, including her correspondence. The second critique is never really made publicly, and can be pieced together only from correspondence and other unpublished writings as well as from her handwritten marginalia in her personal copy of *Reason and Revolution* (Dunayevskaya n.d.).

In her critiques of Marcuse's 1960 preface, Dunayevskaya tends to focus on the following sentence: "I believe it is the idea of Reason itself which is the undialectical element in Hegel's philosophy" (Marcuse 1960, p. xii). Dunayevskaya ([1969] 1981f, p. 4410) writes of "how perverse such a conclusion will sound to dialecticians in general, and to Marxists in particular." She writes elsewhere ([1982] 1991, p. 177) that while Marcuse in the 1941 text of *Reason and Revolution* was working out the relationship of dialectics "to actual revolution," by the 1960 edition "Marcuse added 'A Note on the Dialectic,' which pointed in a very different, 'one-dimensional' direction." In her view, by 1960, Marcuse was not only moving away from the traditional Marxian concept of the working class as subject, but also and even more fundamentally at a theoretical level, from his earlier view of dialectical Reason. To be sure, Marcuse's new dialectic traced its origin to Hegel and Marx, but she argues that the central place it now gave to the "Great Refusal" of avant-garde art was a move away from the Hegelian-Marxian dialectic as developed in the original 1941 text of *Reason and Revolution*.

In several letters to Marxist Humanist colleagues written soon after the appearance of Marcuse's *One-Dimensional Man* in 1964, she sees the 1960 preface as lying somewhere in between his book *Soviet Marxism* (1958), which she had sharply attacked for its relatively uncritical stance toward the Soviet Union, and his present position: "it is his transition point from total pessimism and apologia through the mid-point of the 'Great Refusal' (1960) to the present almost-optimism of 'One Dimensional Man' perhaps working his way out" (Dunayevskaya [1964b] 1981f, p. 13884). She calls this 1960 preface to *Reason and Revolution* "the *philosophic* point that separates us" ([1964c] 1981f, p. 13888). Apparently in order to stress what she regarded as the most radical core of Marcuse's thought (as against his later development), she entitled her review of *One-Dimensional Man* "Reason and Revolution vs. Conformism and Technology" (Dunayevskaya 1964a, Greeman 1968).

In a letter written a year before her death, and just after having deposited her correspondence with Marcuse in the Wayne State University archives, Dunayevskaya sums up her view of the division between Marcuse's 1941 and 1960 concepts of dialectic:

> In 1941, Marcuse was optimistic, saw Marx as Humanism, revolutionary Humanism, inseparable from dialectics of revolutionary categories of development; in 1960 he was pessimistic and was on the way to declaring, not the "negation" of the system so much as "negation" of mankind . . . Dialectic, "negation of the negation," undergoes changed interpretation—or, like Absolute, gets omitted altogether . . . (Dunayevskaya 1986a, p. 3)

Thus, the attack on the 1960 preface is at the same time a great appreciation for the 1941 text.

Her critiques of the 1941 text itself are less frequent, and tend to center on Marcuse's view of Hegel's Absolutes and the Hegel-Marx relationship. Dunayevskaya sees much similarity between Lenin and Marcuse in their reading of the last paragraphs of Hegel's *Science of Logic*. Similar to Lenin in his 1914–15 *Hegel Notebooks*, Marcuse interprets the last paragraph of Hegel's *Science of Logic* as a transition to Nature, ignoring (according to Dunayevskaya) the fact that Hegel mentions there not only a transition to Nature, but also one to Mind. This is important because Lenin had jumped on this mention of Nature to conclude that this was a transition to materialism (Lenin [1914–15] 1961, p. 234). In material added to the 1989 edition of her *Philosophy and Revolution* from some of her last writings (Dunayevskaya ([1973] 1989a) and elsewhere (Dunayevskaya 1989b), she criticizes Lenin's reading of Hegel's final paragraphs as an attempt to jump too quickly toward materialism, and thus a truncation of the dialectic.

In unpublished 1961 notes on Hegel's *Science of Logic*, Dunayevskaya writes that in *Reason and Revolution*, as with Lenin earlier, Marcuse too stresses Hegel's "statement about the Idea releasing itself freely as Nature." At the same time, Marcuse points to the great difficulty of this passage of Hegel's work. Dunayevskaya ([1961] 1981f, p. 2832) complains:

> But he himself doesn't attempt to overcome these difficulties. On the contrary, he disregards them, accepting the idea that it is a closed ontology and the best we can do is take this method and use it as a critical theory.

At one point in her marginal notes to *Reason and Revolution*, Dunayevskaya writes, apparently comparing Marcuse's discussion of the Absolute Idea to

that of Lenin: "Actually HM [Herbert Marcuse] too stops at Nature" alongside a passage where Marcuse is discussing the conclusion of Hegel's *Science of Logic* as a transition to Nature (Dunayevskaya n.d., p. 166). Here
Dunayevskaya (n.d., p. 166) also writes in the margin of Marcuse's text:
"not only Nature but also Spirit [Mind]." She is apparently criticizing Marcuse for ignoring Hegel's *Philosophy of Mind*, one of his most idealistic
works. While avoided by most Marxists as too idealist, this key text forms
the conclusion to Hegel's *Encyclopedia of the Philosophical Sciences*. It was
primarily on the basis of this work of Hegel's, especially its concluding
chapter on Absolute Mind, that she developed the most important aspects
of her own interpretation of Hegel's Absolutes not as closures but as permeated with absolute negativity, and with new beginnings (Dunayevskaya
[1973] 1989a, 1989b).

While agreeing in general with Marcuse that there were both historical
and social as well as purely ontological elements in Hegel's philosophy, at
several points in her marginal notes, she also criticizes Marcuse for stressing the primacy of ontology in some of Hegel's most idealistic categories.
Next to a passage where Marcuse writes that "Hegel's dialectical process
was thus a universal ontological one in which history was patterned on
the metaphysical process of being," Dunayevskaya writes: "No, he derived
it from actual history" (Dunayevskaya n.d., p. 314). She also writes "NO"
over the word "ontological" where Marcuse argues that Hegel's philosophy, although rooted in history, "is constantly overwhelmed by the ontological conceptions of absolute idealism" (Dunayevskaya n.d., p. 161). In
this sense, her position may be closer to that of Jean Hyppolite's ([1955]
1969) treatment of Hegel's relation to history in his discussion of the relationship of the *Phenomenology* to the French Revolution. To Dunayevskaya,
the whole of Hegel's idealistic dialectic, including his Absolutes, is an historically based dialectic of freedom that can have concrete political and
social ramifications.

By the late 1970s, Dunayevskaya sharpens her critique of even the 1941
text of *Reason and Revolution*, writing to a leading British labor activist that
her differences with Marcuse in the 1950s and 1960s were not only over
issues such as the place of the labor movement in postwar capitalism but
also over the dialectic: "Why, however, could I not have made myself so
clear to myself as to see that, much as I learned from Marcuse, we were not
only on different planets 'politically' but philosophically?" (Dunayevskaya

[1978] 1981f, p. 6433). A year before her death she wrote that Marcuse's analysis of Hegel's *Science of Logic* "remained in the Doctrine of Essence, at most reaching the threshold—the threshold only—of the Absolute" (Dunayevskaya [1986b] 1981f, p. 11262).

Thus, Dunayevskaya's critique of *Reason and Revolution* is from a different vantage point not only from that of Colletti but also from that of Kellner. She identifies strongly with the Hegelian Marxism of the 1941 text of *Reason and Revolution*, but develops her own concept of dialectic by going beyond it, taking up whole areas of Hegel's writings that even Marcuse either ignored or tended to dismiss as ontological idealism. Where Marcuse stresses Hegel's concept of negativity in general, Dunayevskaya focuses more specifically on the concept of absolute negativity, the form in which negativity appears in Hegel's Absolutes. As against Marcuse's (1941, p. 163) notion that the abstract character of the Absolute Idea reflects an ultimately conservative "separation of the intellectual sphere from the sphere of material production," Dunayevskaya ([1973] 1989a, pp. 31–32) argues that Hegel's dialectic is at its most critical and revolutionary here where it is most abstract, in his Absolutes, and that Hegel becomes more conservative when he comes down to earth to develop a political philosophy:

> Precisely where Hegel sounds most abstract, seems to close the shutters tight against the whole movement of history, there he lets the lifeblood of the dialectic—absolute negativity—pour in. . . . [H]e has, by bringing oppositions to their most logical extreme, opened new paths . . .

As we have seen, Marcuse's position is similar in that he too regards Hegel's abstract works such as the *Phenomenology* or the *Logic* as more critical and revolutionary than his political philosophy, but he does not accept Dunayevskaya's extensions of this notion to include Hegel's Absolutes. For her part, Dunayevskaya tends to attack Marcuse for, in her view, having moved away from Hegelian Marxism by 1960 toward what she considered to be a non-Marxist concept, the "Great Refusal," while continuing in her own work to draw inspiration from Marcuse's earlier writings on Hegel and Marx in elaborating her own stance, where she considered Hegel's "absolute negativity as new beginning" (Dunayevskaya [1973] 1989a, p. 3).

Conclusion:
Facing the challenge of postmodernism

I am not here suggesting something so simplistic as a notion that Marcuse, in moving away from some aspects of the Hegelian Marxism of the 1941 text of *Reason and Revolution*, ever gave up either Hegel or the dialectic. A few years before his death, Marcuse was asked whether Hegel was dead. The interviewer, Frederick Olafson, wondered, "Is it still possible for living philosophies to be built on the great classical authors?" Marcuse responded strongly in the affirmative:

> I would say definitely yes. And I would definitely say that one of the proofs is the continued existence and development of Marxist theory. ... It is, of course, a greatly modified idealism, but elements of it remain in social and political theory. (Olafson [1974] 1988, p. 103)

While it is thus fairly clear that Marcuse remained a Hegelian Marxist until his death, I believe it is erroneous to ignore the substantial shift in his concept of dialectic from the 1941 text of *Reason and Revolution* to the 1960 Preface and his other writings of the 1960s.

At a time when much of the debate in radical social theory is cast as a duel between, on one hand, the defense by Habermas of liberal Enlightenment reason and, on the other hand, Foucauldean and postmodernist attacks on both liberalism and the Hegelian-Marxian dialectic, Marcuse's *Reason and Revolution* offers us something different: a defense of the dialectic as a critical, rational, and therefore radical perspective.

Of the various French structuralists, poststructuralists, and postmodernists whose theoretical writings have prepared the ground for much of the recent debate in radical social theory, Jacques Derrida stands out as the one who has been the most seriously engaged with Hegel. In a brief look at Derrida's critique of Hegel, I will attempt to show how his critique engages, at least implicitly, some of the positions advanced by Marcuse in *Reason and Revolution*, but that he does not succeed in refuting either Hegel or Marcuse. While Derrida ([1972b] 1981, p. 64) expresses admiration for "the decisive progress simultaneously accomplished by Althusser and those following him" in analyzing "the relationship of Marx to Hegel" ([1972b] 1981, p. 63), he does not apparently endorse Althusser's extreme rejection of Hegel. As is well known, Althusser ([1965] 1969, p. 116) once wrote that a task "more crucial than any other today" would be to "drive the shade of Hegel . . . back into the night" in favor of a return to a de-Hegelianized—*Althusserized?*—Marx.

Instead, Derrida ([1972b] 1981, p. 77) argues: "We will never be finished with the reading or rereading of Hegel." This is no idle statement: it is evidenced in much of Derrida's work. One key example is found in his well-known essay "Différance," where he works with (and against) Hegel, Saussure, Nietzsche, and Freud to develop one of his own most important concepts (Derrida [1972a] 1982; see also Norris 1987). Yet, to Derrida, Hegel is most often a foil, the best example of what is wrong with the Western "logocentric" tradition. This leads Derrida to two points of implicit confrontation with Marcuse's Hegelian Marxism: (1) Derrida's general rejection of the existentialist, radical humanist, and Hegelian Marxist trends, in many respects similar to Marcuse's position, which were so prevalent in French thought after 1945; and (2) Derrida's critique of Hegel's concepts of difference and negativity, the latter perhaps the central dialectical concept developed and elaborated in *Reason and Revolution.*

There was a time lag in translating into English Derrida's major works, most of them published in French in the late 1960s or early 1970s: *L'Écriture et la différence* (1967), *De la grammatologie* (1967), *Marges de la philosophie* (1972), *Positions* (1972). This time lag obscures the political and theoretical context of Derrida's work, the fact that these writings were published at the height of Marcuse's influence, at a time when his books were selling hundreds of thousands of copies in the U.S. and Europe, in the midst of student upheavals in the U.S., France, and Germany. Thus, Marcuse's "best seller" *One-Dimensional Man* (1964) was published only three years before two of Derrida's major works listed above. The time lag in the English-language discussions of Derrida's work obscures Derrida's implicit critique of positions similar to those taken by Marcuse, something that was recognized when Derrida published these books.

This is seen by looking at Derrida's article "The Ends of Man," first delivered as a paper to an international philosophy colloquium in New York in October 1968. Published in 1969 in the American journal *Philosophy and Phenomenological Research*, this paper was for years one of the very few examples of Derrida's work available in English. Over a decade later, in 1982, it appeared in a different translation in his *Margins of Philosophy*. In this often-cited (see, for example, Habermas 1987) paper, Derrida ([1972a] 1982, p. 117) identifies with what he terms "the current questioning of humanism" in French thought. He critiques what he considers to be the "uncontested common ground of Marxism and of Social-Democratic or Christian discourse," all of it grounded in "the anthropologistic readings of Hegel (interest in the *Phenomenology of Spirit* as it was read by Kojève), of Marx (the privilege accorded to the *Manuscripts of 1844*) . . ." In addition to Kojève, Derrida attacks Sartre explicitly, but his targets probably include other left existentialists, Hegelian Marxists, and Hegel scholars such as Maurice Merleau-Ponty, Simone de Beauvoir, Henri Lefebvre, Lucien Goldmann, and Jean Hyppolite. Derrida ([1972a] 1982, p. 121) attacks Hegel for subordinating his philosophy to a Christian eschatology, where the Hegelian "we" is "the unity of absolute knowledge and anthropology, of God and man, of onto-theo-teleology and humanism." He concludes that the creation of a truly radical philosophy "can only come from outside" the Western humanist tradition ([1972a] 1982, p. 134). The best way to do so is "by affirming an absolute break and difference" ([1972a] 1982, p. 135) via recourse to Nietzsche.

There was a formal critique of Derrida's paper immediately after his having delivered it at the 1968 conference in New York, a critique that was also published in 1969 in *Philosophy and Phenomenological Research*. In that critique, the American philosopher Richard Popkin (1969, p. 63) attacks Derrida's recourse to Nietzsche, which he terms "the extremely pessimistic conclusion of the paper." Popkin draws a contrast between, on the one hand, Derrida's anti-humanist, Nietzschean stance and, on the other hand, the radical humanist mentality, which he saw exemplified in the ferment against the Vietnam War and racism then taking place on American campuses.

Popkin also puts forward Marcuse's Hegelian Marxism as an alternative to Derrida's anti-humanist, anti-Hegelian perspective:

> The Marxian Hegel is just beginning to be taken seriously in the form of the current Marcuse boom. We have had perhaps more direct contact with this vibrant, humanistic Hegel than France has had, since many of the leading figures in German thought of the 20's fled to America, or fled to France briefly and then to America. (Popkin 1969, p. 61)

Even though Derrida had not referred specifically to Marcuse's work (which he may not even have read), Popkin was fundamentally right to bring Marcuse into the debate, because Marcuse represented a leading example of the Hegelian and Marxist humanist trends Derrida was attacking in his paper. Thus, from the moment of one of Derrida's first entries into American intellectual debate, the question of Derrida versus Marcuse was posed publicly.

The second point, Derrida's critique of Hegel's concepts of difference and negativity, shows not a general but a specific engagement with precisely those questions that preoccupy Marcuse in *Reason and Revolution* (although, once again, to my knowledge Derrida does not refer explicitly to Marcuse's argument when he critiques Hegel). Derrida's stance with regard to Hegel's concept of negativity, which he often ties to the concept of difference, is especially interesting for an examination of the contemporary relevance of Marcuse's Hegelian Marxism, because negativity is one concept of Hegel's Derrida does not dismiss, but rather attempts to build on while simultaneously attacking what he sees as the limits of Hegel's concept. For example, in *Of Grammatology*, the first of his major works to be published in English, when Derrida ([1967a] 1974, p. 26) attacks Hegel as the prime example of a Western logocentric thinker, "the last philosopher of the book," he simultaneously praises Hegel in the same paragraph as "*also* the thinker of irreducible difference." The British sociologist Gillian Rose (1985, p. 139, see also Rose 1981) writes of "Derrida's equivocation concerning Hegel" in this very passage. Citing Hegel's *Logic* on the dialectical relationship between unity and difference, she argues further: "The alternatives could be avoided by the speculative exposition of *différance* as the 'unity and difference of identity and difference.' But Derrida's eschatological reading of Hegel leaves this out."

Elsewhere, Derrida ([1967b] 1978, p. 259) takes up Hegel's concept of negativity, which he terms the "blind spot of Hegelianism." Following the interpretation of the French Nietzschean Georges Bataille, Derrida argues that for Hegel "negativity is always the underside and accomplice of positivity." While Hegel created a "revolution" in thought by "taking the negative *seriously*," Derrida concludes that Hegel works "convulsively to tear apart the negative side, that which makes it the reassuring *other* surface of the positive." Rose (1985, p. 162) observes astutely with regard to this critique, "It sounds as if Derrida is developing another kind of 'conservative' reading of Hegel's thinking and reserving its radicality for his own thinking." Thus, Derrida ultimately reads Hegel on negativity in a manner similar to Löwith's (1942a) earlier critique of Marcuse, viewing Hegel as fundamentally a philosopher of reconciliation, of positivity.

In this sense, Derrida's equivocation on Hegel's concept of negativity manages to avoid coming to grips with the type of left revolutionary reading of Hegel carried out by Marcuse in *Reason and Revolution*, one that, I have argued here, centers on the concept of negativity. So anxious is Derrida to move beyond humanism and Hegelian Marxism, to affirm an "absolute break and difference" ([1972a] 1982, p. 135), that he avoids coming to grips fully with the critical—even revolutionary—ramifications of Hegel's concept of negativity as defended and appropriated by Marcuse for radical social theory. I would argue that the fact that Marcuse's Hegelian Marxism points to alternatives to the fetishized human relations of modern capitalist society makes it not less, but *more*, radical than the perspective defended by Derrida, who leaves us in the end with no real alternative to existing social structures.

References

Afary, Janet. 1989. "The Contribution of Raya Dunayevskaya, 1910 to 1987: A Study in Hegelian Marxist Feminism." *Extramares* 1(1): 35–55.

Althusser, Louis. [1965] 1969. *For Marx*. New York: Vintage.

Anderson, Kevin. 1986. "Recent Writings of R. Dunayevskaya." *Hegel-Studien* 21: 186–88.

Anderson, Kevin. 1989a. "A Preliminary Exploration of the Dunayevskaya-Marcuse Dialogue, 1954 to 1979." *Quarterly Journal of Ideology* 13(4): 21–28. https://bit.ly/2yTyD6f

_____. 1989b. "Response to Kellner on the Dunayevskaya-Marcuse Dialogue." *Quarterly Journal of Ideology* 13(4): 31–33. https://bit.ly/2yTyD6f

_____. 1990. "The Marcuse-Dunayevskaya Dialogue, 1954-79." *Studies in Soviet Thought* 39(2): 89–109.

Bernstein, Richard. 1988. "Negativity: Theme and Variations." Pp. 13–28 in Pippin et al.

Bloch, Ernst. [1949] 1962. *Subjekt-Objekt: Erläuterungen zu Hegel*. Frankfurt: Suhrkamp Verlag.

Bruun, H. H. 1972. *Science, Values and Politics in Max Weber's Methodology.* Copenhagen: Munksgaard.

Colletti, Lucio. [1969a] 1972. *From Rousseau to Lenin.* London: New Left Books.

_____. [1969b] 1973. *Marxism and Hegel.* London: New Left Books.

_____. 1975. "Introduction." Pp. 7–56 in *Karl Marx: Early Writings.* New York: Vintage.

Derrida, Jacques. [1967a] 1974. *Of Grammatology.* Baltimore: Johns Hopkins University Press.

_____. [1967b] 1978. *Writing and Difference.* Chicago: University of Chicago Press.

_____. [1972a] 1982. *Margins of Philosophy.* Chicago: University of Chicago Press.

_____. [1972b] 1981. *Positions.* Chicago: University of Chicago Press.

Dilthey, Wilhelm. [1905] 1959. *Jugendgeschichte Hegels.* In *Gesammelte Schriften*, Vol. 4. Stuttgart: B. G. Teubner Verlagsgesellschaft.

Dunayevskaya, Raya. [1958] 1988. *Marxism and Freedom: From 1776 until Today.* New York: Columbia University Press.

_____. [1961] 1981f. "Rough Notes on Hegel's *Science of Logic.*" Pp. 2815–33 in *The Raya Dunayevskaya Collection* (microfilm). Detroit: Wayne State University Archives.

_____. 1964a. "Reason and Revolution vs. Conformism and Technology." *The Activist* Fall: 32–34.

_____. [1964b] 1981f. "Letter of June 9 to Eugene Walker." Pp. 13884–85 in *Raya Dunayevskaya Collection.* https://bit.ly/3610Jsy

_____. [1964c] 1981f. "Letter of September 27 to Bessie Gogol and Eugene Walker." Pp. 13888–89 in *Raya Dunayevskaya Collection.* https://bit.ly/3cv5Of1

_____. [1966] 1981f. "Letter of October 20 to Eugene Walker." Pp. 13936–37 in *Raya Dunayevskaya Collection.* https://bit.ly/2WtHlB9

_____. [1969] 1981f. "The Newness of Our Philosophic-Historic Contribution." Pp. 4407–16 in *Raya Dunayevskaya Collection.* https://bit.ly/2AlpSSJ

_____. [1973] 1989a. *Philosophy and Revolution: From Hegel to Sartre, and from Marx to Mao.* New York: Columbia University Press.

_____. [1978] 1981f. "Letter of June 30 to Harry McShane." Pp. 6432–33 in *Raya Dunayevskaya Collection.* https://bit.ly/3cvOxSY

_____. 1979. "Herbert Marcuse, Marxist Philosopher." *Newsletter of the International Society for the Sociology of Knowledge* 5(2): 10–11.

_____. 1980. "Hegel's Absolute Idea as New Beginning." Pp. 163–77 in *Art and Logic in Hegel's Philosophy*, edited by Warren Steinkraus and Kenneth Schmitz. New Jersey: Humanities Press.

_____. [1982] 1991. *Rosa Luxemburg, Women's Liberation, and Marx's Philosophy of Revolution*. Second Edition, with a new Foreword by Adrienne Rich. Urbana: University of Illinois Press.

_____. 1986a. "Letter of April 17 to John Welsh." Held by Raya Dunayevskaya Memorial Fund, Chicago.

_____. 1986b. "Letter of July 13 to John Welsh." Pp. 11262–65 in *Raya Dunayevskaya Collection*. https://bit.ly/3budo9V

_____. 1989b. *The Philosophic Moment of Marxist-Humanism*. Edited by Peter Hudis. Chicago: News & Letters.

_____. n.d. "Marginalia on *Reason and Revolution*." Held by Raya Dunayevskaya Memorial Fund, Chicago.

Dunayevskaya, Raya and Herbert Marcuse. 1989. "Excerpts from the Dunayevskaya-Marcuse Correspondence: 1954–79." Edited by Kevin B. Anderson. *Quarterly Journal of Ideology* 13(4): 3–16. https://bit.ly/2yTyD6f

Durkheim, Émile. [1897] 1951. *Suicide*. New York: Macmillan.

Franzen, Erich. 1942. "Review of *Reason and Revolution*." *American Sociological Review* 7(1): 126–28. https://bit.ly/2y4FZUc

Goldmann, Lucien. 1976. *Cultural Creation in Modern Society*. St. Louis: Telos Press.

Greeman, Richard. 1968. "A Critical Appreciation of Herbert Marcuse's Works." *New Politics* 6(4): 12–23.

Habermas, Jürgen. 1987. *The Philosophical Discourse of Modernity*. Cambridge, Massachusetts: MIT Press.

_____. 1990. "What Does Socialism Mean Today?" *New Left Review* 183: 3–21.

Hegel, G.W.F. [1831] 1969. *The Science of Logic*, translated by A.V. Miller. New York: Humanities Press.

Hyppolite, Jean. [1955] 1969. *Studies on Marx and Hegel*. New York: Harper and Row.

Hook, Sidney. 1941a. "Reason and Revolution." *The New Republic*. 105(July 21): 90–91.

_____. 1941b. "Review of Marcuse, *Reason and Revolution*." *The Living Age* 360 (March-August): 594–95.

Jay, Martin. 1973. *The Dialectical Imagination*. Boston: Little, Brown.

_____. 1984. *Marxism and Totality*. Berkeley: University of California Press.

Johnson, Patricia Altenbernd. 1989. "Women's Liberation: Following Dunayevskaya in Practicing Dialectics." *Quarterly Journal of Ideology* 13(4): 65–74.

Kellner, Douglas. 1984. *Herbert Marcuse and the Crisis of Marxism*. Berkeley: University of California Press.

_____. 1989a. *Critical Theory, Marxism, and Modernity*. Baltimore: Johns Hopkins University Press.

_____. 1989b. "A Comment on the Dunayevskaya-Marcuse Dialogue." *Quarterly Journal of Ideology* 13(4): 29–30.

Kosík, Karel. [1963] 1976. *Dialectics of the Concrete*. Boston: D. Reidel.

Lenin, V.I. [1914–15] 1961. "Abstract of Hegel's Science of Logic." Pp. 85–238 in *Collected Works*, Vol. 38. Moscow: Progress Publishers.

Levine, Donald N. 1985. *The Flight from Ambiguity*. Chicago: University of Chicago Press.

Löwith, Karl. [1941] 1967. *From Hegel to Nietzsche*. New York: Doubleday.

_____. 1942a. "Review of *Reason and Revolution*." *Philosophy and Phenomenological Research*. 2(4): 560–63.

_____. 1942b. "In Reply to Marcuse's Remarks." *Philosophy and Phenomenological Research*. 2(4): 565–66.

Lukács, Georg. [1923] 1971. *History and Class Consciousness*. Cambridge, Massachusetts: MIT Press.

_____. [1947] 1975. *The Young Hegel*. London: Merlin Press.

Lyotard, Jean-François. 1989. "Universal History and Cultural Differences." Pp. 314–323 in *The Lyotard Reader*, edited by Andrew Benjamin. Cambridge, Massachusetts: Basil Blackwell.

MacGregor, David. 1984. *The Communist Ideal in Hegel and Marx*. Toronto: University of Toronto Press.

Marcuse, Herbert. [1932a] 1987. *Hegel's Ontology and the Theory of Historicity*. Cambridge, Massachusetts: MIT Press.

Marcuse, Herbert. [1932b] 1973. "The Foundation of Historical Materialism." Pp. 1–48 in *Studies in Critical Philosophy*. Boston: Beacon Press.

_____. 1941. *Reason and Revolution: Hegel and the Rise of Social Theory*. London: Routledge & Kegan Paul.

_____. 1942. "Rejoinder to Mr. Löwith." *Philosophy and Phenomenological Research* 2(4): 564–65.

_____. 1954. "Epilogue." Pp. 432–39 in *Reason and Revolution*. London: Routledge & Kegan Paul.

_____. 1960. "A Note on Dialectic." Pp. vii-xiv in *Reason and Revolution*. Boston: Beacon Press.

_____. [1964] 1991. *One-Dimensional Man*. With a new introduction by Douglas Kellner. Boston: Beacon Press.

Marx, Karl. [1844] 1968. "Kritik der Hegelschen Dialektik und Philosophie überhaupt." Pp. 568–88 in Marx and Engels, *Werke: Ergänzungsband* I. Berlin: Dietz Verlag.

_____. [1867–75] 1976. *Capital*, Vol. I, translated by Ben Fowkes. London: Penguin Books.

McGill, Vernon J. 1942. "Dialectical Materialism and Recent Philosophy." *Science & Society* 6(2): 150–63.

McGlone, Ted. 1985. "Absolute Negativity, Labor and the Dialectics of Revolution." *Research Papers in Political Economy* 2. Salt Lake City: Department of Economics, University of Utah.

Negt, Oskar. [1963] 1974. *Die Konstituierung der Soziologie zur Ordnungswissenschaft: Strukturbeziehungen zwischen den Gesellschaftslehren Comtes und Hegels*. Frankfurt: Europäische Verlaganstalt.

Noël, Georges. 1897. *La Logique de Hegel*. Paris: Félix Alcan.

Norris, Christopher. 1987. *Derrida*. Cambridge, Massachusetts: Harvard University Press.

Olafson, Frederick. [1974] 1988. "Heidegger's Politics: An Interview with Herbert Marcuse." Pp. 95–104 in Pippin et al.

Ollman, Bertell. 1971. *Alienation*. New York: Cambridge University Press.

_____. 1992. *Dialectical Investigations*. New York: Routledge.

Pippin, Robert. 1988. "Marcuse on Hegel and Historicity." Pp. 68–94 in Pippin et al.

Pippin, Robert, Andrew Feenberg, Charles Webel and Contributors. 1988. *Marcuse: Critical Theory and the Promise of Utopia*. South Hadley, Massachusetts: Bergin and Garvey.

Popkin, Richard. 1969. "Comment on Professor Derrida's Paper." *Philosophy and Phenomenological Research*. 30(1): 58–65.

Rich, Adrienne. 1986. "Living the Revolution." *Women's Review of Books*. 3(12): 1, 3–4.

Rose, Gillian. 1981. *Hegel Contra Sociology*. New Jersey: Humanities Press.

_____. 1985. *Dialectic of Nihilism: Post-Structuralism and Law*. Oxford: Basil Blackwell.

Sabine, George. 1942. "Review of *Reason and Revolution*." *American Journal of Sociology*. 48(2): 258–59.

Schwalbe, Michael. 1986. *The Psychosocial Consequences of Natural and Alienated Labor*. Albany: SUNY Press.

Tillich, Paul. 1941. "Review of *Reason and Revolution*." *Studies in Philosophy and Social Science* 9: 476–78.

Originally published as "On Hegel and the Rise of Social Theory: A Critical Appreciation of Herbert Marcuse's Reason and Revolution, Fifty Years Later," *Sociological Theory* 11:3 (1993), pp. 243-67. Reproduced with permission.

7

Lukács on the young Hegel

In contrast to his classic 1923 book, *History and Class Consciousness*, Georg Lukács's *The Young Hegel* ([1948] 1975) is a relatively neglected work that has been too often underrated or dismissed without a serious confrontation with Lukács's argument. Beyond encompassing a study of Hegel's early writings, as the title would imply, *The Young Hegel* ends with a substantial discussion of Hegel's first great work, *The Phenomenology of Spirit*. Similar to other studies of Hegel and Marx during the 1940s by Herbert Marcuse ([1941] 1960), Jean Hyppolite ([1946] 1974), and Karl Löwith ([1941] 1967), Lukács's concern lies in elaborating and analyzing the affinities between Hegel and Marx, thus overcoming the one-sided views of both conservative Hegel scholars and crudely materialist Marxists. Lukács's view of the relationship of the two thinkers is far more comprehensive and developed than the familiar catechism of Hegel the "idealist" and Marx the "materialist."

Unlike the other studies just cited, which were published under conditions of relative political and intellectual freedom, Lukács wrote much of *The Young Hegel* in Stalin's Russia and had it published while living in Eastern Europe during Stalin's lifetime, a period when the slightest "deviation" could result in imprisonment or death. Therefore, Lukács's references to Stalin's allegedly deep theoretical understanding and his occasional crudely materialist qualifications of Hegel's original insights have to be seen—in part at least—as the forced intellectual conformity of the era rather than as central themes in Lukács's study. This has its amusing aspects as in: "The method of vulgar sociology is built on the belief that an historical phenomenon is adequately explained once its social origins have been uncovered . . . Marx, Engels, Lenin and Stalin never imagined that the substance, the truth-content of a scientific theory could be assessed in terms of its social origins" (Lukács [1948] 1975:510). Such plaudits to Stalin are easily seen through. However, Jean Hyppolite's characterization of these references as "quite beside the point" ([1955] 1969:71) is not quite accurate either, since the capitulation to Stalinism is not entirely unrelated to how Lukács appropriates Hegel's critique of what Lukács terms "irrationalism."

Trying to recover the "revolutionary dialectic" after a long period of crude materialist Marxism, Lukács, from 1923 on, became one of the first to show that the Hegelian dialectic arose not only from confrontation with other philosophers such as Kant, let alone from religion, but also from Hegel's concern, as opposed to a "history of ideas," with concrete human history, from ancient Greece to his own turbulent period of the French Revolution and the Napoleonic wars. Further, Lukács shows that—as seen in Hegel's assessment of the French Revolution as the epochal event in European history—Hegel anticipates Marx in his studies of economics, another instance of their relationship eluding the crude materialist catechism.

Aside from these intertwined interests of Hegel and Marx, a second original insight of *The Young Hegel* concerns the relationship of Hegel to his philosophical contemporaries. Lukács presents Hegel's philosophy and his philosophical development as a critique of German Romanticism and intuitionism (dubbed "irrationalism"), represented by Friedrich Schelling and Friedrich Jacobi, seeing this as of equal significance alongside Hegel's far more frequently discussed critique of the formalism of Immanuel Kant. The Hegelian dialectic thus becomes not only a critique of positivist or Kantian social science and of crude Marxism, but also of such anti-positivist philosophies as intuitionism, mysticism, and existentialism, taken together as "irrationalist" by Lukács. Here, unfortunately, Lukács shows the far deeper harm his capitulation to Stalinism did him than those occasional references to Stalin would imply. While the point that Hegel criticized intuitionism equally with Kantianism is well taken, Lukács's critique of "irrationalism" becomes so broad that he lumps Jean-Paul Sartre and

Hyppolite together with Martin Heidegger, and even Adolf Hitler. Such critiques backfired, discrediting Marxist philosophy in its battle of ideas with French leftwing versions of existentialism.

Finally, the treatment of "tragedy in the realm of the ethical" and the lengthy discussion of Hegel's *Phenomenology of Spirit* toward the end of *The Young Hegel*, which constitute the most original parts of the book, show on the one hand a relationship of the Hegelian dialectic to gender and, on the other, a serious treatment of the *Phenomenology* as a whole. Here Lukács stresses the *Phenomenology's* relationship to the French Revolution, but carries his view of the Hegelian dialectic as revolutionary right through its last chapters on Religion and Absolute Knowledge. At the same time, Lukács stops short of any notion of Hegel's Absolute Spirit yielding "Absolute Negativity," as seen in Marx's 1844 "Critique of the Hegelian Dialectic" (Marx 1967:314–37). Moreover, he never develops anything like a concept of "Absolute Negativity as new beginning," which was placed at the center of a renewed Marxist dialectic by the Marxist-Humanist philosopher Raya Dunayevskaya (1973).

On Hegel's theological writings

In studying Hegel's youthful writings, unpublished for the most part until the early twentieth century, Lukács seeks to minimize their theological content by exhibiting their relationship to the French Revolution and the Enlightenment. This contrasts with the approach of Marcuse, who sees Hegel's interests gradually shifting "from theological to philosophical questions and concepts" ([1941] 1960:35). In a biography of Lukács, George Lichtheim cites this thesis of *The Young Hegel*—to the effect that Hegel never really had a theological period—in order to dismiss the entire book as a Stalinist vulgarization (Lichtheim 1970:115).

Lukács does, however, present enough evidence to suggest that even Hegel's earliest theological writings were shot through with bitter critiques of many aspects of the Christian religion. Furthermore, he finds here concepts like "positivity," which foreshadow mature Hegelian concepts such as alienation.

Because the Enlightenment, which had used Greek society as a critical measure of its own society, including the Church, profoundly influenced Hegel and his contemporaries, Lukács views this period for Hegel as one centered more on Greece than on theology. To this end, he quotes the young Hegel's thoughts while still in his twenties, as preserved in one of his Berne notebooks:

> When opponents of the Christian religion, who, their hearts full of human feelings, contemplate the history of the Crusades, the discovery of America, the contemporary slave-trade—and not merely these outstanding episodes in which Christianity in part performed greatly to its credit, but the whole chain of princely corruption and popular depravity—their hearts will certainly bleed at the sight. And when they compare this with the claims of the teachers and servants of religion to excellence, general utility, and so forth—they must surely be filled with bitterness and hatred of the Christian religion. (cited in Lukács [1948] 1975:66–67)

Here, the attack on Christianity is unrelenting.

Lukács also writes that Hegel compared Jesus unfavorably with Socrates, thus including Jesus in his critique, which was more than a simple tracing of the "corruption" of the Church since Jesus's day, but a sharp attack on the founder of Christianity:

> Jesus took his disciples out of society, out of life, cutting them off and turning them into men whose chief characteristic was precisely their disciplehood. In the case of Socrates his disciples remain social, they stay as they are, their individuality is not remolded artificially. They return therefore into public life enriched. . . . Jesus, however, created a narrow-minded, closed sect; among the Greeks he would have been an object of laughter! (Lukács [1948] 1975:49)

Nevertheless, Lukács criticizes Hegel's looking toward the Greeks for contemporaneous solutions and his "inability to direct his attack at religion per se" (Lukács [1948] 1975:81), instead searching for a new religion for modern Europe along classical lines. The latter point was later developed in great detail by H.S. Harris (1972).

For Lukács, the "economic and political backwardness" of Germany at the time of Hegel causes these "idealistic illusions." He repeats this formula throughout *The Young Hegel* whenever he criticizes Hegel in terms of Marx. At the same time, Lukács views the "backwardness" of Germany as prompting its philosophers to avoid the route of technical solutions, forcing them instead to develop their categories at a very high theoretical level. The Hegelian dialectic, born under these conditions, in this view later enabled Marx to go beyond both the political economists of technologically advanced England and the early utopian socialists of turbulent France.

Marx himself wrote on the Greeks in his youth, as in his doctoral thesis, and even in his "mature" *Grundrisse* had the following to say:

> But the difficulty lies not in understanding that the Greek arts and epic are bound up with certain forms of social development. The difficulty is that they still afford us artistic pleasure and that in a certain respect they count as a norm and as an unattainable model. (Marx 1973:111)

Thus, for Marx, "backwardness" is itself a contradictory notion. In this sense, contra Lukács, it was not necessarily the "backwardness" of Germany that led Hegel to the Greeks. Both Marx and Hegel, of course, criticize, and see as a limitation in Greek society and thought, the fact that it was based on slavery. For example, the mature Hegel writes:

> When individuals and nations have once got in their heads the abstract concept of full-blown liberty, there is nothing like it in its uncontrollable strength, just because it is the very essence of mind . . . The Greeks and Romans, Plato and Aristotle, even the Stoics, did not have it. On the contrary, they saw that it is only by birth (as, e.g., an Athenian or Spartan citizen), or by strength of character, education, or philosophy (—the sage is free even as a slave and in chains) that the human being is actually free. (1971:239–40)

For his part, Marx wrote in *Capital* that Aristotle could not understand human labor as the source of the value of commodities because "Greek society was founded on the labor of slaves, hence had as its natural basis the inequality of men and of their labor-powers" (1976:152). I would therefore argue that Lukács's constant stress on the economic and political backwardness of Germany is not dialectical enough, despite his acknowledgement that Hegel created his dialectic there under those conditions.

Nevertheless, in his discussion of Hegel's early writings, Lukács makes the very important point that his concept of the artificial moralistic precepts of Christianity, which the young Hegel called its "positivity"—as against ancient Greek thought and religion, which he saw as flowing out of daily life rather than being superimposed as a morality to guide life—is a notion of the Christian religion that foreshadows the later concepts of alienation in both Hegel and Marx. In a detailed study of the young Hegel's Berne, Frankfurt, and Jena manuscripts, Lukács shows him moving a bit closer toward mystical Christianity for a time in Frankfurt, but paradoxically forming the Hegelian dialectic there for the first time by placing contradiction at the center of reality.

At a strictly political level, Lukács finds many very enthusiastic statements on the French Revolution among Hegel's writings in this early period, which complement his discussion of Greek democracy. On the French Revolution, one of the most explicit statements Lukács quotes is where Hegel writes of "a people that has armed itself":

> Here the word of command is liberty, the enemy tyranny, the commander-in-chief the constitution, subordination obedience to the representatives of the people. But there is a great difference between the passivity of ordinary military obedience and the ardour of insurrection. (cited in Lukács [1948] 1975:45)

Lukács attacks conservative Hegel scholars who tried to argue on the basis of style that this passage is an extract from a French general and not Hegel's own words. Lukács pointedly remarks that, even if true, this still leaves the question of why Hegel copied down the passage unanswered. Thus, for Lukács, Hegel's youthful writings indicate by no means a simple gradual development from theology toward philosophy.

Lukács may not have proven what he concludes, that Hegel's theological period is a "myth" constructed by "German reactionaries," but as Hyppolite wrote in his review essay on *The Young Hegel*: "Lukács is perhaps not entirely wrong (though he tends to take the opposite extreme) in treating the theme of Hegel's theological period as a reactionary legend" (Hyppolite [1955] 1969:71).

On Hegel's critique of Kant

The cautious and somewhat schematic discussion in *The Young Hegel* on Hegel's critique of Kant does not equal the force of Lukács's earlier treatment of the "Antinomies of Bourgeois Thought" in the central essay on reification in his 1923 *History and Class Consciousness*. There, he had written that by splitting the categories of appearance and essence, for Kant "the resulting ethic becomes purely formal and lacking in content" ([1923] 1971:124).

But even in 1923, Lukács had stopped short of the deeper critique of Kant by the mature Hegel, who wrote in his *Science of Logic*:

> It will always stand out as a marvel how the Kantian philosophy recognized the relation of thought to sensuous reality, beyond which it did not advance as only a relative relation of mere Appearance, and perfectly well recognized and enunciated a higher unity of both in the Idea in general and, for example, in the Idea of an intuitive understanding, and yet stopped short at this relative relation and the assertion that the Notion is and remains utterly separate from reality—thus asserting as *truth* what it declared to be finite cognition, and denouncing as an unjustified extravagance and a figment of thought what it recognized as *truth* and of which it established the specific motion. (Hegel 1969:592)

Here, Kant stands accused of yielding to formalism, and thus stopping short of the really important questions confronting philosophy.

Lukács did in 1923 call for a reconstruction of philosophy as a totality, with the conclusions flowing dialectically out of the facts in the manner of Hegel and Marx, rather than as an ethic superimposed upon them. The "formalistic" ethics of Kant were to be replaced by the reason of proletarian revolt in the manner of Marx's early writings, still unknown to the world in 1923, including to Lukács. In 1844, in a brief critique of Hegel's *Philosophy of Right*, Marx had written:

> Always seeking *fundamentals*, Germany can only make a *fundamental* revolution. The *emancipation of the German* is the *emancipation of mankind*. The *head* of this emancipation is *philosophy*, its *heart* is the *proletariat*. Philosophy cannot be actualized without the transcen-

dence [*Aufhebung*] of the proletariat, the proletariat cannot be transcended without the actualization of philosophy. (Marx 1967:264)

Overall, Lukács's concept of totality is dialectical in the sense that capitalism can only be comprehended from the "standpoint of the proletariat," and not by formal categories out of the head of the philosopher.

Unfortunately, in 1923 these important points are swallowed up by Lukács's espousal in the reification essay of the extension of reification—in an unmediated and unnuanced manner—from the industrial worker of Marx to intellectual and white-collar labor, here influenced by the sociological theories of his teacher Max Weber. Thus, at the very moment Lukács recovers the philosophical roots of Marx's dialectic in the critique of bourgeois thought, his dialectic "perishes." He undermines his concept of the reification of labor by generalizing it to the point where it departs from Marx's notion of the centrality of the worker at the point of production.

The Young Hegel, published a quarter century later under the wary eye of Stalinism, has no such points of affinity with non-Marxist sociology and tends more toward the opposite pole—crude materialism—in its critique of Kant. Here, as in 1923 or today, the whole critique of Kant has far wider dimensions than may be apparent at first. Certainly, Hegel's critique of Kant is fundamental to any Marxist critique of bourgeois thought.

Beyond offering a critique of positivist social science and philosophy, a critique also carried out in the work of the early Adorno and Horkheimer, a consideration of Hegel's critique of Kant also shows the limits of crude Marxism. As Lucien Goldmann writes in his essay "The Dialectic Today":

> This is the radical critique of all positivism (and positivism is not merely a small school, but includes any claim of a rupture between judgements of fact and value judgements). These Hegelian categories are all recovered in Marxism; and it is no accident that they were reactualized in Europe around, say, the years 1917–1923: first by Lenin in the *Philosophic Notebooks*, secondly by Lukács in *History and Class Consciousness*, and thirdly, I believe, somewhat later in Gramsci's concretely philosophic analyses. Furthermore, it is not accidental that in the interim, with Mehring, Plekhanov, Kautsky, Bernstein, and even Lenin at the time he wrote *Materialism and*

Empiriocriticism, Marxism was just as positivistic as academic science. (1976:112–13)

Stalinism, as is well known, returned most of Marxism to such crudely materialist and positivist views for many years. Even Trotsky, despite his political opposition to Stalin, certainly never freed himself from positivist and Kantian categories at a philosophical level.[1]

The treatment of the Kant-Hegel problem is somewhat submerged in *The Young Hegel*, as compared with *History and Class Consciousness*, possibly due to Stalinist pressure and influence. Be that as it may, Lukács justified this relative neglect of Kant by claiming that Hegel did not approach Kant as seriously in his youth as in his mature writings, especially the *Science of Logic*. According to Lukács, the youthful Hegel concerned himself more with critiques of Fichte, Schelling, and Romanticism, and treated Kant in a more off-hand fashion in part because he was never drawn very strongly to Kant. Lukács does however cite an early Hegelian critique of Kant's ethics where he criticized them as formalistic, much in the sense that he at that time regarded the Christian religion as artificial and "positive," as discussed above.

In his first published work, *The Difference Between the Fichtean and Schellingian Systems of Philosophy* (1801), Hegel criticizes not only Fichte but also Kant and the intuitionist Jacobi. He defends Schelling and, along with him, seeks to develop a philosophy of objective idealism, where subject-object identity becomes the goal. Lukács writes:

> There can only be an objective-idealist dialectics (a) if we may assume the existence of something that goes beyond the consciousness of individuals but is still subject-like, a kind of consciousness, (b) if amidst the dialectical movement of the objects idealism can discern a development which moves towards a consciousness of itself in this subject, and so (c) if the movement of the world of objects achieves an objective and subjective, real and conscious union with knowledge. ([1948] 1975:270)

Here the idea becomes part of the objective reality being analyzed, some-

---

1. Raya Dunayevskaya (1977) has argued that this in turn limited Trotsky's political critique of Stalinism, as in his reluctant defense of the 1939 Hitler-Stalin Pact, and thus truncated his overall theoretical contribution.

thing Schelling reached through a conception of "intellectual intuition" and which Hegel sought to derive rationally.

The importance and timeliness of this problem is seen in the work of Theodor Adorno. Philosophically somewhere between Kant and Hegel, Adorno concludes his *Negative Dialectics* with the phrase "metaphysics must know how to wish." However, he continues, "the wish is a poor father to the thought," as shown by the dashed hopes of humanity since the Enlightenment, especially in the twentieth century concentration camps ([1966] 1973:407). Nevertheless, even so resigned a philosopher as Adorno concludes: "But thinking, itself a mode of conduct, contains the need—the vital need, at the outset—in itself. . . . Yet the need in thinking is what makes us think" ([1966] 1973:408). Thus Adorno, who certainly sees no solution to the crisis of philosophy or of society, still pinpoints in "the need" or "the wish" what is at the heart of Hegel's objective idealism as opposed to the more formalistic rationality of Kant. These statements must of course be seen in light of Adorno's explicit rejection of subject-object identity.

As Lukács argues at great length, the Hegelian critique of Kant and Fichte emerged along with an attack on the intuitionist Romantic Jacobi, even at a time when Schelling had some influence on him. While this is certainly well argued by Lukács, it is harder to accept his view that the early Hegel was not overly concerned with Kant, and was never a Kantian. H.S. Harris's lengthy study of Hegel's early development certainly documents an important concern with Kant from the outset, with Hegel's initial critiques having a religious basis, while at other times Hegel used Kantian categories to criticize Christianity. Harris also sees no conflict between his own view of a Hegel preoccupied with religion and Lukács's view of him as a "proto-Marx" (Harris 1972:157).

Lukács claims questionably that Hegel gave his critique of Kant great attention only after his break with Schelling and the Romantics. Nonetheless, Lukács is truly original in seeing Hegelianism as emerging as much from a critique of Schelling and Romanticism as from a critique of Kant, a topic to which I now turn.

Hegel's critique of Schelling and Romanticism

In contrast to his own *History and Class Consciousness* (1923), where he passed it over almost in silence, Lukács gives great attention in 1948 in

The Young Hegel to the Hegelian critique of what Lukács now calls "irrationalist" philosophy. For the Lukács of 1923, positivism and neo-Kantianism were his intellectual antagonists, with his critique of the antinomies of bourgeois thought centering on Fichte, Kant, and neo-Kantians such as Heinrich Rickert. In 1923, Lukács largely ignores Schelling, Jacobi, and the Romantics. But after the rise of fascism, Lukács began to see Romanticism and existentialism, the latter especially in its Heideggerian form, as equally important intellectual defenses of bourgeois society.

Very few other scholars of Hegel—Marxist or non-Marxist—have given much attention to the Hegelian critique of intuitionism. To his credit, Lukács sees Hegel's dialectic emerging fully only after a critical assessment of Schelling's philosophy and the related themes of Romanticism and intuitionism. Unfortunately, this original point is seriously undercut by the overly broad nature of Lukács's attack on "irrationalism." As mentioned above, this one-sidedness has led many to dismiss *The Young Hegel* entirely. Such rejections of the book are problematic, because they have led to a lack of attention to some very important points Lukács makes concerning Hegel's critique of Romanticism and intuitionism.

Lukács is at pains to show that Hegel was never a follower of Schelling, even in the period when their work converged and there was no public difference between them (that is, the Jena period of 1802 through 1807). Hegel's first public critique of Schelling, aside from some remarks in class to his students at the University of Jena, came only in 1807 in the *Phenomenology of Spirit*. Lukács points to numerous passages, especially in the Preface to that work, which contain criticism of Schelling, especially of the latter's concept of "intellectual intuition." Lukács writes:

> "Intellectual intuition" goes hand in hand with an aristocratic theory of knowledge. Schelling repeatedly argues that authentic philosophical truth, knowledge of the absolute, is attainable only by a few chosen people, by geniuses. One part of philosophy, the most important part, simply could not be acquired by learning . . . [quoting Schelling—KBA] "the element of poetry in philosophy." ([1948] 1975:430)

Hegel's own attitude toward the public differed sharply from this, despite the supposed obscurity of his philosophy. Thus, he addresses "the public" rather than "the critics" in the Preface to the *Phenomenology of Spirit*:

> But in this connection the public must often be distinguished from those who pose as its representatives and spokesmen. In many respects the attitude of the public is quite different from, even contrary to, that of these spokesmen. Whereas the public is inclined good-naturedly to blame itself when a philosophical work makes no appeal to it, these others, certain of their own competence, put all the blame on the author. The effect of such a work on the public is more noiseless than the action of these dead men when they bury their dead. (1977:44–45)

This passage distinguishes Hegel not only from Schelling but also from many later thinkers, including academic philosophers.

The Hegelian category of mediation forms another dividing line separating him from Schelling. Both agreed that their "objective idealism" must embrace all knowledge as a totality, as against Kant's concept of an unknowable area, the thing-in-itself. But with Schelling's "intellectual intuition," knowledge of these areas, absolute knowledge, came immediately and not as a process of reflection and understanding.

Hegel ridicules such an attitude in the *Phenomenology of Spirit*, where, in an apparent reference to Schelling, he writes,

> ... least of all will it be like the rapturous enthusiasm which, like a shot from a pistol, begins straight away with absolute knowledge, and makes short work of other standpoints by declaring that it takes no notice of them. (1977:16)

Thus, rather than an arbitrary construct like Schelling's or a concept like Kant's that "stops short" and limits its terrain of inquiry from the beginning, Hegel's dialectical concept of concrete totality, where the whole flows out of the particular contents, and at the same time is a great deal more than mere summation of the parts, emerges now in its first full statement in the *Phenomenology of Spirit*.

Lukács distinguishes Hegel from all of his contemporaries and predecessors for his joining together of dialectics with logic:

What Hegel, and he alone, perceived was that the existing content of even the most abstract categories makes it possible to discern and portray them in movement; that in consequence the absence of content in traditional formal logic is merely a borderline case, just as repose is only a borderline case of movement. ([1948] 1975:442)

Lukács continues, "It is abundantly clear, then, that the method of the *Phenomenology* evolves out of Hegel's attacks on Schelling's philosophy" ([1948] 1975:445). In this view, Hegel's philosophy is a sharp break, especially with Schelling, and Lukács separates himself from other scholars who see Hegel in a continuity, whether with Kant, with German Romanticism, or with German idealism as a whole.

Just as in the *Phenomenology of Spirit*, evidence of the importance of a critique of intuitionism in Hegelian thought is widespread in his later writings as well. In the last edition in 1827 of the shorter *Logic* from the *Encyclopedia*, he devotes an entire chapter to each of three "Attitudes Toward Objectivity" before presenting his own position (Hegel 1970). The first attitude involves religious faith, the second the rationalism or "subjective idealism" of Kant and Fichte, and the third the German Romantic Jacobi. Hegel's *Science of Logic*, first published in 1812 and 1816, likewise contains many critiques of Jacobi. Since Jacobi did not have the importance in German intellectual life by this time that he had once had, this continuing attention to him by Hegel shows intuitionism to have been an important and recurrent preoccupation. In fact, he called it a "retrogression."

As with the critique of Kant, Hegel's critique of Schelling and Jacobi has many implications for today. Lukács uses it to attack fascism and existentialism: not only the pro-Nazi Martin Heidegger's, but also leftwing postwar existentialists such as France's Hyppolite and Sartre. As Lukács writes in the new Preface to the 1954 East German edition of *The Young Hegel*: "The attempts made in France to 'modernize' Hegel in an existential, irrationalist sense—above all in the well-known book by Jean Hyppolite—have not given me any cause to amend my arguments or even to supplement them" ([1948] 1975:xi). This was written in the same period that saw Lukács's attacks on modernism in literature and the arts.

For example, in a 1955 essay "On the Responsibility of Intellectuals," which includes some of the main arguments from his book *The Destruction of Reason*, Lukács creates an astonishing amalgam of proto-fascists that includes the theorist of anti-Semitism Georg Simmel:

> One cannot find in Hitler one word which had not already been stated by Nietzsche or Bergson, Spengler or Ortega y Gasset ("on a high level") . . . It is therefore absolutely necessary and a great task of the progressive intelligentsia to unmask this entire ideology . . . to show that from Nietzsche to Simmel, Spengler and Heidegger, *et. al.*, a *straight* path leads to Hitler. (Lukács 1973:268–69)

This type of crude amalgamation is the opposite of Hegel's dialectic. Lumping together in this way French leftist existentialists, German Romantics, and fascists as "irrationalists" certainly weakens the argument of *The Young Hegel*. A similar thing happens with Lukács's 1947 essay on "Existentialism" with its crude Stalinist attacks on Sartre (Lukács 1973). However, unlike the slightly later period of *The Destruction of Reason*, at this time, also that of *The Young Hegel*, Lukács is still developing much that is original and important, despite the crudity and one-sidedness of many of his arguments.

One of the few other Hegelian Marxists to emphasize Hegel's critique of intuitionism was Raya Dunayevskaya. She provides a far more balanced view of Hegel's critique of intuitionism, emphasizing Jacobi rather than Schelling. Dunayevskaya's argument can be found in her *Philosophy and Revolution*, where she writes:

> To comprehend fully the movement of "pure thought," we must see why Hegel singled out Jacobi. He did so first in his Observations on Being, and then, more than a decade later, devoted the entire Third Attitude to Objectivity to Jacobi's Intuitionism. Obviously, though in 1812 he had referred to Jacobi's views as "perhaps already forgotten," by 1827 he had decided that such an attitude to objectivity would always recur *when*, in the process of battling contradiction, the Subject becomes impatient with the seemingly endless stages of negation it must suffer through, and therefore, instead, slides backward into Intuition. (1973:20)

For Dunayevskaya, this aspect of Hegel's dialectic also forms the basis of a critique of Maoism and parts of the New Left of the 1960s. In her critique of Maoism, Mao is seen to be zigzagging from the Great Leap Forward in the 1950s to the Cultural Revolution of the 1960s, and from being the implacable foe of the United States to Nixon's host in Beijing. Dunayevskaya (1973) analyzes all of this in terms of Hegel's "Third Attitude Toward Objectivity," his critique of undialectical, intuitionist "leaps" by Jacobi and others.

In contrast to Lukács and Dunayevskaya, Marcuse in *Reason and Revolution* downplays both Hegel's split with Schelling and his critique of intuitionism. Like Lukács, Marcuse seeks to separate Hegel from fascism, but he confines his critique to avowedly fascist Hegelians such as Giovanni Gentile, and simply quotes from several Nazi spokesmen to show their hostility to Hegel, including one statement that on the day Hitler came to power, "Hegel, so to speak, died" (Marcuse [1941] 1960:419)

For his part and in contrast to Lukács, Hyppolite finds some existentialist and Romantic themes in the writings of the young Hegel:

> Hegelianism developed against the background of romanticism. Like Schelling or Hölderlin, Hegel wished to express in philosophical form the infinite life which expresses itself through a multitude of determinate living forms . . . As Hegel puts it in a passage from his *Jenenser System*, man is a sick animal; he is aware of his death and to the degree that he is conscious of it he becomes *for himself* what life is unalterably *in itself*. ([1955] 1969:26)

While Lukács is no doubt correct to emphasize the importance of the break with Schelling and intuitionism, he weakens his case both by the previously discussed overly sweeping and crude polemics against "irrationalism," and by an implacable refusal to acknowledge any Romantic or religious phase in the young Hegel, even to the point of denying any basic affinity between Hegel and Schelling, including during the period when they worked closely together.

To this writer, Hegel seemingly experienced a period of affinity with Schelling and Romanticism, but he had clearly broken with that by the time he wrote the *Phenomenology of Spirit*. Goldmann writes perceptively that "the problematic of Stalinism" permeates the work of Lukács in this period, and that Hegel's own grappling with Napoleonic and Jacobin dictatorships was for Lukács a mirror for his own capitulation to the political realities of Stalinism (Goldmann 1976:109). It is in this light that we must view a large part of Lukács's critique of "irrationalism" in the 1940's and 1950's.

Hegel on economics and labor

Lukács portrays Hegel as more concerned with economic and social questions than any of his German contemporaries. He sees English political economy in particular as playing a major role in Hegel's development. Hegel's economic studies resulted not in abstract formulas but in an analysis of the labor process as one of both human self-development and alienation. Lukács quotes Hegel: "Man makes tools because he is rational and this is the first expression of his *will*. This will is still abstract will—the pride people take in their tools" (cited in Lukács [1948] 1975:322). Thus, tool-making is one of the earliest rational activities of human beings for Hegel, but the thought precedes the deed, at least conceptually in Hegel's presentation of the problem. In his 1831 Preface to the new edition of his *Science of Logic*, Hegel writes:

> Nowadays we cannot be too often reminded that it is *thinking* which distinguishes man from the beasts. . . . logic must certainly be said to be the supernatural element which permeates every relationship of man to nature, his sensation, intuition, desire, need, instinct, and simply by so doing transforms it into something human. (1969:31–32)

Despite his interconnecting of the problems of work and thought, Hegel never quite unites them into something like Marx's conception of labor as praxis, as free, creative, thinking activity that is uniquely human.

In *Capital*, Marx transcends Hegel's notion of "thinking" and labor and takes the problem to a new level:

> We presuppose labor in a form in which it is an exclusively human characteristic. A spider conducts operations which resemble those of the weaver, and a bee would put many a human architect to shame by the construction of its honeycomb cells. But what distinguishes the worst architect from the best of bees is that the archi-

tect builds the cell in his mind before he constructs it in wax. At the end of every labor process, a result emerges which had already been conceived by the worker at the beginning, hence already existed ideally. (1976:283–84)

On the very next page Marx cites a phrase from Hegel's *Logic* on the "cunning" of reason, as he begins to speak of alienated labor, thus also acknowledging his debt to Hegel.

Of course, the Marxist concept of labor includes the more prevalent form of alienated labor, for Marx the principal form of labor under capitalism. The parallel between Hegel and Marx on labor extends to this area as well. Hegel's Jena lectures, which he never published and which were unknown to Marx, contain some striking passages on alienated labor in the new factory system:

> By using machines ... to manipulate nature, he does not escape the necessity for work, but only defers it, removes it further from nature, no longer confronts nature as one living being confronting another ... Work becomes even more absolutely dull . . . the skill of the individual becomes infinitely more limited, and the consciousness of the factory workers is reduced to complete apathy. (cited in Löwith [1941] 1967:263–64; partially in Lukács [1948] 1975)

For Karl Löwith, who quotes it more fully than Lukács, this passage means Hegel sees work with machines as serving "to remove man from any living connection with nature" ([1941] 1967:263).

Marx's concept of alienated labor is, of course, more specific historically to capitalism, but it should be noted that Hegel, likewise, views machine production, the characteristic mode of labor under capitalism, as alienated labor. The actual difference between the two thinkers lies not in their concept of the degradation of labor so much as in Marx's additional concept of the working class as the living negation of capitalism, who are to overthrow it and create a new communist society.

During Hegel's lifetime, industrial strife between labor and capital did not dominate the scene as it did later on, and Hegel never returned to the problem of alienated labor in such detail. In his later writings he saw state intervention from above, with a state that he saw as embodying the universal interests of society, rather than workers' revolt, or even democracy, as the source of the needed "resolution" of the problems of labor and economics.

Lukács includes most of these points in *The Young Hegel*, but his biggest concern is to show the extent of Hegel's studies of economics and their limits, due to an idealization of the state as a body that is neutral and above classes. In so doing, Lukács makes the important point that the problem of labor is central to the first stages of self-consciousness in the *Phenomenology of Spirit*. There, Hegel not only includes slavery as part of his beloved Greek civilization, in his famous dialectic of the master and the slave, but he also makes the problem of slavery central to the whole Greco-Roman epoch.

In Hegel's discussion of slavery, although the master dominates the relationship, and appears to do the thinking at the highest level, ultimately the human spirit advances through the slave, who "through work . . . becomes conscious of what he truly is." Hegel continues, "it is precisely in his work wherein he seemed to have only an alienated existence that he acquires a mind of his own" (1977:118, 119). For his part, Lukács writes:

> Hegel sees quite clearly that the labor of man is sheer drudgery with all the drawbacks that slavery entails for the development of consciousness. But despite all that the advance of consciousness goes through the mind of the servant and not that of his master. In the dialectics of labor real self-consciousness is brought into being, the phenomenological agent that dissolves antiquity. The "configurations of consciousness" which arise in the course of this dissolution: skepticism, stoicism, and the unhappy consciousness (primitive Christianity) are without exception the products of the dialectics of servile consciousness. ([1948] 1975: 327)

Thus, for Lukács, the problem of work is the starting point for the *Phenomenology of Spirit*'s "shapes of consciousness" on their way toward "Absolute Knowledge."

On gender: *Tragedy in the Realm of the Ethical*

Before he turns to a detailed treatment of the *Phenomenology of Spirit* as a whole, Lukács writes a brilliant and suggestive chapter on Hegel's theory of tragedy entitled "Tragedy in the Realm of the Ethical." He takes this title from one of Hegel's unpublished early manuscripts. Lukács views this early version of Hegel's famous theory of tragedy and "ethical action"—in relationship particularly to Sophocles's *Antigone*—as a perceptive anticipation of theories of matriarchy developed later by Friedrich Engels and Johann Bachofen.

For Hegel, the female protagonist Antigone represented the "nether world" of family, ethical, and religious ties that historically preceded (and continued within) the rational world of "light," as represented by Creon in his espousal of the Greek society of cities and laws made by human beings for themselves. This new work of "light" is nevertheless an alienated world. While Hegel certainly ultimately favors Creon's world of "light" over Antigone's "nether world," his scrupulously objective theory of tragedy sees the great merit of both sides as the source of the greatness of Sophocles's tragedy.

Thus, while favoring Creon in the end as the representative of a higher stage of the human spirit, Hegel's account of *Antigone* and the relation of brother and sister gives a hint of the stateless tribal society that Marxists and feminists have argued preceded "civilization." Lukács writes:

> Hegel had no more idea of the nature of tribal society than any other scholar of his time. He believed, however, and rightly so, that the state must have been preceded by a stateless society. . . . In a sense he anticipates the discussion of the *Oresteia* by Bachofen and Engels. ([1948] 1975:411)

Lukács concludes that while "Hegel had no conception of tribal society or matriarchal systems," he "anticipates these future discoveries." Today, one might add that Hegel and Lukács have anticipated some of today's debates over gender and revolution.

In a similar vein, Judith Shklar writes in her study of the *Phenomenology of Spirit* that Creon "must assert the rules of the realm of light, indeed of reason, the human law made by human beings." The ethical relation of brother and sister, as exemplified by Antigone and Polynices, is overthrown by Creon's "universal law." However, Shklar continues, the social web is now broken and the new society results in "war between the sexes, a concomitant of democratic societies that Hegel was exceptionally sensitive to have recognized" (1976:80).

Hegel wrote at a later point in the *Phenomenology of Spirit* that the highest and most equal relationship between man and woman was between brother and sister, a relationship where "they are free individualities with regard to each other." Their recognition of each other is "pure and unmixed with any natural desire," and because of this "equilibrium," he continues, "the loss of a brother is irreparable to the sister, and her duty towards him is the highest" (Hegel 1977:274–75). The latter sentence is footnoted to *Antigone* in Hegel's text.

While it is certainly questionable whether the relationship between brothers and sisters is totally free of sexual aspects, it remains one of the most equal social relationships between men and women, especially when compared with women's relationships with fathers and husbands. One can only think of the way in which brothers and sisters can unite against parents, or other authority figures.

Hegel palpably senses something "lost" to humanity with the rise of the completely patriarchal society of laws and cities as represented by Creon. Because what is "lost" is a sense of "equilibrium" between men and women, his theory of tragedy and the family anticipates not only nineteenth century discoveries about tribal and matriarchal societies as Lukács writes, but also, one might add today, the quest for totally new human relations as seen in today's worldwide feminist movement. While that movement certainly concerns itself with changing laws, it has called for changes in "life" as well. None of this is meant to suggest that Hegel's philosophy is free of sexism; rather, that the penetrating character of his dialectic method often enabled him to go beyond the prejudices of his day, and to see man-woman relations quite truthfully, as seen in this remarkable discussion of *Antigone*.

According to Lukács, Hegel employs similar concepts in his theory of tragedy and in his treatment of the French Revolution, which is so crucial to the *Phenomenology of Spirit*. Summing up, Lukács writes of Hegel's profound objectivity:

> [Hegel makes an] extraordinarily impartial analysis of the historical rights and wrongs of the tragic conflict and his demonstration of the dialectical "rightness" of the opposing sides. He can see the historical justification of Creon's point of view and the necessity underlying it: the inevitable triumph of the state. At the same time

he can recognize the ethical superiority of Antigone and the state of society for which she speaks. This impartiality not only results in a brilliant analysis; it also expresses that contradictory view of progress. ([1948] 1975:412)

In that same sense, with that same objectivity that enabled his theory of tragedy to come close to a theory of matriarchy developed only much later by others—in that same *contradictory* sense—Hegel also approaches the French Revolution and the resultant rise of capitalist society with all of its contradictions.

Hegel's *Phenomenology of Spirit* as a whole

Although Hegel's personal views never became as fervently supportive of the French Revolution as did those of some other German intellectuals, Lukács emphasizes the fact that he never repudiated the French Revolution later on, but retained it as the epochal event of his era, which determined the whole capitalist civilization that followed.

While Hegel's critique of the French Revolution in the chapter on "Absolute Freedom and Terror" in the *Phenomenology of Spirit* certainly can be read (and has been) as part of the conservative reaction that followed the Revolution in much of European thought, Lukács reads it instead as an anticipation of the contradictions of the capitalist civilization it brought into being when it swept away feudalism. As with Hyppolite's work, Lukács sees the French Revolution as the turning point of the *Phenomenology of Spirit*.

Lukács argues that Hegel admired Napoleon at the time of the publication of the *Phenomenology of Spirit* and that he continued to do so for long afterward, as shown by his private correspondence. Hegel devotes the entire section on "Spirit in Self-Estrangement"—a substantial part of the whole book—to the Enlightenment and the French Revolution. Here "we find ourselves in the midst of history as it really happened," writes Lukács ([1948] 1975:486).

The period before the French Revolution is that of the breakdown of French society. Hegel writes that the "disintegrated consciousness" embodied by the cynical views of Diderot's *Rameau's Nephew*, whose utterances are "the absolute and universal alienation of the actual world and thought . . . pure culture" (1977:316). Hyppolite discusses this in his essay on the *Phenomenology of Spirit* and the French Revolution:

> But in this case truth is on the side of the Bohemian, for he describes everything in the social world for what it is, that is to say, the opposite of what it appears to be: "Money is everything, but we should not say so." The noble consciousness and the base consciousness are in reality the opposite of what they should be, the good is evil and the evil is good. The Bohemian lays bare the comedy of a social order which has lost its foundations in any substantial reality. ([1955] 1969:48–49)

For his part, Lukács remarks that Hegel offers no "reconciliation" of these two opposed attitudes; they must fight to the death. As with the slave's superiority to the master in the famous dialectic of the master and the slave, the new comes from unexpected quarters.

Lukács sees Hegel's analysis of French society's breakdown as relevant not only to that period of history but also to the crises of capitalism that later concern Marx and, to some extent, Hegel himself:

> For this reason we may say that the aspect of capitalism that stands in the forefront of attention today has been much more successfully defined here from the standpoint of social morality than in those passages where Hegel brings about a "reconciliation" of opposites. ([1948] 1975:497)

Of course, Hegel had a critique of the actions of the French revolutionaries, but the germ of a critique of capitalism is also involved here in his general view of an epoch in crisis. The "absolute freedom" where, according to Hegel, society becomes merely the ruthless struggle of factions with no group looking to the general interest of society, certainly contains not only a critique of the Jacobin period in the French Revolution but it also functions as a preview of the individualism of nineteenth century competitive capitalist civilization and its contradictions.

Although the Enlightenment triumphs over the old society in the French Revolution, it only brings forth a "self-alienated spirit," Hegel writes (1977:363). Lukács argues that Hegel saw this type of division potentially overcome in the next stage, that of the Napoleonic order, but that is debatable. Nevertheless, Lukács has drawn out an Hegelian theory of social crisis that is relevant to many social structures, including Napoleon's attempted empire.

Some remarks by Hegel could be seen as also criticizing the Napoleonic order, as in his phrase "in place of rebellion appears arrogance" (1977:315). This passage occurs in a description of the breakdown of feudalism proper in prerevolutionary France and the rise of the opulent court of Louis XIV, where the "heroism of the deed" is replaced by the "heroism of flattery," but the passage could certainly be construed more generally. As noted earlier in the discussion of the theory of tragedy, Hegel makes a remarkably objective presentation of both sides of each contradiction, and there is no reason why the phrase "in place of rebellion appears arrogance" cannot be applied to Napoleon, whether Hegel meant to or not, and despite his initial admiration for the French general.

For Hegel, as Lukács sees him, progress is contradictory. A more "advanced" consciousness often emerges in a cynical form judged to be "base" or "depraved" by society, but its "depravity" is merely a reflection of the sickness of the entire social order. While it is important to be aware of the historical period Hegel refers to at each stage of *Phenomenology of Spirit*, it must be remembered also that these are "shapes of consciousness," which recur in different forms in different periods. For that reason, Hegel's philosophy has enduring relevance, and there have been many Hegel revivals during or after periods of great crisis in society.

Lukács also gives detailed treatment to the *Phenomenology of Spirit's* climax in "Absolute Knowledge":

> Absolute Knowledge, Hegel's designation for the highest stage of human knowledge, has a definite idealistic significance: the reintegration of "externalized" reality into the subject, i.e., the total supersession of the objective world. ([1948] 1975:513)

But he continues:

> Here, however, this distance from history is transformed into the attempt to abolish reality's character as real, to transmute objectivity into something posited by the subject and into an identity of subject and object, in short to complete the transformation of substance into subject. ([1948] 1975:514)

Thus, Hegel's "annulment" of objective reality has certain ambiguities. On one hand, it constitutes the ultimate "reconciliation" of all contradictions at the level of thought. On the other hand, Hegel has, according to Lukács, "the whole dilemma" of the contradictory character of reality, which he has recognized throughout his philosophy "recurring at the end of his system in a more acute form than ever" ([1948] 1975:532).

For her part, Dunayevskaya has denied—even more forcefully than has Lukács—that the contradictions cease even at the level of Hegel's "Absolute Knowledge." She instead develops the concept of "absolute negativity as new beginning":

> In truth, as we see, we have reached not heaven, but the Golgotha of the Absolute Spirit! Hegel tries softening the shock of reaching death at the very pinnacle, Absolute Knowledge. . . . Absolute Knowledge was not, after all, the end. . . . And now that we have reached the final chapter, he keeps reiterating over and over again, as we saw, about the "movement," the "transforming" of Substance into Subject. The "ultimate" turns out to be *not the Absolute, which has suffered its Golgotha, but a new beginning, a new point of departure.* (1973:17–18)

According to this view, subjectivity does not here negate the world in any "mystical" sense, but moves forward with the world. For Dunayevskaya, Hegel begins here anew from this in his next work, the *Science of Logic*.

While Lukács stops short of this type of argument in *The Young Hegel*, Marcuse had caught some of its implications seven years earlier in his *Reason and Revolution*, a work to which Lukács does not refer. Marcuse rightly sensed implications of Hegel's "Absolute" for an age of totalitarianism. In a remark that also foreshadows his later one-dimensionality thesis, he writes that in Hegel's "Absolute," "at the end of the road, pure thought again seems to swallow up living freedom" (Marcuse [1941] 1960:120).

Dunayevskaya's concept of "absolute negativity as new beginning" is explicitly related to an age faced with concentration camps and nuclear terror, which she terms one of "absolute terror." Unlike Marcuse's "one-dimensionality," however, Dunayevskaya's concept of "absolute negativity as new beginning" reveals a positive within the negative—a sense of powerful movements for human emancipation developing as determinate negations to ever-newer forms of domination of destruction.

Lukács, possibly on the verge of confronting Hegel's "Absolute" in relation to our totalitarian age, and specifically the Stalinist form under which he resided at the time, retreats hastily to safer ground. He launches instead a lengthy critique of Hegel's concept of religion after only a brief look at "Absolute Knowledge."

Conclusion

Despite its flaws in some areas, *The Young Hegel* addresses many important issues in Hegel's philosophy and its relationship to Marx. Far from a mere Stalinist exercise, it contains some very original insights totally incompatible with the reigning dogma in the USSR. Lukács hints at the way he accommodated to Stalinism at one point when he quotes the poet Henrich Heine on his impression of the politically "resigned" mature Hegel. Heine studied with Hegel in Berlin in the early 1820s and maintained that his teacher's outlook had remained revolutionary and that he also was secretly an atheist who gave

> very obscure and abstruse signs so that not everyone could decipher them—I sometimes saw him anxiously looking over his shoulder for fear that he had been understood. ... When once I expressed disapproval of his assertion "everything which exists, is rational" he gave a strange smile and said that one might equally say "everything which is rational, must exist." (cited in Lukács [1948] 1975:462)

Lukács probably exaggerates in accepting Heine's account of Hegel as a secret atheist, but the notion of the mature Hegel as still seeing the "rational" pulling reality forward in a possibly revolutionary manner is most intriguing. One also wonders if the above anecdote, as recounted in the context of 1948 by Lukács, was a sly evocation of his own outward accommodation for many years to Stalinism. (It should also be noted that this was followed by his courageous break during the Hungarian Revolution of 1956, three years after Stalin's death and eight years after *The Young Hegel*.)

The most exciting and original parts of *The Young Hegel* occur in the discussion of Hegel's theory of tragedy and in the eighty-page "Synoptic

View" of the *Phenomenology of Spirit*. The latter could stand easily by itself. In the flawed but still very important discussion of Hegel's critique of Schelling and intuitionism, Lukács has also covered ground that few others have ventured into, while in the discussion of the *Phenomenology of Spirit* he has surpassed the accounts of many others in an area frequently traversed. The study of Hegel and economics and his theological writings also have much interest.

In the case of the treatment of Hegel on economics, it is possible that Lukács is making too much of this in order to "legitimate" Hegel in the eyes of crudely materialist party ideologues who were looking over his shoulder. He does show that Hegel read widely in economic literature, especially Adam Smith, but the relationship of this to Marx's work, especially *Capital*, is probably at a much more general level than Lukács suggests. Marx took over Hegel's dialectic as a whole, and not just the parts on economics, master and slave, or other seemingly more "relevant" sections. Lukács of course points this out repeatedly, as in his frequent statements that Hegel's dialectic is more revolutionary when it is abstract, and that his conclusions often become more conservative the more empirical and contemporary they become.

When Lukács points with great insight to Hegel's grasp of "the contradictory character of reality" or when one looks at the entire *Phenomenology of Spirit* as the overthrow of one "shape of consciousness" by another arising from within it—even if that shape happens to be religion or "absolute knowledge"—it is in this sense that Hegel's dialectic is revolutionary.

Hegel did not develop this only by reading economic literature, but, as Lukács shows at length, by studying periods of crisis in the history of human civilization, from his youthful notebooks on the fall of Rome and Greece and the "positivity" of the Christian religion to his concentration on the Enlightenment and the French Revolution in the *Phenomenology of Spirit*. The revolutionary character of Hegel's dialectic lies in its capturing the contradictory character of reality, which enables it to look critically and yet with great objectivity at society and its thought, not least on gender.

Finally, Lukács has shown that Hegel's polemics against Kant in the *Science of Logic*, or against Schelling and Jacobi earlier on, constitute an integral part of his dialectical philosophy, and not merely tangential points. Hegel certainly had an encyclopedic grasp of his subject matter, which was itself wide indeed, but his philosophy was no summary of previous thinkers. Instead, his thought develops and clarifies itself out of that polemical movement, critically appropriating from others and rooting itself in concrete historical reality as no previous philosopher had done.

References

Adorno, Theodor. [1966] 1973. *Negative Dialectics*, trans. E.B. Ashton. New York: Seabury Press.

Dunayevskaya, Raya. 1973. *Philosophy and Revolution: From Hegel to Sartre, and from Marx to Mao.* New York: Delacorte.

_____. 1977. "Leon Trotsky as Man and as Theoretician." With a comment by Ernest Mandel. *Studies in Comparative Communism*, Vol. X:1-2 (Spring/Summer):166–83.

Goldmann, Lucien. 1976. *Cultural Creation in Modern Society*, trans. Bart Grahl. St. Louis: Telos Press.

Harris, H.S. 1972. *Hegel's Development: Toward the Sunlight 1770–1801*. London: Oxford University Press.

Hegel, G.W.F. 1969. *Science of Logic*, trans. A.V. Miller. New York: Humanities Press.

_____. 1970. *Hegel's Logic* [Shorter Logic], trans. William Wallace from the *Encyclopedia of Philosophical Sciences*. London: Oxford University Press.

_____. 1971. *Philosophy of Mind*, trans. William Wallace. London: Oxford University Press.

_____. 1977. *Phenomenology of Spirit*, trans. A.V. Miller. London: Oxford University Press.

Hyppolite, Jean. [1946] 1974. *Genesis and Structure of Hegel's Phenomenology*, trans. Samuel Cherniak. Evanston: Northwestern University Press.

_____. [1955] 1969. *Studies on Marx and Hegel*, trans. John O'Neill. New York: Harper and Row.

Lichtheim, George. 1970. *Georg Lukács*. New York: Viking.

Löwith, Karl. [1941] 1967. *From Hegel to Nietzsche*, trans. David E. Green. New York: Doubleday.

Lukács, Georg. [1923] 1971. *History and Class Consciousness: Studies in Marxist Dialectics*, trans. Rodney Livingstone. Cambridge: MIT Press.

_____. 1973. *Marxism and Human Liberation*, edited by E. San Juan, Jr. New York: Dell.

_____. [1948] 1975. *The Young Hegel: Studies in the Relations between Dialectics and Economics*, trans. Rodney Livingstone. London: Merlin Press.

Marcuse, Herbert. [1941] 1960. *Reason and Revolution: Hegel and the Rise of Social Theory*. Boston: Beacon Press.

Marx, Karl. 1967. *Writings of the Young Marx on Philosophy and Society*, edited by Lloyd Easton and Kurt Guddat. New York: Doubleday.

_____. 1973. *Grundrisse*, trans. Martin Nicolaus. New York: Pelican.

_____. 1976. *Capital*, Vol. I, trans. Ben Fowkes. Baltimore: Pelican.

Shklar, Judith. 1976. *Freedom and Independence: A Study of the Political Ideas of Hegel's Phenomenology of Mind*. London: Cambridge University Press.

[Written in 1980. I would like to thank Michael E. Brown, the late Raya Dunayevskaya, and Teru Kanazawa for comments in that period.]

PART III

Dialectics today

8

Dialectical reason and its critics

The crucial point is not only that for every stage of phenomenolog-ical development there is a corresponding historic stage, but also that thought molds its experience in such a manner that it will never again be possible to keep these two opposites in separate realms. . . . No matter what the phenomena are, thought molds the form of experience in a way that determines both the experience and "the ways in which consciousness must know the object as itself."—Raya Dunayevskaya[1]

... Hegelian categories are all recovered in Marxism; and it is no accident that they were reactualized in Europe around, say, the years 1917–1923 ... And if after 1923 this renaissance of dialectical thought subsequently ended, it was because the revolutionary period was clearly over ... —Lucien Goldmann[2]

The modern and postmodern anti-dialectic

We do not live in one of those periods, of the type Lucien Goldmann

---

1.   Raya Dunayevskaya, *Philosophy and Revolution: From Hegel to Sartre, and from Marx to Mao* (New York: Columbia University Press, 1989, orig. 1973, pp. 9, 13.

2.   Lucien Goldmann, "The Dialectic Today" (1970) in his *Cultural Creation in Modern Society*, trans-lated by Bart Grahl, with an Introduction by William Maryl (St. Louis: Telos Press, 1976), pp. 112–13.

describes, of recovery of the Hegelian dialectic in Marxism and radical thought. Instead, we are in an epoch when the dominant intellectual currents all, in one way or another, reject the dialectic of Hegel and of Marx. This is true even of critical and leftist thought nowadays, as discussed below.

The crude materialism of sociobiology and evolutionary biology

In his widely discussed book *Consilience*, Edward O. Wilson, the founder of sociobiology—now more often called evolutionary biology—wants to speak of the unity of all human knowledge, albeit in a positivist sense. The example of dialectical thinking he singles out for attack is Kant's famous statement to the effect that "there is in man a power of self-determination, independent of any coercion through sensuous impulses." In language that could as easily have been used against Hegel, Wilson writes condescendingly that "this formulation has a comforting feel to it, but it makes no sense at all in terms of either material or imaginable entities." Wilson concludes his brief treatment of German idealism by suggesting that if these thinkers had "known modern biology or experimental psychology they would [not] have reasoned as they did."[3]

Other evolutionary biologists are somewhat less conservative, for example, Richard Dawkins. The author of a best-selling attack on religion, *The God Delusion* (2006), Dawkins writes in terms of "selfish genes," not individuals. Therefore, individuals might act in a selfless manner if that protects their gene pool; this is because we are programmed by biology to sacrifice for the group, in order to protect not ourselves as individuals, but our gene pool (children, siblings, etc.). Not only is Dawkins less Hobbesian than Wilson; he also directs his aim against conservative religious fundamentalists, whether Christian, Islamic, or based on other religious traditions. However, it should be noted that this kind of Enlightenment secularism has some major limitations. First, it easily falls into ethnocentrism and even racism when it is deployed against minority religions, like Islam in Europe and the U.S. Second, it can be used to validate science and its "progress" as inherently positive, an anachronistic position in the

---

3.   Edward O. Wilson, *Consilience: The Unity of Knowledge* (New York: Knopf, 1998), pp. 248–49.

age of nuclear weapons and ecological destruction. Here, progressive religious standpoints—like theology of liberation in Latin America or Black liberation theology in the U.S.—are more critical and radical than this kind of secularism.

Utterly reactionary ideas continue to try to base themselves upon evolutionary biology, however, sometimes in unexpected quarters. Take the case of Lawrence Summers, who had to resign from his position as President of Harvard University after suggesting in a public forum in 2005 that women's lower scores in mathematics might be based in biological difference. Summers called for more research in this area, referring to recent studies in evolutionary biology. The outcry was so great, with women scientists and other scholars speaking out forcefully against such biologistic determinism, that Summers was forced to resign 18 months later, in 2006. Sadly, this did not stop Obama from appointing Summers a top economic adviser a couple years later, in the wake of the Great Recession, whereupon Summers kept up a defense of neoliberalism. This suggested that the rankest sexism could be tolerated not only in the Trump-dominated Republican Party, but also inside the liberal establishment. [Note added in 2020: In retrospect, Summers's appointment — and the way in which his biologistic sexism has been nearly forgotten — was a harbinger of the misogyny that undermined the 2016 presidential campaign of Hillary Clinton, herself a longtime member of the neoliberal establishment whose lack of sensitivity to the politics of class left the road open for Trump's rightwing populist appeals to white America.]

Sociobiology/evolutionary biology denies historical materialism's notion that human consciousness grows and develops through history, which is a product of the self-creation of human beings. Although sociobiology/evolutionary biology is a materialism, and thus fights against religious obscurantism, it is a non-dialectical, non-historical materialism. It falls into what Marx, in probably describing Wilson's and Dawkins's intellectual hero Charles Darwin, had already called the "abstract materialism of natural science, a materialism which excludes history and its process."[4] This passage from *Capital*, Vol. I is not as well known, even among Marxian scholars, as it should be, in no small part because Engels—himself not

---

4.   Marx, *Capital*, Vol. I, trans. by Ben Fowkes (London: Pelican, 1976), p. 494.

free of positivism—spoke of Darwin and Marx as equivalent thinkers in his famous oration at Marx's funeral in 1883.

The heritage of structuralism and poststructuralism

A second line of anti-dialectical thought that is influential today can be discerned, this time among oppositional and leftist thinkers; I refer to those theorists and philosophers who have been influenced by structuralism and poststructuralism.

The famous French sociologist Pierre Bourdieu represents a version of the French structuralist tradition, even though he denied that label. Bourdieu organized an intellectual network supporting the workers during the great 1995–96 strikes against a conservative government. In a 1998 manifesto, "For a Leftist Left," he and other French intellectuals counterposed the movement of immigrants and unemployed in the streets to those who accepted the logic of the world market. Their attack targeted not only the right but also social democracy. However, Bourdieu also kept his distance from Marxism, and was in addition extremely hostile to all forms of idealism and humanism, even revolutionary ones. This can be seen in how Bourdieu attacked the existentialist philosopher Jean-Paul Sartre, who had carried out an uncharacteristically fine dialectical analysis of working-class consciousness at one point in *Being and Nothingness* (1943):

> For it is necessary to reverse the common opinion and acknowledge that it is not the harshness of a situation or the sufferings it imposes that lead people to conceive of another state of affairs in which things would be better for everybody. It is on the day that we are able to conceive of another state of affairs, that a new light is cast on our trouble and our suffering and we *decide* they are unbearable."[5]

Here, Sartre is arguing for the crucial importance of conceptualizing the idea of freedom as the precondition for a genuinely revolutionary transformation. In his critique, Bourdieu points correctly to the problematic

---

5. Cited in Pierre Bourdieu, *Outline of a Theory of Practice*, trans. by Richard Nice (New York: Cambridge University Press, 1977, orig. French edition 1972), p. 74. The only published English translation of Sartre's *Being and Nothingness* by Hazel Barnes (NY: Washington Square Press, 1966, p. 561), garbles this passage, and it had to be translated anew for Bourdieu's book.

nature of Sartre's concept of "choice," but then dismisses Sartre's entire statement as a form of idealism that is "totally devoid of *objectivity*."[6]

In a similar and one-sidedly objectivist manner, Bourdieu defines his central category, the "habitus," as "the durably installed generative principle of regulated improvisations." The habitus "produces practices which tend to reproduce the regularities immanent in the objective conditions . . . while adjusting to the demands inscribed as objective potentialities in the situation" (p. 78). In a direct attack on Hegel, Bourdieu puts forward the habitus as an alternative to the notion of "the future conceived as 'absolute possibility' (*absolute Möglichkeit*), in Hegel's sense" (p. 76).

Bourdieu's notion of habitus is supposed to be less one-sided than Lévi-Strauss's or Althusser's "structures," but is not really as different from structuralism as Bourdieu's adherents claim it to be.[7] For example, even when Bourdieu discusses dialectics, he is so dismissive of freedom, consciousness, and the human subject that the only time he can bring himself to refer to freedom is as "conditioned and conditional freedom" (p. 95). Thus, he emphasizes the structures of domination, not their inner contradictions or how to overcome them, an odd position for a leftist thinker. This creates a cul-de-sac for the left.

From a related but different camp, that of poststructuralism, philosophies of radical difference rooted in Nietzsche and Derrida were put forward during the 1980s as alternatives to Marxism and dialectics, which were attacked as totalizing modes of thought that were oppressive and false. A striking example of the philosophy of difference that emerged from poststructuralism can be found in a 1987 injunction from Daniel Cohn-Bendit and Gilles Deleuze that was all too characteristic of the period:

> The goal is . . . what we call a *culture of dissensus* that strives for a deepening of individual positions and a resingularization of individuals and human groups. What folly to claim that everyone—immigrants, feminists, rockers, regionalists, pacifists, ecologists, and hackers—should agree on a same vision of things!

---

6. Bourdieu, *Outline of a Theory of Practice*, p. 74. Further page references are directly in the text.

7. For a critical discussion of Bourdieu from inside the French Left that places him as a structuralist, see François Dosse, *History of Structuralism*, Vol. 2 (Minneapolis: University of Minnesota Press, 1997), pp. 66–75.

We should not be aiming for a programmatic agreement that erases their differences.[8]

How the various spheres of the left, even if taken seriously in each of their particular manifestations, could eventually come together with enough force to challenge the rule of capital is probably not advanced by such a formulation. It should also be noted that Cohn-Bendit and Deleuze conspicuously leave aside the labor movement from their list of movements, and capitalism from their conception of what to oppose.

Moving in another direction, but still strongly influenced by poststructuralism, Antonio Negri and his frequent collaborator Michael Hardt have undermined such a philosophy of difference. They have helped to refocus critical theory on capitalism as the underlying mechanism of domination and the main force of oppression. In so doing, they became leading theorists of the anti-capitalist and global justice movements. Negri and Hardt have synthesized Marx and Deleuze/Foucault into a new radical theory of domination and resistance, but they do so from an openly Nietzschean and anti-dialectical perspective. In their celebrated *Empire* (2000), they attack Hegel as a theorist of capitalism and colonialism. They target as well all forms of dialectic, including Marxian dialectics, as part of "logic of modern domination." This is because of the dialectic's "relegating the multiplicity of difference to binary oppositions and its subsequent subsumption of these differences in a unitary order."[9] They are referring, of course, to the type of procedure in Hegel's *Logic* where identity breaks down into difference but then difference is subsumed by contradiction. Negri and Hardt attack Hegel's theory of contradiction, also a core part of Marxian dialectics, for allegedly subsuming difference into totality and teleology. Because of this, they conclude that "the postmodernist project must be nondialectical," a project they nonetheless see as in sync with both Marx and Lenin (p. 140).

Pragmatism and "everyday life" versus dialectics

Members of a third strand of contemporary theory are dissatisfied with

---

8.   Cited in John Sanbonmatsu, *The Postmodern Prince* (New York: Monthly Review Press, 2004, p. 14.)

9.   Michael Hardt and Antonio Negri, *Empire* (Cambridge: Harvard University Press, 2000), p. 140.

the one-sided emphasis on structure by Bourdieu and other structuralists. They say we need to look also at "agency." In 1998, the American sociologists Mustafa Emirbayer and Anne Mische summed up some of these critiques of Bourdieu when they criticized him for giving "selective attention to the role of habitus and routinized practices" and for viewing "human agency as habitual, repetitive, and taken for granted." While Emirbayer and Mische wish to focus on "the constitutive creativity of action," the alternative they espouse is not the dialectic of Hegel or Marx, which they do not even mention. Instead, they identify with American pragmatism, which, they claim, grasps human creativity by focusing on everyday life as a process of self-constitution.[10]

Of course, we need to remember that, alongside their belief in incremental change and pragmatic discourse rather than revolutionary ruptures, the late nineteenth century founders of pragmatism first embraced and then broke decisively with Hegel. William James, for example, in his famous book *A Pluralistic Universe*, singled out Hegel's absolute for particular attack. He termed Hegel's philosophy a form of "vicious intellectualism" because of Hegel's search for truth as opposed to the multiple truths of a relativistic worldview. For his part, John Dewey wrote of "absolutism versus experimentalism."[11] In the continuing hostility today to all absolutes, including even Hegel's absolute idea, we can still feel the effects of these century-old arguments.

The late Richard Rorty, a more recent pragmatist philosopher who was influenced by Heidegger and poststructuralism as well, also attacked the dialectic throughout his career. Rorty summed up much of the recent academic criticism of the dialectic—and of totality, and of essences—in his 1992 article "The Intellectuals and the End of Socialism." With characteristic bluntness, Rorty offered a rather bizarre take on and agenda for radical philosophy right after the collapse of statist communism in Russia and Eastern Europe:

> I hope we have reached a time when we can finally get rid of the conviction common to Plato and Marx, the conviction that there must be large theoretical ways of finding out how to end injustice,

---

10.   Mustafa Emirbayer and Anne Mische, "What Is Agency?" *American Journal of Sociology* 103:4 (January 1998), pp. 963, 969.

11.   For a summary of this history, see Richard J. Bernstein, "Why Hegel Now?" *Review of Metaphysics* 31:1 (September 1977), pp. 29–60.

as opposed to small experimental ways. I hope we can learn to get along without the conviction that there is something deep—such as the human soul, or human nature, or the will of God, or the shape of history—which provides a subject matter for grand, politically useful theory.[12]

Rorty, of course, saw postmodernists as sharing his critique of totality, essences, and dialectic. But he also cited Habermas, who had moved from dialectical thinking to pragmatism, especially in his critiques of the "philosophy of consciousness."[13] For his part, Rorty wanted to uproot not only Marxist dialectics, but also, in Heideggerian fashion, the whole tradition of critical, dialectical thinking from Plato onwards. Rorty concludes that no "alternative to capitalism" exists and therefore, "The only hope for getting the money necessary to eliminate intolerable inequities is to facilitate the activities of people like Henry Ford ... and even Donald Trump"![14] Such were the depths into which academic radicalism had sunk in the neoliberal 1990s.

However, it should also be noted that pragmatism, this particularly American form of philosophy, was never uncontested in the U.S., any more than structuralism and poststructuralism have been uncontested in France. As Raya Dunayevskaya once noted, in the period "of the 1930s .. . , far from pragmatism and American thought being one and the same, Marxian dialectics was very much on the scene."[15]

Dialectical perspectives

Marcuse's dialectics of negativity: A critique of pragmatism and positivism

In terms of alternatives to pragmatism at the height of its influence,

---

12. Richard Rorty, "The Intellectuals and the End of Socialism," *The Yale Review*, Vol. 80:1/2 (April 1992), p. 4.

13. Jürgen Habermas, *The Theory of Communicative Action*. Two volumes. Translated by Thomas McCarthy. Boston: Beacon Press, 1984–91.

14. Richard Rorty, "The Intellectuals and the End of Socialism," p. 4.

15. Raya Dunayevskaya, *The Myriad Global Crises of the 1980s and the Nuclear World Since World War II* (Chicago: News & Letters, 1986), p. 5.

Dunayevskaya may have been referring to Herbert Marcuse's *Reason and Revolution*, first published in 1941. At that time, John Dewey's influence in American philosophy remained quite strong. *Reason and Revolution* was the first Hegelian Marxist book to appear in English. In addition, it holds the important distinction of being the first systematic analysis of Hegel's major works from a Marxist standpoint in any language.[16] *Reason and Revolution* views the entirety of Marx's writings as grounded in Hegel's concept of dialectic. Theoretically, Marx's work is presented as a critique not only of capitalism but also, at least implicitly, as the foundation for a critique of Stalinist communism. Not only does Marcuse's book contain a critical analysis of Hegel's major works—such as the *Phenomenology of Mind* and the *Science of Logic*—but it also includes the first serious treatment in English of Marx's *Economic and Philosophical Manuscripts of 1844*. This Hegelian-Marxian heritage is counterposed to what Marcuse considered to be the essentially conservative world-view of positivism, which teaches people "to view and study the phenomena of their world as neutral objects governed by universally valid laws."[17]

However, Marcuse attacks not only positivism, but also pragmatism, at least in veiled form. In his discussion of Hegel's *Phenomenology of Mind*, Marcuse shows the limitations of the world of common sense and even that of everyday experience, if it is not mediated by dialectical reason. For Hegel, writes Marcuse, "The world in reality is not as it appears, but as it is comprehended by philosophy" (1941, p. 93). Furthermore, Hegel develops the ground from which to attack the naive perspectives of everyday life and commonsense experience: "Knowledge begins when philoso-

---

16. This point often startles my European Marxist friends, who usually suggest the prior work of Lukács. It is true that Lukács's germinal *History and Class Consciousness* was published in 1923, but it did not explore Hegel's writings as a whole. Although he seems to have completed it as a doctoral dissertation in Russia in 1938, his second major book on dialectics, *The Young Hegel*, which offered an analysis of Hegel's thought up through the 1807 *Phenomenology of Spirit*, did not appear in print until 1948. This was seven years after the publication of Marcuse's book. To be sure, the Stalinist purges and then the war were key factors in delaying publication of *The Young Hegel*. But this is part of the larger fact that during World War II, the center of Marxist theoretical debate moved to the U.S., as most of Europe suffered under the stifling atmosphere of fascism or Stalinism. The most important discussions of Marxist theory were thus carried forth in the U.S. by émigré as well as local scholars, among them most of the key members of the Frankfurt School (Marcuse, Erich Fromm, Franz Neumann, Theodor Adorno, Max Horkheimer), as well as figures like Karl Korsch, Raya Dunayevskaya, C.L.R. James, Grace Lee Boggs, W.E.B. Du Bois, Paul Mattick, Sidney Hook, Oskar Lange, Paul Sweezy, and Paul Baran.

17. Herbert Marcuse, *Reason and Revolution: Hegel and the Rise of Social Theory* (London: Routledge & Kegan Paul, 1955, originally published in 1941), p. 326. Further page references are directly in the text.

phy destroys the experience of daily life." The latter is only "the starting point of the search for truth" (1941, p. 103), which is ultimately based on a critique of commonsense notions of reality. Thus, Marcuse identifies strongly with the specifically Hegelian critique of commonsense experience, putting him at odds with pragmatism. It is likely that he did not make this critique as explicit as he might have done because of his vulnerable position as a philosopher in exile in a land where pragmatism had enormous influence.

It should also be noted that on the eve of Hitler's coming to power, Marcuse had published a lengthy article on Marx's *1844 Manuscripts* immediately after they appeared for the first time in German in 1932. In this article's conclusion, Marcuse quotes the following passage from the young Marx's Hegel critique:

> The outstanding achievement of Hegel's *Phenomenology* and of its final result, *the dialectic of negativity as the moving and creative principle*—is thus that Hegel conceives the self-creation of the human being [*des Menschen*] as a process ...[18]

In this 1932 essay on the young Marx, one of the last Marxist essays to be published in Germany until after 1945, Marcuse already points to the above as illustrating "the 'positive meaning' of negation."[19] Nearly a decade later, in *Reason and Revolution*, Marcuse spells out explicitly the centrality to Marx of Hegel's concept of negativity, arguing that here, in this 1844 text, lie "the origins of the Marxian dialectic" (p. 282). He writes further: "For Marx, as for Hegel, the dialectic takes note of the fact that the negation inherent in reality is 'the moving and creative principle.' The dialectic is the 'dialectic of negativity.'" Negativity is important to Marx in part because: "Economic realities exhibit their own inherent negativity" (p. 282).

Marcuse's emphasis on Hegel's concept of negativity is new and original. It is, of course, at variance with the interpretations of more conservative Hegel scholars, who tend instead to stress categories such as reconciliation and mediation. But it also differs from the emphasis on

---

18. Marx, Karl, "Kritik der Hegelschen Dialektik und Philosophie überhaupt," in Marx and Engels, *Werke: Ergänzungsband* I (Berlin: Dietz Verlag, 1968), p. 574, emphasis added.

19. Marcuse, "The Foundations of Historical Materialism," in *Studies in Critical Philosophy*. (Boston: Beacon Press, 1973), p. 46.

the category of totality in Lukács's *History and Class Consciousness*, written before Marx's 1844 discussion on Hegel's concept of negativity as "the moving and creative principle" had been published in any language.

Even after the *1844 Manuscripts* were published, however, Russian Stalinists were generally hostile to any emphasis on the concept of negativity, viewing it as a trace of idealistic Hegelianism. In the 1950s, for example, the Soviet ideologist V. A. Karpushin tried to banish the issue of negativity from Marxism, arguing in a discussion of the *Manuscripts* that Marx opposed the notion of "some kind of negativity which allegedly inherently clings to things, as Hegel put it."[20]

In his discussion of Hegel's *Science of Logic* in *Reason and Revolution*, Marcuse addresses some of the consequences of the dialectic of negativity. He discusses what he terms "Hegel's concept of real possibility" (p. 151). He writes that in Hegel's concept of essence, the "possible and the real are in a dialectical relation" (p. 150). This leads Marcuse, as a Marxist, to write that for Hegel "a new [social] system is really possible if the conditions for it are present in the old" (p. 152).

Kosík's dialectical critique of the "Pseudoconcrete"

The crude materialism of sociobiology/evolutionary biology, the anti-dialectics of structuralism/poststructuralism, and the concentration on common sense in pragmatism each exemplify, albeit in different ways, what the Czech Marxist Humanist Karel Kosík called the false world of the pseudoconcrete. All three of these currently dominant perspectives not only avoid the specific historical circumstances of human thought and action but also (and more importantly) deny that "thought molds its experience" in a liberatory manner, as Raya Dunayevskaya once wrote.[21]

During the Prague Spring of 1968, the workers and intellectuals of what was then Czechoslovakia tried to develop a "socialism with a human face," but after eight months of moving in that direction, they were repressed by the Russian military and its Eastern European allies. Kosík was the most original philosopher of Marxist humanism in Czechoslovakia in the 1960s. Among his greatest contributions was that concept of the pseudocon-

---

20. Cited in Dunayevskaya, *Marxism and Freedom: From 1776 Until Today* (New York: Columbia University Press, 1988, original edition 1958), p. 62.

21. Dunayevskaya, *Philosophy and Revolution*, p. 9.

crete. In the famous discussion with which he begins his book *Dialectics of the Concrete*, first published in Czech in 1963, Kosík calls the pseudo-concrete "the collection of phenomena that crowd the everyday environment and the routine atmosphere of human life." This is the world "of man's fetishized praxis (which is not identical with the revolutionary-critical praxis of mankind)."[22] Of course, Kosík is no Platonist, and recognizes, as does Hegel in his discussion of "illusory being" [*Schein*] in the *Science of Logic*, that there are links between the fetishized world of the pseudoconcrete and the dialectically concrete.

However, Kosík warns us that dialectics is "the opposite of doctrinaire systematization or romanticization of routine ideas" and "therefore has to *abolish* the apparent autonomy of the world of immediate everyday contacts" (p. 6).

Dunayevskaya's Hegelian Marxist humanism

Kosík and Marcuse develop dialectics as a critique of the pseudoconcrete worlds of positivism, pragmatism, and Stalinism. Yet their work does not explicitly answer anti-dialectical thinkers from the poststructuralist and pragmatist camps of today on one of their major points, the notion that dialectics as a totalizing perspective is incapable of conceptualizing particularity and difference, which ever since Plato it allegedly tends to swallow up into totality. Specifically, dialectics is charged with not having room for the perspectives of oppressed racial and ethnic minorities, of women, or other marginalized groups, since it can only grasp grand totalities like capitalism or progress.

Dunayevskaya, building on both Marx and Lenin, took over from Lenin the dialectical notion that a new stage of capitalism—imperialism—unleashed a new stage of opposition: the national liberation movements. These anti-colonial, anti-imperialist movements were not necessarily proletarian, but they were allies of the working classes of the imperialist countries. In dialectical terms, as developed in Lenin's Hegel Notebooks of 1914–15 (which Dunayevskaya was the first to translate into English), national liberation was the new dialectical contradiction within the larger and stronger capitalist system of the era of imperialism. This

---

22.   Karel Kosík, *Dialectics of the Concrete*, trans. by Karel Kovanda with James Schmidt (Boston: D. Reidel Publishing, 1976, orig. Czech edition 1961), p. 2. Further pagination directly in the text.

meant that a new force of opposition was coming onto the scene, not part of the old duality capital/labor, but somewhat outside it, upsurging from the peripheries of capitalism, inside the colonial and semi-colonial countries like India and China. Not unrelated to this issue in Lenin's eyes—a point of view later shared by Trotsky—were the aspirations for liberation by oppressed minorities like Black people in the U.S.

After Lenin's death, as Central European capitalism developed into fascism during the 1930s, new dialectical contradictions emerged among the resistance movements to fascism and militarism. Elsewhere, the Chinese revolution gained strength from both a national liberation struggle against Japanese imperialism and resistance to the capitalist military dictatorship of the Chinese Nationalists. In the U.S., the contradictions of capitalism in the post-World War II era were analyzed by Dunayevskaya as including not just the proletariat or working class as a single force of revolution and opposition but rather four forces of revolution: rank-and-file workers, Blacks, women, and youth. In her book *Women's Liberation and the Dialectics of Revolution* (1985), she spelled out this dialectic in terms of a revolutionary feminism, but unseparated from Marxist dialectics and a critique of the capitalist mode of production.

Dunayevskaya also addressed the notion of totality within dialectics. In 1958 in *Marxism and Freedom*, she had considered the absolute idea in Hegel's *Logic* more as a totality, as the unity of theory and practice. She was stressing Hegel's statement at the beginning of the absolute idea chapter in the *Science of Logic* to the effect that "the Absolute Idea has shown itself to be the identity of the theoretical and the practical idea. Each by itself is still one-sided . . . "[23] But by the 1970s, with *Philosophy and Revolution* (1973), her emphasis is different. She focuses not so much on unity as on contradiction, diremption, and opposition right within the absolute idea itself. Indeed, she begins her Hegel Society of America lecture of 1974 (reprinted in *Power of Negativity*) by noting that Hegel's absolute idea is "so totally infected with negativity"[24] that Hegel begins the absolute idea chap-

23.   Hegel, *Science of Logic*, translated by A. V. Miller (New Jersey: Humanities Press, 1969), p. 824; see also Dunayevskaya, *Marxism and Freedom*, p. 42.

24.   Dunayevskaya, *The Power of Negativity: Selected Writings on the Dialectic in Hegel and Marx*, edited by Peter Hudis and Kevin B. Anderson (Lanham, MD: Lexington Books, 2002), p. 163.

ter by telling us that the Absolute "contains the highest opposition within itself."[25]

But even that point, opposition and negativity within the Absolute, is not the whole of what Dunayevskaya wants to convey in that 1974 lecture. Far from it, for she then writes:

> The same first paragraph of the Absolute Idea that riveted our attention to the highest opposition, cautioned against imposing an old duality on the new unity of opposites reached—the Theoretical and Practical Idea. "Each of these by itself is still one-sided . . ." The new, the highest opposition, rather, has to self-develop.[26]

Here, Dunayevskaya's stricture (which she says is Hegel's own) "against imposing an old duality on the new unity of opposites reached" refers to the fact that the opposition within the absolute idea is not a return to the old type of opposition between the practical idea and the theoretical idea. That former opposition has by now been transcended or sublated [aufgehoben], and new types of opposition will emerge, again and again. Dunayevskaya then writes—paraphrasing Marx in 1844—of "the power of the negative which is the creative element" and points over and over again to "fresh beginning[s]" that Hegel develops in that absolute idea chapter.[27]

In one sense, Dunayevskaya in her 1974 lecture holds onto the Hegelian concept of totality, first singled out in the Marxist dialectical tradition by Lukács in 1923 in *History and Class Consciousness*. But Dunayevskaya claims very explicitly that it is not the closed totality that Hegel's critics allege to be the case. She reinterprets totality to encompass the absolute idea as absolute negativity rather than as any kind of ultimate metaphysical rest in a closed totality. This allows the dialectic to connect to the richness and variety of movements for change in the post-World War II era—workers, students, gay and lesbian movements, women's movements, movements of oppressed ethnic and national minorities—without giving up the notion of a universal drive toward liberation. By creating a unifying point through a dialectical vision of a new society, free of the domination of capital and its value form, and also of sexism, racism, and heterosexism,

---

25.   Hegel, *Science of Logic*, p. 824.

26.   Dunayevskaya, *Power of Negativity*, p. 165.

27.   Dunayevskaya, *Power of Negativity*, p. 167.

she avoids the pseudoconcrete that envelops so many of the postmodern philosophies of difference.

Concluding remark

We cannot recover and develop the dialectical critique of society and thought today without taking a plunge into the fullness of Hegel's dialectic, which Marx called "the source of all dialectics."[28] The rejection of, or silence toward, Hegel and the dialectic in so much of contemporary thought makes it extremely difficult for radical philosophy to advance beyond the traps in which it finds itself today. We need to open ourselves anew to the dialectic, to be unafraid to allow it to mold our experience in a critical, revolutionary manner. But this has to be a reinterpreted dialectic, not one that emphasizes totality to the exclusion of the problems of identity and difference.

Dialectical thinking needs not only to engage and critique the recent forms of anti-dialectical philosophy. It also needs to appropriate critically into the dialectics of the 21st century some of the insights from postmodernism and pragmatism, although probably not evolutionary biology. We need to examine some of the questions raised since Marx or Lukács, especially on difference, particularity, gender, and sexuality. Otherwise, dialectics could atrophy into a "classical" perspective, like that of Plato or Confucius, rather than continuing as a living and critical philosophy for today.

[Originally presented at Marxist-Humanist conference in Chicago in 2009]

---

28.   Marx, *Capital*, Vol. I, p. 744.

9

Derrida on Marx:
Return or deconstruction?

After he stunned an international Marx conference in Riverside, California with his call for a return to Marx, something that also marked a major "turn" in his thought, Jacques Derrida's book *Specters of Marx* was eagerly awaited by a broad spectrum of the intellectual Left.[1] The book is, in fact, a much-expanded version of that April 1993 lecture.

The vicissitudes of deconstruction

Derrida and the philosophico-literary school of "deconstruction" that he represents have long been associated with an intense theoretical radicalism rooted in abstruse linguistic/textual analysis. He and his numerous followers, along with the whole cultural movement termed postmodernism, have tended to disparage not only liberal thought, but also Marx's thought, as essentially Eurocentric, phallocentric, and full of humanist illusions and delusions.

In place of Marx, Nietzsche and Heidegger are often invoked as the truly radical philosophers, something that drew Derrida into an embarrassing (for him) dispute with the American leftist philosopher Thomas Sheehan in the *New York Review of Books* in 1993 over Derrida's attempt to

---

1. Originally appeared in News & Letters, November 1994, with which I was then affiliated.

suppress the English translation of some of his own statements, which seemed to excuse Heidegger's anti-Semitism.

At a directly philosophical level, Derrida's most prominent colleague in the United States, Gayatri Spivak, has, while using Marx's theory of exploitation, pointed proudly to "deconstruction's share in the undoing of the dialectic" as well as its opposition to all forms of "transcendence" of the given.[2] Derrida himself, in one of his first essays in English, originally published in 1968, attacked humanist readings of Marx as forms of "onto-theo-teleology," calling instead for "an absolute break and difference" from/ with the Western humanist tradition, Marx included, via a return to Heidegger and Nietzsche.[3]

Derrida's own work has often been more complicated and interesting than that of his followers. For example, while some of his American followers support crude forms of Third Worldism, and others hesitate from openly defending women's rights against Islamic fundamentalism, Derrida himself strongly supports human rights movements. He is a prominent member, for example, of the French committee to support the persecuted anti-fundamentalist Bangladeshi feminist writer Taslima Nasreen.

On the urgency of Marx for today

The opening pages of Derrida's book are full of praise for Marx. In the first chapter, he writes: "Upon rereading the *Manifesto* and several other great works of Marx, I said to myself that I knew of few texts in the philosophical tradition, perhaps none, whose lesson appears more urgent *today*."[4] Derrida mourns the fact that today the name of Marx "has disappeared" (p. 5) from philosophical and political debate, but he declares that the specter of Marx still haunts our post-1989 world. There are many provocative literary allusions with regard to the notion of the specter, not only to the first sen-

2.   Gayatri Spivak, "Limits and Openings of Marx in Derrida," in her *Outside in the Teaching Machine* (New York: Routledge, 1993), p. 119.

3.   Derrida, "The Ends of Man," in *Margins of Philosophy*, trans. by Alan Bass 109–36 (Chicago: University of Chicago Press, 1982), pp. 134–35.

4.   Derrida, *Specters of Marx: The State of the Debt, the Work of Mourning and the New International*, trans. by Peggy Kamuf (New York: Routledge, 1994), p. 13. Further pagination directly in the text, translation occasionally modified.

tence of the *Communist Manifesto* about the specter of communism haunting Europe, but also to Hamlet's haunting by his murdered father's ghost.

Derrida's point is not to introduce or reintroduce Marx into what he calls the "great canon of Western political philosophy" (p. 32) but rather to make Marx actual, to challenge the new *"dominant* discourse," which has become an "incantation" to the effect that "Marx is dead, communism is dead, very dead, and along with it its hopes, its discourse, its theories, and its practices. It says: long live capitalism, long live the market, here's to the survival of economic and political liberalism!" (p. 52). Further, Derrida argues that it is necessary to *"assume the [heritage] of Marxism"* in such a way that this "heritage is never a *given*, it is always a task" to be worked out for the future (p. 54).

These gestures toward Marx for today do not mean, however, a return to the humanism and dialectic of Hegel and Marx. There are enough hints, even on these early pages praising Marx, of where Derrida will go later. For one still finds silence about the *1844 Essays*, and an effort to separate the "spirit" of Marxism from "Marxism as ontology, philosophical or metaphysical system, [or] as 'dialectical materialism'" (p. 68).

Then, a bit later, a little over halfway through the book, Derrida announces, "What is certain is that I am not a Marxist" (p. 88). It becomes clearer that the "spirit" of Marx that he wants to evoke is that of a radical critique of capitalism, but not the "dialectical method," the concept of "totality" or other philosophical aspects of Marxism, which he explicitly opposes (p. 88).

It is beginning to sound more familiar, as if Derrida wants to use some of Marx's socio-economic analysis without embracing the core of Marxism—the dialectic—and that he wishes instead to substitute his own deconstructionism for the Hegelian-Marxian dialectic. Deconstruction, he tells us, is an "attempted radicalization of Marxism" (p. 92). It is necessary to use deconstruction to overcome some of Marxism's worst flaws which include its "anthropo-theology" rooted in Hegel's *Phenomenology of Spirit* (p. 144), its "untenable" humanism (p. 145), and its concept of the "whole" (p. 146).

Diverging from Marx

In the closing pages of the book, Derrida takes up the famous section on commodity fetishism from chapter one of *Capital*, Vol. I. In an intricate and original reading of this key text, he seems to agree with Marx that under capitalism the products of human labor take on a life of their own, assuming a fetishized, mystical form while (at the same time) the human being is dehumanized, and relations between people, Marx writes, take on "the fantastic form of a relation between things."[5] All those who are oppressed by this racist, sexist, homophobic, classist system know well this feeling of being reduced to an object, a thing, (some)thing less than human.

But it is at this crucial juncture that Derrida diverges in an important way from Marx. He seems to make a serious misreading of Marx when he avers that "as soon as there is production, there is fetishism" (p. 166). Derrida probably knows full well that for Marx, precapitalist societies with their more openly expressed forms of social hierarchy did not need commodity fetishism, and were therefore more socially transparent. Also, he no doubt is aware (but does not mention) that Marx saw the growing self-organization of the workers and other revolutionary groups as pointing toward a future society of freely associated labor where human rationality would take hold of and uproot commodity fetishism.

Derrida seems to argue instead for the permanence of fetishism, and mentions the "general question of fetishization" as something he will return to in a "work to come" (p. 167). He apparently considers Marx's critique of commodity fetishism under capitalism to be nothing more than an attempted exorcism of the fetish. Or, putting it more accurately, he thinks that dialectical reason—in the sense of unmasking, critiquing, and going beyond the fetish—itself has no rational basis.

He suggests that Marx may be grounded in a set of "messianic" beliefs, which includes, Derrida writes, an "exorcism at the beginning of *Capital*," which is linked to a great "revolutionary promise" for the future (p. 163). Derrida does not therefore dismiss Marx, because even such an "exorcism" would not "discredit" Marx, and he points to the possibility of a form of messianism without theology. However, he does write that Marx is a "critical but predeconstructive" thinker (p. 170). But this does not mean any easy assimilation of Marx into deconstruction, for "Marx has not yet been received" and he remains even today a clandestine "immigrant" in

---

5. Marx, *Capital*, Vol. I, trans. by Ben Fowkes (New York: Vintage, 1976), p. 165. Further pagination directly in text.

Western thought (p. 174). The latter point offers a remarkable insight into Marx's marginality as an immigrant intellectual and political refugee in London, something many scholars miss as they essentialize this trilingual, cosmopolitan as a "German" thinker. Derrida's perspicacity here may be rooted in his own life experience as a Jewish North African living in Paris.

Diverging from Derrida

Let us look more closely for a moment at Marx's own text to get a better grasp of Derrida's critique. Derrida himself (p. 164) quotes the following passage on commodity fetishism from *Capital*: "The whole mystery of commodities, all the magic and necromancy that surrounds the products of labor on the basis of commodity production, vanishes therefore as soon as we come to . . . other forms of production" (p. 169).

Derrida never, however, quotes any of Marx's historico/dialectical analysis that follows, wherein precapitalist social formations such as European feudalism had "no need for labor and its products to assume a fantastic form different from their reality" (p. 170), because the exploitation of the peasantry was open, brutal, and direct. In a different way, the liberatory society of the future to which Marx also points will dispense with commodity fetishism because in a society based upon "freely associated" labor, human relations would assume not only a "transparent" but also a "rational" form (p. 173). It is these very notions of transparency and of dialectical reason that Derrida questions, however.

To be sure, in today's retrogressive climate, it is hard to see the actuality of dialectical reason as negation of the negation, as the positive in the negative of this crisis-ridden world. Yet, without such a perspective, on what basis can we really go beyond the capitalist order?

Still, Derrida's critique is more interesting than that of the structuralist Louis Althusser a generation ago. Althusser tried to banish Hegel, humanism, and dialectical reason from Marx, which was ultimately impossible to do given Marx's own writings. Derrida, however, is seriously engaged with Hegel throughout his writings. Although he too is an anti-humanist, he acknowledges Marx's humanism, yet urges us to return to Marx.

Two decades before *Specters of Marx*, in her *Philosophy and Revolution*, the Marxist-Humanist philosopher Raya Dunayevskaya wrote that in the reified [thingified] and fetishized world of capitalism, "the reification of human relations is a fact so overpowering that it dominates the whole of society, including . . . *the thought of the period*."[6] Is this not the trap Derrida has fallen into, in assuming fetishism to be permanent? Is this not in large part because deconstruction lacks an historical dimension?

Perhaps this problem is related to another one also found in deconstruction and in postmodern theory generally, the tendency to reject subjectivity. Dunayevskaya addresses this problem in a later discussion of fetishism. There, she stresses that post-Marx Marxists tended to discuss fetishism, if at all, only as an "objective" feature of capitalism, one that weighed down upon us, and not as something that also generated "subjective" yearnings for freedom on the part of the oppressed: "The objective may outweigh the subjective, but, unless we see the unity of the two and grapple with the truth of both, we will never be free. And freedom is what all the striving is about."[7]

The importance of Derrida's return to Marx

But none of this should obscure the uniqueness of what Derrida has wrought. In raising Marx as the thinker for today, Derrida may have opened up some important space for debate on Marx, Hegel, and the dialectic among youth, feminists, and radical intellectuals generally.

Furthermore, Derrida has put forth most forcefully the notion that Marx's own writings, by now over a century old, are still, as cited earlier, "urgent" for "today." Perhaps some of this will inspire the generation of radical youth who have been influenced by Derrida to confront Marx directly and to connect Marx to their fight against sexism, racism, ethnocentrism, homophobia, war, and imperialism. It is interesting that Derrida is the only one of today's internationally prominent philosophers to advocate a return to Marx.

He is taking the opposite tack to that of other "radical" philosophers such as Richard Rorty or Jürgen Habermas. Why has he done so? Why now?

---

6. Raya Dunayevskaya, *Philosophy and Revolution: From Hegel to Sartre, and from Marx to Mao* (New York: Columbia University Press, 1989, orig. 1973), p. 88, emphasis added.

7. Dunayevskaya, *Rosa Luxemburg, Women's Liberation, and Marx's Philosophy of Revolution* (Urbana: University of Illinois Press, 1991, orig. 1982), p. 144.

Something is rotten[8] in a European civilization that allows genocide to continue unchecked in Bosnia, that greets another genocide of up to a million people by the French-financed Rwandan regime with near silence, and that allows a "normal" fascism, as in the "neo" fascists who are part of the Italian government, to become simply an accepted part of political life. All the while this same civilization, of which America is the sole super-power, closes its borders ever tighter against people of color.

It is perhaps this rot, this decadence, this retrogression, that has drawn one radical French philosopher—one who as a teenager in Algeria was forced to wear the yellow star under the Nazi Occupation—to return to the greatest of Europe's revolutionary philosophers, Karl Marx, as the one who is most "urgent" for us today.

[Originally appeared in *News & Letters*, November 1994, with which I was then affiliated.]

---

8. In a recent review of the book in France, Alain Guillerm writes: "We can thank Derrida for hav-ing written such a book during a period of rottenness," *L'Homme & la Société*, No. 111–12 (Jan–June 1994).

10

Resistance vs. emancipation: From Marx to Foucault

Introductory note to the 2019 Spanish translation

This article appeared in 2013, amid the wave of radical movements that burst forth in the wake of the Great Recession and the Arab Revolutions of 2011.[1] In the next few years, those revolutions were mainly crushed by the old regimes, and we have also witnessed the coming to power in several countries of far-right populism, from the U.S. to India, from Hungary to Brazil. By 2019, however, the revolutionary wave returned as significant uprisings broke out in Hong Kong and Sudan, then in Algeria, Chile, and Lebanon.

During the same period, 2013–19, Marxist thought experienced a global resurgence, while the fortunes of Foucault's philosophy experienced something of a decline. At a direct level, this decline was sparked by criticisms by younger intellectuals about Foucault's silence in the face of the rise of neoliberalism in the years before his 1984 death or, worse, his possible support of neoliberalism. The decline also seemed to be related, in dialectical fashion, to the Marxian revival.

Nonetheless, Foucault's thought remains an important frame of refer-

---

1. This article originally appeared as Kevin B. Anderson, "Resistance versus Emancipation: Foucault, Marcuse, Marx, and the Present Moment," *Logos: A Journal of Modern Society & Culture* 12:1 (Winter 2013. Reproduced here with permission.

ence for many critical and leftist social philosophers and activists, among them a number of anarchists. Some anarchists—and the somewhat related Antifa movement in the U.S.—have, like Foucault, emphasized resistance at the expense of articulating a positive, humanist alternative, even if the direct recourse to Foucault has diminished in frequency. Many serious intellectuals also admire—and rightly so—Foucault's critiques of the modern prison and of the apparatus [dispostif] of sexuality. In addition, many of his adherents continue to occupy important positions in leading universities, especially in the U.S. and the U.K., where they sometimes espouse forms of radicalism supposedly to the left of Marx.

For all the above reasons, my 2013 critique of Foucault may still be of some interest.

The changed world of 2011–12

We live in a far different world than just a few years ago. Not only have we suffered the greatest economic downturn since the 1930s but we have also witnessed the emergence of new forms of mass struggle. Foremost among these have been the 2011–12 Arab revolutions, still ongoing. Not since 1848 has the world experienced such a wave of revolutions crossing borders in such a short period. Moreover, unlike some of the other democratic upheavals of this century (Iran 2009, Ukraine 2004, Serbia 2000), the Arab revolutions have articulated not only political demands but also economic ones. The spread of these revolutions to countries whose governments boasted of their anti-imperialist credentials, like Libya and Syria, has also tested those on the Left who place opposition to U.S. imperialism ahead of everything else.[2] Several other key struggles have emerged in the wake of the Arab revolutions, among them the summer 2011 British youth uprising triggered by minority youth, a serious challenge to racially-based state/police oppression and austerity economics. We have also witnessed serious movements against austerity and economic oppression, above all in Greece (begun before 2011), but also in Spain and Israel, as well as the labor upheaval in Wisconsin. In the U.S. and U.K., the 2011–12 Occupy Movement has galvanized a new generation of young radicals, most notably in Oakland, California, where they were able to shut down

---

2.   For elaboration, see Anderson (2012).

of one of the world's largest ports in alliance with dockworkers, while also linking their movement to earlier protests against the murder of an African American youth, Oscar Grant, by local transit police. One could make a number of critiques of these new movements concerning their organizational practices or their political stances. In the discussion below, however, I concentrate on a philosophical orientation that influences contemporary radical movements, centered on the all-too-common preoccupation with notions of "resistance."

Foucault and resistance

Over the past decade or so, poststructuralist currents of thought have often merged with anarchism and some elements of Marxism to produce new notions of resistance. These notions include resistance to power, resistance to the state, resistance to surveillance, resistance to cultural hegemony, and resistance to capital.

To be sure, this constitutes an advance over earlier forms of intellectual radicalism—from Althusser to Adorno—that stressed hegemony almost to the exclusion of resistance. But this advance has come at a price, as will be discussed below.

Before going there, however, it must be asked, where does this twenty-first century usage of the term *resistance* originate? Not, seemingly, in the broad-based national resistance movements against fascism during World War II. One can instead trace the term's current usage to a more recent source: the writings of Michel Foucault on power and resistance. Although resistance is not emphasized in his earlier writings, by 1976 Foucault famously takes up resistance as well as power. By then, he sketches power as a "relation," "not something that is acquired, seized, or shared" (Foucault 1978: 94). This notion of power as relational was surely meant as an allusion to—and perhaps as a sublation or supersession of—Marx's notion of capital as a social relation, not a thing (Marx 1976: 932).

Foucault (1978: 95–96, translation altered based on French original) writes further:

> Where there is power, there is resistance, and yet, or rather consequently, this resistance is never in a position of exteriority in relation to power. . . . [Power relationships' very] existence depends on

a multiplicity of points of resistance. . . . Hence there is no single locus of great Refusal, no soul of revolt, source of all rebellions, or pure law of the revolutionary. Instead there are specific cases of resistance. . . . They are "the other" in the relations of power; they inscribe themselves as irreducible in relation to it.

Note—and I touch on this below—Foucault's explicit attack on Herbert Marcuse's notion of a Great Refusal, one of the French philosopher's rare direct engagements with the Critical Theory of the Frankfurt School.

Critique of Foucault's concept of resistance

Why has this term *resistance* largely replaced "emancipation," "liberation," "a society free of exploitation," "a society free of alienation," and the like, and at what cost?

At the level of political activism, one obvious cost of adopting or even adapting Foucault's notion of resistance is linked to the fact that not all forms of resistance are equivalent.

Is resistance to state power by the Right the same as that by Marxists or anarchists?

Is resistance to Western imperialism by religious fundamentalists the same as that by national liberation movements?

Is the Catholic Church's resistance to state-sponsored contraception in the U.S. equivalent to the labor movement?

Are women religious fundamentalists who seized the Red Mosque in Islamabad, Pakistan in 2007 in order to crack down on free expression similar to socialist feminists in the same society like Malala Yousafzai, whom those with politics similar to the former tried to assassinate?[3]

This sort of problem lay at the root of Foucault's embarrassing support for Ayatollah Khomeini's leadership during the Iranian Revolution of 1978–79, when he dismissed worries expressed by Iranian feminists. As Khomeini assumed power in 1979, Foucault wrote about Islamic resistance to imperialism, this after mockingly referring to Marxist-Leninist notions like "the struggle of classes, of the armed vanguards" (Afary and Anderson 2005: 239) as outdated and misplaced:

---

3.   For an interesting discussion of Yousafzai's politics, see Weinberg (2012).

Thus, it is true that as an "Islamic" movement, it can set the entire region afire, overturn the most unstable regimes, and disturb the most solid ones. Islam—which is not simply a religion, but an entire way of life, an adherence to a history and a civilization—has a good chance to become a gigantic powder keg, at the level of hundreds of millions of men. Since yesterday, any Muslim state can be revolutionized from the inside, based on its time-honored traditions. (Afary and Anderson 2005: 241)

A second problem is that Foucault's concept of resistance lacks a notion of emancipation. As the autonomist Marxist John Holloway (2002: 40) argues, "in Foucault's analysis, there are a whole host of resistances which are integral to power, but there is no possibility of emancipation. The only possibility is an endlessly shifting constellation of power-and-resistance."

In their 2011 introduction to a volume of Herbert Marcuse's writings, Douglas Kellner, Clayton Pierce, and Tyson Lewis (2011: 63) raise a similar point, albeit in a more philosophical vein:

With the rise of postmodernism and the discourse of power—in particular Foucault's critique of the Great Refusal—it has become fashionable to replace revolution with the terms *resistance*—or even with *micro-resistance*. Resistance is here internal to power, and ultimately produced by power, thus challenging power from the inside.

Kellner *et al.* go on to quote Slavoj Žižek's criticism that such a concept of resistance "does not allow for the radical gesture of the thorough restructuring of the hegemonic symbolic order in its totality" (Kellner, Pierce, and Lewis 2011: 63).

Marcuse's great refusal

What did Marcuse actually mean by the "Great Refusal"? In his 1964 book *One-Dimensional Man*, which sold quite widely in France in the years before the publication of Foucault's *History of Sexuality* in 1976, Marcuse (1964: 260–61) located revolutionary opposition to modern capitalist society not in the employed parts of working classes but among bohemians, the unemployed, and racial minorities who refused "the rules of the game":

> Underneath the conservative popular base is the substratum of the outcasts and outsiders, the exploited and persecuted of other races and other colors, the unemployed and the unemployable. . . . Their opposition is revolutionary even if their consciousness is not. Their opposition hits the system from without and is therefore not deflected by the system . . . The critical theory of society possesses no concepts which could bridge the gap between the present and its future; holding no promise and showing no success, it remains negative. Thus it wants to remain loyal to those who, without hope, have given and give their life to the Great Refusal. (Marcuse 1964: 256-57)

However much it was expressed in a language of deep pessimism about the human prospect, it is clear that Marcuse's revolutionary vision encompassed the need to overturn totally the capital relation, the class society upon which it was based, and its noxious byproducts, from aggressive militarism to stultifying social conformity in the consumer society. In short, a total uprooting was needed, however unlikely that might seem as a concrete historical possibility.

Marcuse's key difference with Foucault was as follows: unless these forms of resistance became forms of emancipation, linked to a vision of new human relations, they would founder and achieve little or nothing except the gesture of a Great Refusal.

To a considerable extent, Marcuse's Great Refusal was rooted in the Hegelian notion of negativity, of absolute negativity or double negation, wherein a positive is constructed even as the old is being negated. This was also what Marx had meant in the 1844 *Manuscripts* when he termed negativity the "moving and creating principle" of Hegel's philosophy (Marx 1961: 176).

But Marcuse's Great Refusal also carried overtones of the Kantian "ought," wherein the normative and the descriptive undergo a radical separation. This can be seen in Immanuel Kant's rather abstract critique of war. Where Hegel's universals were concrete—in the sense of being linked to real possibilities in the given world—Kant's were more abstract, sometimes just panaceas like "perpetual peace" that he advised warring nations to adopt from his perch as a philosopher, without mapping out any real social forces capable of making such a change.

The generalized "scream" against injustice and oppression with which Holloway (2002: 9) begins *Change the World without Taking Power* may also suffer from some of these problems, as when he writes:

> The loss of hope for a more human society is not the result of people being blind to the horrors of capitalism, it is just that there does not seem to be anywhere else to go, any otherness to turn to. ... So perhaps we should not abandon our negativity but, on the contrary, try to theorize the world from the perspective of the scream.

Dunayevskaya, Marcuse, and Foucault

When viewed from the vantage point of Foucault's unending constellation of power-resistance-power, Marcuse's Great Refusal holds some similarities to the critique of twentieth century Marxism articulated by my mentor, the Marxist-Humanist philosopher Raya Dunayevskaya: "Without such a vision of new revolutions, a new individual, a new universal, a new society, new human relations," and "without a philosophy of revolution activism spends itself in mere anti-imperialism and anti-capitalism, without ever revealing what it is *for*" (Dunayevskaya 1982: 194).

Dunayevskaya also conceptualized some very specific oppositional social forces and groups—rank-and-file labor, youth, women's liberation (as it was called then), Blacks and other racial minorities, and Third World national liberation movements—that would be, if self-mobilized and united, powerful enough to give life to the aspiration for a new society. In contrast, Marcuse's emancipatory politics in the form of the Great Refusal remained more of an existential attitude without much of a serious possibility of its realization, because its form of negation was indeterminate rather than determinate or specific.[4]

Moreover, by leaving his Great Refusal at such a high level of indeterminateness, Marcuse opened himself up to the very type of critique that those like Foucault would level at him and, more generally, at the eman-

---

4. On the lack of a concept of determinate negation in Marcuse's thought, see Kellner (1984).

cipatory Marxism of the 1960s. According to Foucault, the Great Refusal was a lot of hot air mixed with noble sentiments, as also seen in many of the political pronouncements of other radical philosophers like Jean-Paul Sartre. To Foucault, such philosophers were always ready to take a stand but not to do the intellectual labor necessary to develop real expertise. Recall his evocation of the specific intellectual rather than the generalist one like Sartre, something Foucault practiced in his prisoner support work of the 1970s during which he researched and wrote an important book on the prison, *Discipline and Punish*. Of course, that book also came with a lot of limitations, especially in how it minimized the emancipatory currents running through the modern Western prison system in the 1970s, as witnessed most dramatically in the Attica prison uprising of 1971.

Marx and concrete universals: The dialectics of race, ethnicity, and class

Does Marx's work—and that of his philosophical mentor Hegel—take us beyond the conundrum left us by Foucault and even Marcuse and Holloway? Does Marx offer us emancipatory universals that are really concrete? Even if this is the case, do his universals still speak to us today and can they still guide our practice?

As I argued in my book *Marx at the Margins*, Marx's critique of capital was both global and local, both universalizing and particularizing. Over four decades, Marx examined the relationship of race, ethnicity, and nationalism to revolution, particularly in Poland, the U.S. during the Civil War, and Ireland. These writings belie the notion that Marx's conceptualization of capitalist modernity constitutes a "totalizing" grand narrative under which the particulars of race, ethnicity, and nation are subsumed.

Take, for example, his writings on Ireland of 1869–70, where he connected class with nationalism, race, and ethnicity—a discussion that began with his writings on Poland and on the American Civil War. Inside the First International, Ireland was a major reason behind Marx's break with the anarchist Mikhail Bakunin, who did not want the International to get involved in "non-class" issues like the defense of Irish political prisoners. For his part, Marx thought that this issue was intimately connected to the class struggle in Britain. All of this led him to some important theoretical reflections.

By 1870, Marx saw the Irish independence struggle as deeply linked to the struggles of British workers against capital. This is seen in the "Confidential Communication" of March 1870, a rejoinder to Bakunin that he drafted on behalf of the General Council of the International. English working-class consciousness, Marx wrote, was attenuated by anti-Irish prejudice, in a dynamic similar to that of white racism in the U.S.:

> The average English worker hates the Irish worker as a competitor who lowers wages and the *standard of life*. . . . He views him similarly to how the *poor whites* of the Southern States of North America viewed Black slaves. This antagonism among the proletarians of England is artificially nourished and kept up by the bourgeoisie. It knows that this split is the *true secret of maintaining its power*. (Marx 1985: 120, trans. slightly altered on basis of the French original)

Moreover, the Irish independence struggle could, Marx wrote in this argument with Bakunin, become the "lever" that could pry apart British and thus global capitalism as part of an international revolutionary struggle:

> Although revolutionary initiative will probably come from France, England alone can serve as the *lever* for a serious economic Revolution. . . . It is the only country where the *capitalist form*, that is to say, combined labor on a large scale under the authority of capitalists, has seized hold of almost the whole of production. . . . The English have all the *material* conditions for social revolution. What they lack is *a sense of generalization* and *revolutionary passion*. It is only the General Council [of the International] that can provide them with this, that can thus accelerate the truly revolutionary movement in this country, and consequently *everywhere*. . . . If England is the *bulwark* of landlordism and European capitalism, the only point where official England can be struck a great blow is *Ireland*. (Marx 1985: 118–19, translation slightly altered)

The last sentence about landlordism referred to Ireland's revolutionary peasantry, whose opposition to the system was enhanced by a national factor: that the landlord class in Ireland was to a great extent British, not

Irish. Ireland was also where the landed aristocracy, part of the British ruling class alongside the industrial capitalists, had important holdings. It is notable that this period was also marked by the emergence inside Ireland of the Fenian Movement, a revolutionary nationalist movement with a strong class dimension directed against Irish as well as British landlords.

Marx: Productive forces and leisure time

Of course, Marx's core writings examined the capital relation and its overcoming more than national emancipation. But this was connected to his discussion of Irish and British labor, of Ireland's national emancipation and Britain's working-class revolution, both of them only potentialities. All of this also rested upon the conquests of the capitalist era, especially the building up of the productive forces. As Marx wrote at length in the *Grundrisse*, these new productive forces created the possibility of creative leisure time for all in place of stultifying toil, if and when capitalism could be overcome:

> *The creation of a large quantity of disposable time* apart from necessary labor time for society generally and each of its members (i.e. room for the development of the individuals' full productive forces, hence those of society also), this creation of not-labor time appears in the stage of capital, as of all earlier ones, as not-labor time, free time, for a few. What capital adds is that it increases the surplus labor time of the mass by all the means of art and science. . . . It is thus, despite itself, instrumental in creating the means of social disposable time, in order to reduce labor time for the whole society to a diminishing minimum, and thus to free everyone's time for their own development. (Marx 1973: 708)

Eventually, Marx maintained, this unrealized potential challenges capitalism itself, and the workers move to overthrow it:

> Once they have done so . . . the development of the power of social production will grow so rapidly that . . . *disposable time* will grow for all. For real wealth is the developed productive power of all indi-

viduals. The measure of wealth is then not any longer, in any way, labor time, but rather disposable time. (Marx 1973: 708)

For Marx, however, this painful pathway through the capitalist mode of production was not one that all societies had to follow, now that a few key ones had developed those productive forces, albeit amid all the exploitation and alienation of capitalism.

Marx: Multilinear pathways of development and revolution

Near the end of his life, Marx examined the issue of whether Russia and the large agrarian societies of Asia were inevitably destined to modernize in the Western capitalist manner. In his well-known 1881 letter to the Russian revolutionary Vera Zasulich, he concluded that alternate pathways of development were possible. He based his judgment in large part upon the marked differences between the social structure of the Russian village (and often its Asian counterparts)—with its communal property and production relations—and the village under Western European feudalism's somewhat more individualized social relations. He added that his recent studies of Russian society "convinced me that the commune is the fulcrum for a social regeneration in Russia" (Shanin 1983: 124). In the 1882 preface to the Russian edition of the *Communist Manifesto*, Marx and Engels suggested that a local uprising sparked by these communal social formations in Russia could form the starting point for a global communist revolution, if such an uprising could link up with the revolutionary labor movement in the Western capitalist lands.

Moreover, Marx made a key philosophical point during one of these discussions, one that challenges the postmodernist accusation (by Jean-François Lyotard and others) that Marx's work constitutes yet another universalizing "grand narrative" or totality in which all particulars are swallowed up. This is also relevant to Foucault's point about "specific cases of resistance" versus an overarching Great Refusal. It is a point that takes us back as well to the difference between an abstract universal in the Kantian manner and the Hegelian type of concrete universal.

In an 1877 letter responding to a discussion of *Capital* by the Russian writer N. K. Mikhailovsky, Marx defended himself from the charge of unilinearism, of the notion that Russia had to follow the pathway of Britain, first building up its productive forces and only then being able to contemplate concretely the possibility of a truly emancipated, socialist society. In response to his critics, and to his supporter Mikhailovsky's ham-handed attempt to defend him by ascribing to him just such a formalistic theory, Marx denied explicitly that he had developed "a historico-philosophical theory of the general course fatally imposed on all peoples" (Shanin 1983: 136). This also reversed Marx's position in his 1853 *New York Tribune* writings on India, where he implicitly supported British colonialism as a necessary stage in the modernization of Asia, a position he and Engels also took with regard to China in the *Communist Manifesto* of 1848.

Thus, by the 1880s, Marx was theorizing concretely about Russia's revolutionary possibilities, in all their specificity, while at the same time linking the Russian peasant-based revolutionary movement to that of the radical labor movement in the West. He was also sketching this philosophically by explicitly denying the need for "a historico-philosophical theory of the general course fatally imposed on all peoples."

Hegel's concrete universals

All of this was rooted in the most critical and revolutionary side of Hegel's legacy, which was found not in his more conservative texts like *Philosophy of Right* or *Philosophy of History*, but in his most abstract works like *Phenomenology of Spirit*, *Science of Logic*, and *Philosophy of Mind*. As Dunayevskaya has noted: "Precisely where Hegel sounds most abstract, seems to close the shutters tight against the whole movement of history, there he lets the lifeblood of the dialectic—absolute negativity—pour in" (Dunayevskaya 1973: 31–32).

But, like Marx, Hegel also avoids abstract universals of the Kantian sort; in fact, he harshly critiques them. Hegel famously attacked "abstract universality," as exemplified by those who presented things as "the night in which, as the saying goes, all cows are black" (Hegel 1977: 9 [¶16]). Hegel's barb was directed against those kinds of Enlightenment reason that he regarded as overly formalistic, which conceptualized human experience via categories that neglected historical or cultural variety and particularity. In short, the universal had swallowed up the particular.

At the same time, Hegel's particulars often point in the direction of the universal. Thus, the slave develops a "mind of his own" in the famous discussion of Lordship and Bondage in the *Phenomenology*, and this is an important step in the development of human consciousness, part of the road of absolute negativity. At the same time, the master's self-satisfied willfulness and exaggerated sense of self-importance constituted a cul-de-sac on that same road to the emancipation of human consciousness.

Moreover, with Hegel, the universal can sometimes exert a pull on the particular, steering it toward universal human emancipation. This is not an easy process, and there are many stops and starts. Some of them are gigantic failures, like the Great Terror, which, as Hegel saw it, devoured the French Revolution because it tried to leap too quickly toward absolute freedom. Here, Hegel offers a critique *avant la lettre* of modern totalitarianism and its show trials and purges, from Stalin's Russia to Nazi Germany to Mao's China.

The pull of the universal, of the emancipatory future, is always there, even if for the moment driven deep down, beneath the surface of society. For example, at one point —in a statement that infuriates empiricists and realists—Hegel (1969: 477) writes, "The fact *is*, *before it exists*." C.L.R. James (1980: 79) later articulated this in Marxist terms in his well-known expression "the future that is in the present."

Marx and human emancipation

Hegel's notion of the concrete universal is undoubtedly related to Marx's own concept of human emancipation. In 1859, Marx (1977: 264) famously described capitalism as merely a part of the "prehistory of human society." This of course rested upon a concept of socialism, and of the emancipation of labor. Such themes can be found throughout his work, as in his youthful *German Ideology* (co-authored by Engels) with its vision of communist existence as one where the individual would perform both mental and manual labor, gathering food and also philosophizing. It marks as well his mature theorizing in *Critique of the Gotha Programme* (1875) about overcoming "the antithesis between mental and physical labor" (Marx 1989: 87).

Marx alludes to this notion of a fully emancipated human existence not only in various shorter texts, but also throughout the central works of his critique of political economy, from the *Grundrisse* to *Capital*, as Peter Hudis has shown in his *Marx's Concept of the Alternative to Capitalism* (2012). In the *Grundrisse*, Marx (1973: 488) writes:

> When the limited bourgeois form is stripped away, what is wealth other than the universality of individual needs, capacities, pleasures, productive forces etc., created through universal exchange? The full development of human mastery over the forces of nature, those of so-called nature as well as of humanity's own nature? The absolute working-out of his creative potentialities, with no presupposition other than the previous historic development, which makes this totality of development, i.e. the development of all human powers as such the end in itself, not as measured on a *predetermined yardstick*? Where he does not reproduce himself in one specificity, but produces his totality? Strives not to remain something he has become, but is in the absolute movement of becoming?

A decade later, in *Capital*, Marx (1976: 165–66) elaborates his concept of commodity fetishism, wherein human relations are like those between things, totally objectified and instrumentalized:

> The labor of the private individual manifests itself as an element of the total labor of society only through the relations which the act of exchange establishes between the products, and, through their mediation, between the producers. To the producers, therefore, the social relations between their private labors appear as what they are, i.e. they do not appear as direct social relations between persons in their work, but rather as material [*dinglich*] relations between persons and social relations between things.

To be sure, this is a distorting lens, but it is also a form of reality, for under capitalism that is what human relations *really are*. A most chilling passage. And while Marx contrasts the subtle and hidden commodity fetish to the open brutality of feudal domination over the peasantry, his most important contrast is to the not-yet-society that is growing inside the structures of capitalism. This is where the veil of the fetish that hides the reality of social relations is to be swept away by the self-activity of the working class: "The veil is not removed," he writes, until the production process changes, "until it becomes production by freely associated human beings, and stands under their conscious and planned control" (Marx 1976: 173, translation slightly altered). This requires, according to Marx, a "material foundation" that has been developed through a long and painful process, over many centuries.

Free and associated labor is also the term Marx used to describe the Paris Commune of 1871 in the *Civil War in France*. There, Marx (1986: 334) wrote that the Commune constituted "the political form as last discovered under which to work out the economical emancipation of Labor." Similarly, as early as 1843, he had elucidated the difference between merely political and fully human emancipation: "Political emancipation is not the completed, contradiction-free form of *human* emancipation" (Marx 1994: 34).[5]

Such a dialectical, prefigurative standpoint is a far cry from Foucault's concept of a plurality of "resistances," a concept that fails to present a vision of a future in which such resistances might no longer be necessary.

To be sure, Marx also mentioned "resistance" from time to time, for example, in his discussion of labor's struggle, against the voracious demands of capital, for a shorter working day: "As soon as the working class, stunned at first by the noise and turmoil of the new system of production, had recovered its senses to some extent, it began to offer resistance, first of all in England, the native land of large-scale industry" (Marx 1976: 390). But he tied it to a broader concept of human emancipation.

Even Holloway, one of Foucault's most incisive critics from the Left, does not fully elaborate such an emancipatory future at a philosophical level, grounded as he is in a form of dialectical negativity (that of Theodor Adorno) in which the positive in the negative is sidelined if not rejected outright. As Arvind Ghosh and Peter Hudis (2005) write:

> What Holloway fails to single out, however, is that for Marx mere negativity by itself does not surmount the fetishism of commodities. In chapter 1 of *Capital*, Marx does not say that . . . the spell of commodity fetishism can be broken simply through "everyday resistance" or pure negativity. He instead says that the spell of fetishism is broken when we have "for a change, an association of freely associated men."

---

5. For a recent treatment of the early Marx's concept of emancipation, *see* Comninel (2012); *see* also my *Marx at the Margins* (2016: 52) for a discussion of the limitations of Marx's essay's characterizations of Jews and Judaism.

This points to a limitation in Holloway's notion of the "scream," as mentioned above.

Concluding points

1. The theories of resistance found in Foucault, and also in many contemporary debates, exhibit several problems; among these are notions of resistance that fail to distinguish among different types of resistance to power, whether reactionary or emancipatory.

2. Another problem is that the notion of resistance often implies a sort of circularity or permanence of resistance—and of power—which occludes the possibility of an actual overcoming of capital and the state in a positive, emancipatory manner.

3. The Great Refusal of Marcuse, which Foucault unjustly attacks, is a key example of a truly emancipatory politics. At the same time, however, Marcuse's Great Refusal is too abstract, with vestiges of Kantian formalism, thus providing an opening to the kind of critique Foucault makes.

4. A return to Marx after these debates over resistance and emancipation shows that his general dialectic—rooted in Hegel—is not one of abstract universalism but has plenty of room for the specificities of nation, ethnicity, and race, issues on which he makes important and original contributions. Marx's theorization of race, ethnicity, and nationalism in relation to class and to revolution remains topical, as seen for example in the British youth uprising of 2011.

5. Especially in his later writings, Marx theorizes Indigenous forms of opposition to capital and their need to connect to the working classes of more technologically developed sectors (and vice versa). The persistence of these issues can be seen most prominently today in parts of Latin America like Bolivia.

6. Finally, Marx's entire intellectual project is guided by a vision of an emancipated human future. This is the vantage point from which he measures, critiques, and attempts to sublate or tran-

scend capitalist society.

References

Afary, Janet, and Kevin B Anderson. 2005. *Foucault and the Iranian Revolution: Gender and the Seductions of Islamism*. Chicago: University of Chicago Press.

Anderson, Kevin B. 2012. "Year Two of the Arab Revolutions." *Logos: A Journal of Modern Society & Culture* 11 (2–3).

————. 2016. *Marx at the Margins: On Nationalism, Ethnicity, and Non-Western Societies*. Expanded edition. Chicago, London: University of Chicago Press.

Comninel, George. 2012. "Emancipation in Marx's Early Work." Pp. 73–91 in *Marx for Today*, edited by Marcello Musto. New York: Routledge.

Dunayevskaya, Raya. 1973. *Philosophy and Revolution: From Hegel to Sartre, and from Marx to Mao*. NJ: Humanities Press.

————. 1982. *Rosa Luxemburg, Women's Liberation, and Marx's Philosophy of Revolution*. Atlantic Highlands, NJ: Humanities Press.

Foucault, Michel. 1978. *The History of Sexuality*, Vol. 1. *An Introduction*. Trans. Robert Hurley. New York: Pantheon Books.

Ghosh, Arvind, and Peter Hudis. 2005. "Can We Change the World without Taking Power? A Critique." *The International Marxist-Humanist*. (October 19).

Hegel, G.W.F. 1969. *Science of Logic*. Trans. A V Miller. New York: Oxford University Press.

————. 1977. *Phenomenology of Spirit*. Trans. A V Miller. Oxford, New York, Toronto, Melbourne: Oxford University Press.

Holloway, John. 2002. *Change the World without Taking Power: The Meaning of Revolution Today*. London: Pluto Press.

James, C. L. R. 1980. "Dialectical Materialism and the Fate of Humanity." In *Spheres of Existence: Selected Writings*. London: Allison & Busby.

Kellner, Douglas. 1984. *Herbert Marcuse and the Crisis of Marxism*. Berkeley: University of California Press.

Kellner, Douglas, Clayton Pierce, and Tyson Lewis. 2011. "Introduction: Herbert Marcuse, Philosophy, Psychoanalysis and Emancipation." Pp. 1-75 in *Collected Papers of Herbert Marcuse, Volume Five*, edited by Douglas Kellner and Clayton Pierce. New York: Routledge.

Marcuse, Herbert. 1964. *One-Dimensional Man: Studies in the Ideology of Advanced Industrial Society*. Boston: Beacon Press.

Marx, Karl. 1961. "Critique of Hegel's Dialectic and General Philosophy." Pp. 169–96 in *Marx's Concept of Man*, trans. T B Bottomore. New York: Frederick Ungar.

———. 1973. *Grundrisse*. Trans. Martin Nicolaus. New York: Random House.

———. 1976. *Capital: A Critique of Political Economy*, Volume One. Translated by Ben Fowkes. London: Penguin.

———. 1977. "A Contribution to the Critique of Political Economy." Orig. 1859. Pp. 257-417 in Marx & Engels, *Collected Works*, Vol. 29. New York: International Publishers.

———. 1985. "Confidential Communication." Pp. 112-124 in Marx & Engels, *Collected Works*, Vol. 21. New York: International Publishers.

———. 1986. "The Civil War in France." Pp. 307-359 in Marx & Engels, *Collected Works*, Vol. 22. New York: International Publishers.

———. 1989. "Critique of the Gotha Programme." Pp. 75-99 in Marx & Engels, *Collected Works*, Vol. 24. New York: International Publishers.

———. 1994. "On the Jewish Question." Pp. 25-56 in *Marx: Early Political Writings*, Trans. and edited by Joseph O'Malley and Richard A Davis. Cambridge: Cambridge University Press.

Shanin, Teodor. 1983. *Late Marx and the Russian Road: Marx and "The Peripheries of Capitalism."* New York: Monthly Review Press.

Weinberg, Bill. 2012. "Will American Left Betray Heroine Malala Yousafzai?" *Countervortex: Resisting the Downward Spiral*. October 12, 2012.

[First appeared online in *Logos: A Journal of Modern Society & Culture* 12:1 (Winter 2013)][6]

---

6.   I thank the following individuals for comments and corrections: Richard Abernethy, Paul Buhle, Greg Burris, Corrie Ellis, Anton Evelynov, and Mir Yarfitz.

11

Class, gender, race, and colonialism

An abstract, general theory of capital and labor

"Proletarians [*Proletarier*] of all countries, unite!" It is with these ringing words that Marx and Engels famously conclude their *Communist Manifesto* in 1848 (MECW 6: 519, MEW 4: 493, sometimes my translation). This exhortation suggests a broad class struggle involving millions of workers across national and regional boundaries against their collective enemies: capital and landed property. In that same *Manifesto*, Marx and Engels also write, in another well-known passage, that "the workers have no country," and further, that "national differences and antagonisms between peoples [*Völker*] are daily shrinking more and more" with the development of the capitalist world market (MECW 6: 502–03, MEW 4: 479).

In the *Manifesto*, we are presented with large social forces—the proletariat or working class and its opponents—contending with each other on an international scale, where differences of culture, nationality, and geography have been overturned, or are being overturned, as capital is coming to rule the world and the workers are organizing their resistance to it. Marx and Engels are writing here at a very high level of generality, abstracting from the specificities of the life experience of Western European and North American workers, and predicting that their lot will soon become that of the world's working people, at that time mainly peasants laboring in predominantly agrarian societies.

It is in this sense that Marx and Engels also write that capitalism has "through its exploitation of the world market given a cosmopolitan character to production and consumption in every country." They add: "National one-sidedness and narrow-mindedness become more and more impossible" (MECW 6: 488). Capital creates a world culture alongside its world market, forcing itself into every corner of the globe. They go so far as to applaud, in terms imbued with Eurocentric condescension, how capitalism "draws all, even the most barbarian, nations into civilization" as it "batters down all Chinese walls" and forces these "barbarian" nations "to adopt the bourgeois mode of production" (MECW 6: 488). While pain is produced as old societies are destroyed, capital is carrying out its historic mission, the creation of "more massive and more colossal productive forces than have all preceding generations put together" (MECW 6: 489).

Two decades later, in the 1867 preface to *Capital*, Vol. I, Marx writes, with a similar logic emphasizing abstraction, that the "value form" that is at the core of capitalist production cannot be studied only empirically with regard to specific commodities produced. He adds: "Why? Because the complete body is easier to study than its cells." Therefore, to analyze capitalism and its value form properly and fully, one must resort to the "power of abstraction" in order to examine commodity production as a whole (Marx 1976: 90).

There is clearly a universalizing pull under capitalism, a globalizing system whose extension homogenizes, regularizes, and flattens the world, uprooting and changing it as needed to maximize value production, a quest that forms the soul of a soulless system. That same universalizing pull creates a deep contradiction, the revolutionary opposition of the modern working class, "united and organized by the very mechanism of the capitalist process of production" (Marx 1976: 929).

The experience of the working class is similarly homogenized. Shorn of its means of production (land, tools, etc.) and reduced to a group of propertyless wage laborers, prototypically in giant industrial factories, Marx's working class is both alienated and exploited in ways specific to capitalism. As early as the 1844 *Manuscripts*, he wrote of alienated labor, a concept deepened in *Capital* in the section on commodity fetishism. In the capitalist production process, human relations are fetishized because the

products of labor come to dominate their producers, the workers, in a jar-
ring subject-object reversal. These workers then experience that domination as the impersonal power of capital, which is itself produced by their
labor. Capital lords it over them, turning human relations into "relations
between things," with the working class objectified to the extreme (Marx
1976: 166). Raya Dunayevskaya is among the few to emphasize Marx's additional statement to the effect that these relations "appear [*erscheinen*] as
what they are" (Marx 1976: 166, MEW 23: 86, Marx 1994: 607). The German
verb *erscheinen* [like the word *apparaissent* he uses at this point in the
French edition] is not a false or "mere" appearance and it differs from
scheinen [French: *paraissent*], which means "appear" in the sense of sem-
blance or even false appearance. Thus, we are not dealing with a false
appearance that conceals "true" and humanistic human relations, but a
new and unprecedented reality based upon "the necessity of that appearance because, that is, *in truth*, what relations among people are at the point
of production" in a capitalist system (Dunayevskaya 1958: 100). In the long
run, of course, such a thing-like human relationship is false in the sense
that it will be rejected and uprooted by the working class, which seeks a
society controlled not by capital but by free and associated labor. But it
remains utterly real while we are under the sway of the capitalist mode of
production.

At the same time, the workers suffer harsh material exploitation, as the
surplus value they create in the production process is appropriated by capital, in a system characterized by the greatest gulf in history between the
material lot of the dominant classes and those of the working people. This
"exploitation grows" in both absolute and relative terms as capital cen-
tralizes and develops further technologically, in the process of the greatest quantitative increase in the development of the productive forces in
human history (Marx 1976: 929).

Marx pulls together these two concepts, exploitation and alienation,
in his discussion of capital accumulation, wherein "the capitalist system"
turns the labor of the worker into stultifying "torment," serving to "alien-
ate" from the worker "the intellectual potentialities of the labor process,"
while at the same time, the rate of exploitation increases: "the situation of
the worker, be his payment high or low, must grow worse" relative to the
vertiginous accumulation of surplus value by capital (Marx 1976: 799).

Marx's concrete dialectic

The kind of analysis presented above shows Marx as our contemporary, not least his grasp of the limitless quest for surplus value by capital and the concomitant deep alienation and exploitation that it visits upon the working people, from factories to modern call centers.

At the same time, these kinds of statements, especially when read out of context, have been used for decades by Marx's critics, both conservative and leftwing, to portray him as a thinker whose abstract model of capital and labor occludes national differences, race, ethnicity, gender, and other crucially important aspects of human society and culture.

On the one hand, these critics are wrong because capitalism is in fact a unique social system that overturns and homogenizes all previous social relations, tending toward the reduction of all human relations to that of capital vs. labor. Thus, one cannot fully understand contemporary family and gender relations, ethno-racial and communal conflict, or ecological crisis without examining the underlying relationships described above. For the family, the ethnic tableau, and the natural environment are all conditioned by the underlying fact of a capitalist mode of production.

On the other hand, these critics pose questions that make us look more carefully at Marx's theoretical categories. It is very important in this regard to realize, if one wants truly to appreciate Marx's originality, that his concept of capital and labor was posed not only at a high level of abstraction, but that at other levels it encompasses a far wider variety of human experience and culture. As Bertell Ollman (1993) has emphasized, Marx operated at varying levels of abstraction.

The present essay centers on three related points.

First, Marx's working class was not only Western European, white, and male: from his earliest to his latest writings, he took up the working class in all its human variety.

Second, Marx was not an economic or class reductionist, for throughout his career, he considered deeply various forms of oppression and resistance to capital and the state that were not based entirely upon class, but also upon nationality, race and ethnicity, and gender.

Third, by the time of Marx's later writings, long after the *Communist Manifesto*, the Western European pathway of industrial capitalist development out of feudalism was no longer a global universal. He saw that alternate pathways of development were indeed possible, and these connected to types of revolutions that did not always fit the model of industrial labor's overthrowing capital.

In terms of a concrete dialectic, Marx follows in the wake of Hegel. This is true from his earliest writings to *Capital*, Vol. I, where he writes of "the Hegelian 'contradiction,' which is the source of all dialectics" (Marx 1976: 744). One striking feature of Hegel's dialectical framework, despite its overall universalizing thrust, is its rejection of abstract universals, while also avoiding a mere empiricism. No previous philosopher had drawn history and social existence into philosophy in this way, as seen especially in Hegel's *Phenomenology of Spirit*, a book so crucial to our understanding of the present moment that two new English translations appeared in 2018. Again and again in this work, Hegel rejects the abstract universal as "the night in which, as the saying goes, all cows are black" (Hegel 2018: 10, §16). The concreteness of his universals is also seen in the ascending concrete forms of consciousness that develop along the universal pathway toward the freedom of the human spirit, from ancient Rome to the Reformation and the French Revolution of his own time, each of them limited by their historical, social, and cultural context. Of course, Marx also rejects aspects of Hegel's idealism, especially his emphasis on the growth of human consciousness as the most important result of the dialectics of history, as opposed to the actuality of human freedom and healthy development in a society that has been revolutionized from below. In short, Hegel's dialectic, while social and historical, remains somewhat dehumanized.

Such emphasis on the concrete universal in no way negates my earlier citation, where Marx writes that one needs the "power of abstraction" to get at what is really crucial about capitalism, its value form, and the dehumanized fetishized existence experienced by those who live under its domination. No, the solution has to be approached from both directions. The abstract rests upon the concrete, but at the same time the abstract concept has to concretize itself, to become determinate. However, Marx equally rejects what Karel Kosík called the "pseudoconcrete," a type of concrete that cannot think beyond the immediately given under capitalism. As against such false or distorted forms of consciousness, dialectics "dissolves fetishized artifacts both of the world of things and the world of ideas, in order to penetrate to their reality" (Kosík 1976: 7).

Thus, Marx is hostile to mere empiricism, embracing a dialectical form of totality. He at the same time castigates, as did Hegel, the abstract universals of traditional idealist philosophy and of modern liberalism, with its human and civil rights that are so often little more than formulaic to those at the bottom of society. Yet, at the same time, Marx embraces what he and Hegel called the concrete universal, a form of universality that was rooted in social life and yet pointed beyond the given world of the pseudo-concrete.

One example of the concrete universal can be glimpsed in how Marx argues that we cannot adequately measure the world of capitalist exploitation and alienation either in its own terms (the pseudoconcrete) or solely by comparing it—as important as such comparative analysis—to past forms of domination like Western European feudalism, the ancient Greco-Roman world, or the "Asiatic" mode of production. Most importantly, he measures capitalist society against a different yardstick, the unrealized but potentially realizable horizon of a communist future of free and associated labor, as has been emphasized in two recent studies (Hudis 2012, Chattopadhyay 2016). But this is not merely an imagined republic, as Niccolò Machiavelli characterized the abstract and schematic models of the good society found in ancient Greco-Roman thinkers like Socrates. Marx's vision of the future was based upon the aspirations and struggles of an actually existing social class, the proletariat, to which his writings sought to give a more universal and concrete form.

The working class in all its human variety

From the outset, Marx saw Britain as the country where the capitalist mode of production was the most developed, far ahead of any other country. This can be seen especially in *Capital*, where British examples of both capital and labor predominate. But the British working class was by no means homogenous. As the Industrial Revolution surged in Manchester, the cutting-edge city of nineteenth-century capitalism, it did so by harshly exploiting a working class with deep ethnic divisions between English and Irish workers. Engels discusses this issue at length in his 1845 book, published just after he and Marx began to collaborate, *The Condition of the Working Class in England*. Marx regarded this book as one of Engels's greatest contributions, citing it more than any other of his friend's writings in *Capital*.

Most prominently in *Capital,* Marx himself took up the Irish potato famine of the 1840s as a tragedy rooted in the process of capital accumulation, He wrote as well about Irish workers in Britain, especially in 1869–70, at a time when the First International was substantially engaged with supporting Irish revolutionaries. While he was able to convince the International to support the Irish in some important ways, it was a difficult battle. At the same time, this was a battle that needed to be fought and won, because it got to the heart of why, despite its largescale industrialization and organized working class, Britain had not seen the level of class struggle predicted in texts written at an abstract level like the *Communist Manifesto.* He offered an explanation in a "Confidential Communication" of the International issued in early 1870:

> [T]he *English bourgeoisie* has not only exploited Irish poverty to keep down the working class in England by *forced immigration* of poor Irishmen, but it has also divided the proletariat into two hostile camps. . . . The common English worker hates the Irish worker as a competitor who lowers wages and the *standard of life.* He feels national and religious antipathies for him. He views him similarly to how the *poor whites* of the Southern States of North America viewed Black slaves. This antagonism among the proletarians of England is artificially nourished and kept up by the bourgeoisie. It knows that the preservation of this split is the *true secret of maintaining its power.* (MECW 21: 120, trans. slightly altered on basis of French original)

Marx also saw this antagonism based upon the double oppression of the Irish workers, as both proletarians and as members of an oppressed minority, in deeply dialectical terms. As I discuss below, he viewed the Irish as sources of revolutionary ferment that could help spark a British revolution. Thus, we have here the analysis of an actually existing working class at a specific point in time—Britain in 1870—as opposed to the more general and abstract manner in which he and Engels conceptualized the working class in the *Manifesto.*

Marx viewed the racially divided working class of the U.S. in similar terms. He strongly opposed slavery and advocated abolitionism within the working-class movement, attacking those like Proudhon who were more ambiguous on the subject of slavery.

He conceptualized African slavery as central to capitalist development, writing as early as the *Poverty of Philosophy* (1847):

> Direct slavery is just as much the pivot of bourgeois industry as machinery, credits, etc. Without slavery you have no cotton; without cotton you have no modern industry. It is slavery that gave the colonies their value; it is the colonies that created world trade, and it is world trade that is the precondition of large-scale industry. (MECW 6: 167)

During the 1861–65 Civil War in the United States, Marx strongly, albeit critically, supported the North against the slaveholding South. He regarded the war as a second American revolution that had created some real possibilities for the working class. He intoned in *Capital*:

> In the United States of America, every independent workers' movement was paralyzed as long as slavery disfigured a part of the republic. *Labor in a white skin cannot emancipate itself where it is branded in a black skin.* However, a new life immediately arose from the death of slavery. The first fruit of the American Civil War was the eight hours agitation, which ran from the Atlantic to the Pacific, from New England to California, with the seven-league boots of the locomotive. (Marx 1976: 414, emphasis added)

At this point, Marx noted that a large national labor congress took place in the U.S. in 1866, one year after the end of the Civil War, where that demand for the eight-hour day was put forward.

Here, the abolition of slavery is seen as the precondition for a real working-class movement in the racialized capitalism of the U.S.

If Marx's working class was not exclusively white, nor was it exclusively male. In her study of Marx and gender, Heather Brown concludes that in the parts of *Capital* devoted to the life experience of the workers, "Marx not only traces out the changing conditions of the male worker, but also gives significant emphasis to the role of women in this process." While he sometimes lapsed into "echoing paternalistic or patriarchal assumptions" in his descriptions of female workers, it is hard to argue, as some have, that he ignored working women in his most important book (Brown 2012: 91).

This can also be seen in Marx's dialectical discussion of changes to the family and gender relations brought about by capitalist industrialization, which has "dissolved the old family relationships" among the workers, as women and children were forced into horribly exploitative paid employment outside the home:

> However terrible and disgusting the dissolution of the old family ties within the capitalist system may appear, large-scale industry, by assigning an important part in socially organized processes of production, outside the sphere of the domestic economy, to women, young persons and children of both sexes, does nevertheless create a new economic foundation for a higher form of the family and of relations between the sexes. (Marx 1976: 620–21)

Marx returned to gender and the family as a major research topic at the end of his life, as seen in his *Ethnological Notebooks* of 1880–82 (Krader 1974) and other notebooks from that period. In these notebooks, he explored gender relations across a number of societies, from preliterate Native Americans and Homeric Greeks, to precolonial Ireland and contemporary Australian aborigines. Some of these notes became the basis for Engels's *Origin of the Family*. Although that work contains many important insights, it treats the rise of gender oppression in an economic and class reductionist manner that was far less subtle than the notes Marx left behind and that Engels used as source material (Dunayevskaya 1982, Anderson 2016, Brown 2012). These notebooks are also concerned deeply with colonialism, an issue discussed below that Engels did not engage.

Sources of oppression and revolutionary subjectivity outside the working class

Marx's interest in gender issues was not limited to the study of working-class women. From his earliest writings, he pointed to gender oppression as a crucial, foundational form of social hierarchy and domination. In the *1844 Manuscripts*, he wrote:

The direct, natural, necessary relationship of human being [*Mensch*] to human being is the *relationship of man* [*Mann*] *to woman* [*Weib*]. . . . Therefore, on the basis of this relationship, we can judge the whole stage of development of the human being. From the character of this relationship it follows to what degree the *human being* has become and recognized himself or herself as a *species being*; a *human being*; the relationship of man to woman is the *most natural* relationship of human being to human being. Therefore, in it is revealed the degree to which the *natural* behavior of the human being has become *human* . . . (cited in Plaut and Anderson 1999: 6, in my translation; see also MECW 3: 295–96 for an earlier translation)

Here, Marx is concerned not only with working class women, as discussed above, but also with other strata of women, and across the full trajectory of human society and culture, not just modern capitalism. He takes up the oppression of modern women outside the working class in his 1846 text "Peuchet on Suicide," where he focuses on middle and upper-class French women driven to suicide by gender-based oppression from husbands or parents, writing at one point of "social conditions . . . which permit the jealous husband to fetter his wife in chains, like a miser with his hoard of gold, for she is but part of his inventory" (Plaut and Anderson 1999: 58). These concerns did not end with Marx's youth. In 1858, he wrote movingly in the *New York Tribune* about Lady Rosina Bulwer-Lytton, who had been confined to a mental institution by her British politician husband for having attempted to speak out on political issues (Dunayevskaya 1982, Brown 2012).

Nor did Marx focus on the industrial working class to the exclusion of the peasantry, which he saw as an oppressed and potentially revolutionary class. Considerable attention has been paid to his characterization of the French peasantry as somewhat conservative in *The Eighteenth Brumaire of Louis Bonaparte* (1852). In other contexts, though, he discussed the revolutionary potential of peasants, for example, during the sixteenth century Anabaptist uprising in Germany. Concerning his own time, in the *Critique of the Gotha Programme* (1875), he castigated Ferdinand Lassalle for labeling the "peasants" as inherently conservative, since Lassalle's organization had written off "all other classes" besides the working class as "one reactionary mass" (MECW 24: 88–89).

And while condemning racist and imperialist forms of nationalism, Marx also strongly supported nationalist movements that exhibited a clear emancipatory content. Long before Lenin articulated a concept of national liberation, in an 1848 speech on Poland Marx drew a distinction between what he termed "narrowly national [*étroitement national*]" movements and national revolutions that were "reforming and democratic," i.e., ones that put forth issues like land reform even when it targeted the upper classes of the oppressed nation itself rather than only a foreign enemy or occupying power (Marx 1994: 1001, my translation from the French original; see also MECW 6: 549).

Even in the *Communist Manifesto*, where, as discussed above, Marx and Engels had written that national differences were disappearing, they posed it at a general, abstract level. For when it came down to concretizing the principles in terms of a set of immediate goals and slogans in the final section of the *Manifesto*, "Position of the Communists in Relation to the Existing Opposition Parties," Polish national emancipation from Russian, Austrian, and Prussian occupation was nonetheless singled out specifically: "In Poland they support the party that insists on an agrarian revolution as the prime condition for national emancipation, that party which fomented the insurrection of Cracow in 1846" (MECW 6: 518). Marx continued to support a Polish national revolution until the end of his life. He greeted the Polish uprising of 1863 with enthusiasm and, in his writings celebrating the Paris Commune of 1871, he singled out the important contribution of Polish exiles in the military defense of revolutionary Paris. Fittingly, in venerable Père Lachaise Cemetery in Paris, the graves of the Communards include that of Polish General Walery Wróblewski, only steps away from those of Marx's French descendants.

In the above-cited 1870 Confidential Communication on Ireland, the peasantry and the national movement were also intertwined as revolutionary elements. An equally prominent point in this text is Marx's defense of the International's public support of Irish national emancipation, including appeals to Queen Victoria to stop the execution of Irish militants. On this issue, Marx and the International's General Council in London had come under attack by the anarchist Mikhail Bakunin's faction, which took a class-reductionist position, rejecting "any political action which does not have as its *immediate and direct* aim the triumph of the workers' cause against Capital" (cited in MECW 21: 208). In response, Marx wrote in the Communication:

> In the first place, Ireland is the *bulwark* of English landlordism. If it fell in Ireland, it would fall in England. In Ireland this is a hundred times easier because *the economic struggle there is concentrated exclusively on landed property,* because this struggle is at the same time *national,* and because the people there are more revolutionary and angrier than in England. Landlordism in Ireland is maintained solely by *the English army.* The moment the forced Union between the two countries ends, a social revolution will immediately break out in Ireland . . . (MECW 21: 119–20, translation slightly altered on basis of French original in Marx 1966: 358–59)

Moreover, Marx hinted that such a process could also break the impasse in which British workers were stuck:

> Although revolutionary initiative will probably come from France, England alone can serve as the *lever* for a serious economic Revolution. . . . It is the only country where the *vast majority of the population consists of wage laborers.* . . . The English have all the *material conditions [matière nécessaire]* for social revolution. What they lack is *a sense of generalization* and *revolutionary passion.* It is only the General Council that can provide them with this, that can thus accelerate the truly revolutionary movement in this country, and consequently *everywhere.* . . . If England is the *bulwark* of landlordism and European capitalism, the only point where official England can be struck a great blow is *Ireland.* (MECW 21: 118–19, translation slightly altered on basis of French original in Marx 1966: 356–57)

Marx conceptualized more explicitly this notion of the Irish struggle for independence as a detonator for a wider British and European working-class revolution in a letter to Engels of December 10, 1869:

> For a long time, I believed it would be possible to overthrow the Irish regime by *English working class ascendancy.* I always took this viewpoint in the *New-York Tribune.* Deeper study has now con-

vinced me of the opposite. The English *working class* will *never accomplish anything before it has got rid of Ireland.* The lever must be applied in Ireland. This is why the Irish question is so important for the social movement in general. (MECW 43: 398)

Here Marx acknowledges explicitly a change of position, from an earlier one where he had seen proletarian revolution spreading from the core industrial nations to the periphery. At this point, he is starting to develop the notion of a transnational communist revolution beginning in the more agrarian, colonized peripheries of capitalism, and then spreading into the core nations. During the last years before his death in 1883, this was to become a major concern with respect to societies outside Western Europe and North America.

The late Marx:
Multilinear pathways of development and revolution, in India, Russia, and beyond

In the *German Ideology* of 1846, Marx and Engels conceptualized in Euro-centric terms several successive stages of historical development, later called modes of production: (1) clan or tribal, (2) slave-based ancient Greco-Roman, (3) serf-based feudal, (4) formally free wage-labor-based bourgeois or capitalist, and, it was implied, (5) freely-associated-labor-based socialist. A decade later, in the *Grundrisse* of 1857–58, Marx took up modes of production originating in Asia, especially India (the "Asiatic" mode of production) as a type of precapitalist system that did not fall easily under either (2) or (3). It represented something qualitatively different, without as much formal slavery, and with communal or collective property and social relations continuing in the villages for a very long time under class society.

For Marx, this addition constituted a more global and multilinear theory of history, with premodern Asian societies on a somewhat different pathway of development than Western Europe, especially ancient Rome. In *Capital*, Vol. I, he referred to "the ancient Asiatic, Classical-antique, and other such modes of production," where commodity production "plays a subordinate role" as compared to the modern capitalist mode of production (Marx 1976: 172). Marx's distinction between Asian and European precapitalist societies was banned in Stalinist ideology, which clung to the slavery-feudal-bourgeois model of successive modes of production, something that required mental gymnastics to fit societies like Mughal India or Confucian China into the "feudal" or "slave" modes of production. Even as late as the 1970s, the noted anthropologist and Marx scholar Norair Ter-Akopian was dismissed from the Marx-Engels-Lenin Institute in Moscow for having published a book on the Asiatic mode of production.

In notes from his last years not published until after Stalin's death, Marx summarized and commented upon his young anthropologist friend Maxim Kovalevsky's *Communal Property* (1879), especially its treatment of precolonial India. Although appreciative of much of Kovalevsky's analysis, Marx inveighed against his attempts to treat Mughal India, with its highly centralized state system, as feudal: "Kovalevsky here finds *feudalism* in the Western European sense. Kovalevsky *forgets*, among other things, *serfdom*, which < is > not in India, and which < is > an essential moment." Marx concludes that concerning "feudalism," "as little is found in India as in Rome" (appendix to Krader 1975: 383). These notes, available in English since 1975, did not find their way into the Marx-Engels *Collected Works*. Nor can any of the notes on Kovalevsky or other late texts on India be found in the most recent collection of Marx's India writings (Husain 2006). However, Irfan Habib's comprehensive introduction to this volume does mention briefly the late Marx's notebooks on India and his "objection to any designation of the Indian communities as 'feudal'" (Husain 2006: xxxv).

All this would be only an academic topic had Marx not tied these issues to the contemporary problems of colonialism and world revolution. In the years 1848–53, Marx tended toward an implicit support of colonialism, whether on the forcing of a traditionalist China into the world market, as quoted above from the *Communist Manifesto*, or in his 1853 articles on India, which celebrated what he saw as modernizing and progressive aspects of British rule. In 1853, he portrays India as backward in socio-economic terms, incapable of real change from within, and unable to mount serious resistance to foreign invasion due to its social divisions. Therefore, he could write that year in his *Tribune* article, "The British Rule in India," that British colonialism was carrying in its wake "the greatest, and to speak the truth, the only *social* revolution ever heard of in Asia" (MECW 12: 132). To be sure, Edward Said and others have caricatured his 1853 India articles as completely pro-colonialist, ignoring another major one a few weeks later, "The Future Results of British Rule in India," which attacks the "barbarism" of British colonialism and applauds the possibility of India being able one day "to throw off the English yoke altogether" (MECW 12: 221). Nonetheless, some of Said's criticisms are on target with regard to the Eurocentrism and ethnocentrism of the 1853 writings.

By the time of the *Grundrisse* of 1857–58, with its discussion of precolonial India being on a different historical trajectory than ancient Rome, Marx was also coming out publicly, again in the *Tribune*, in support of both the anti-British Sepoy Uprising in India and Chinese resistance to the British in the Second Opium War. But his support for this anti-colonial resistance remained at a rather general level. Marx did not embrace the overall political aims or perspectives of the Chinese or Indians resisting imperialism, which seemed to be neither democratic nor communist (Benner 2018). This differs from his late writings on Russia, which saw emancipatory communist movements emerging from that country's communal villages, where the peasants were supported by the students and intellectuals of the leftwing Populist movement. Thus, Marx's thinking on these issues seems to have evolved further after 1858.

Marx never finished volumes two and three of *Capital*, although he reworked volume one painstakingly for the French edition of 1872–75, altering several passages that could have implied that societies outside the narrow band of industrializing capitalism would inevitably have to modernize in the Western industrial sense. In the original 1867 edition, he had written: "The country that is more developed industrially only shows, to the less developed, the image of its own future" (Marx 1976: 91). Even the usually careful scholar Teodor Shanin viewed this passage as an example of "unilinear determinism" (Shanin 1983: 4), therefore drawing a sharp distinction between *Capital* (determinist) and Marx's late writings on Russia (open-ended and multilinear). But Shanin and other scholars who taxed Marx for this passage did not notice that in the subsequent 1872–75 French edition, the last version of *Capital*, Vol. I that Marx himself saw to publication, he recast this passage: "The country that is more developed industrially only shows, to those that follow it up the industrial ladder [*le suivent sur l'échelle industrielle*], the image of its own future" (Marx 1976: 91, my translation; see also Anderson 2016). In this way, Marx removed any hint of unilinear determinism and, more importantly, suggested that the future of societies outside Western Europe might follow a different pathway.

Marx made a much more explicit statement concerning his multilinear approach to the historical possibilities of agrarian societies outside Western Europe in the draft of an 1877 letter, where he criticized strongly any idea of "transforming my historical sketch [in the "Primitive Accumulation" section of *Capital*—KBA] of the genesis of capitalism in Western Europe into a historico-philosophical theory of the general course fatally imposed on all peoples, whatever the historical circumstances in which they find themselves placed," a letter in which he quoted the French edition of *Capital* (Shanin 1983: 136).

Marx also returned at length to the subject of India in his above-cited 1879 notes on Kovalevsky (appendix to Krader 1975), his *Notes on Indian History* (1960), and his 1880–82 *Ethnological Notebooks* (Krader 1974). During these last years, he wrote of Russian peasant "primitive communism" as a locus of resistance to capital and of possible linkages to the revolutionary working-class communist movement in the West. This is seen in a famous passage from his last published text, the 1882 preface he and Engels contributed to a new Russian edition of the *Communist Manifesto*: "If the Russian revolution becomes the signal for a proletarian revolution in the West, so that the two complement each other, then the present Russian common ownership [*Gemeineigentum*] may serve as the point of departure [*Ausgungspunkt*] for a communist development" (Shanin 1983: 139, see also MECW 24: 426, and MEW 19: 296, trans. slightly altered).

In his late writings on Russia and notebooks on South Asia, North Africa, Latin America, and a number of other agrarian, pastoral, or hunter-gatherer societies, Marx is deeply concerned with the rise of gender and social hierarchy during the decline of communal social formations. (Some of these notebooks are still unpublished and will appear in the *Marx-Engels Gesamtausgabe* or MEGA, but aspects of them have been discussed in Brown 2012, Pradella 2015, and Anderson 2016.) It is also very likely that he was interested in South Asian, North African, and Latin American villages, like the Russian ones, as possible loci of resistance to capital and therefore potential allies of the working classes of Western Europe and North America.

For example, in Marx's notes on Kovalevsky's lengthy discussion of India, he traces in great detail the shift from kin-based communal village organization to one grounded more in mere residency. At this stage, Marx has clearly rejected his earlier notion of an unchanging Indian village system until the arrival of capitalism via the British. However, as against his writings on Ireland, as in his 1869 letter to Engels on Ireland cited above, he never explicitly acknowledges this change of perspective on India.

Of course, we have less information on Marx's thinking in his last years. By 1879, Engels, his most regular intellectual interlocutor, was no longer in faraway Manchester receiving Marx's letters (he had moved to London in 1869), but a neighbor who visited almost daily but without leaving much of paper trail of their conversations. Marx's letters to Kovalevsky were also burned by his friends in Russia, who went to his home to do so, out of fear of their falling into the hands the police, which could have endangered the young anthropologist.

As seen above, as early as the 1857 Sepoy Uprising, Marx seems to have moved away from his previously held notion of India as a passive civilization that did not offer much resistance to foreign conquest. He again recorded detailed data on Indian resistance in another set of notes taken around 1879, on British colonial official Robert Sewell's *Analytical History of India* (1870), published in Moscow as Marx's *Notes on Indian History* (1960) without awareness that this volume consisted mainly of passages excerpted from Sewell's book. In these notes, Marx records dozens of examples of Indian resistance to foreign invaders and domestic rulers, from the earliest historical records right up through the Sepoy Uprising. Moreover, Marx's notes now present Mughal, British, and other conquests of India as contingent rather than the product of ineluctable social forces.

But Marx's main focus in these late notebooks on South Asia, North Africa, and Latin America is the structure and history of communal social relations and property in these regions and on how colonialism uprooted these earlier social relations. At the same time, as a dialectical thinker, Marx also notes the persistence of remnants of these communal social forms even after they had been greatly undermined by colonialism. Did he come to believe that the Indian, Algerian, or Latin American village could become a locus of resistance to capital, as he theorized in 1882 concerning the Russian village? That is what I have concluded after years of study of these notebooks.

To be sure, Marx never said such a thing explicitly. Moreover, in his late writings on Russia, in the drafts of his 1881 letter to Vera Zasulich, he even noted a key difference with India, that Russia had not "fallen prey, like the East Indies, to a conquering foreign power" (Shanin 1983: 106).

Still, I find it hard to believe that Marx engaged in such a deep and extended study of the communal social formations in precolonial and even colonial South Asia, North Africa, and Latin America without an aim beyond purely historical research. As the Italian Marx scholar Luca Basso notes, Marx was (in his late writings on Russia and other non-Western societies) operating on "two planes"—that of "historical-theoretical interpretation" and that of "the feasibility or otherwise of a revolutionary movement"—in the context of what he was studying (Basso 2015: 90). The fact that Marx undertook this research in the years just before his clarion call in the 1882 preface to the *Manifesto* about an uprising in Russia's communal villages as the "starting point for a communist revolution," one that would link up with the Western proletariat, suggests the connectedness of all of this research on primitive communism. As Dunayevskaya argued in the first work that linked these notebooks to modern concerns with revolution and women's liberation: "Marx returns to probe the origin of humanity, *not* for purposes of discovering new origins, but for perceiving new revolutionary forces, *their* reason . . . " (Dunayevskaya 1982: 187).

As we view Marx on his 200th anniversary, it is important to see both his brilliant generalizations about capitalist society and the very concrete ways in which he examined not only class but also gender, race, and colonialism, and what today would be called the *intersectionality* of all of these. His underlying revolutionary humanism was the enemy of all forms of abstraction that denied the variety and multiplicity of human experience, especially as his vision extended outward from Western Europe. For these reasons, no thinker speaks to us today with such force and clarity.

References

Anderson, Kevin B. 2016. *Marx at the Margins: On Nationalism, Ethnicity, and Non-Western Societies*. Expanded edition. Chicago: University of Chicago Press.

Basso, Luca. 2015. *Marx and the Common: From* Capital *to the Late Writings*. Trans. David Broder. Leiden: Brill.

Benner, Erica. 2018. Reprint edition. *Really Existing Nationalisms: A Post-*

Communist View from Marx and Engels. New York: Oxford University Press.

Brown, Heather. 2012. *Marx on Gender and the Family*. Leiden: Brill.

Chattopadhyay, Paresh. 2016. *Marx's Associated Mode of Production*. New York: Palgrave.

Dunayevskaya, Raya. 1958. *Marxism and Freedom*. New York: Bookman Associates.

_____. 1982. *Rosa Luxemburg, Women's Liberation, and Marx's Philosophy of Revolution*. Sussex: Harvester Press.

Hegel, G.W.F. 2018 *Phenomenology of Spirit*. Trans. Michael Inwood. New York: Oxford University Press.

Hudis, Peter. 2012. *Marx's Concept of the Alternative to Capitalism*. Leiden: Brill.

Husain, Iqbal, ed. 2006. *Karl Marx on India*. New Delhi: Tulika Books.

Kosík, Karel. 1976. *Dialectics of the Concrete*. Trans. Karel Kovanda and James Schmidt. Boston: D. Reidel.

Krader, Lawrence. 1974. *The Ethnological Notebooks of Karl Marx*. Second Edition. Assen: Van Gorcum.

_____. 1975. *The Asiatic Mode of Production: Sources, Development and Critique in the Writings of Karl Marx*. Assen: Van Gorcum.

Marx, Karl. 1960. *Notes on Indian History (664–1858)*. Moscow: Progress Publishers.

_____. 1966. "Le conseil générale au conseil fédérale de la Suisse romande." *General Council of the First International 1868–1870. Minutes*. Moscow: Progress Publishers.

_____. 1976. *Capital: A Critique of Political Economy*. Vol. 1. Trans. Ben Fowkes. New York: Penguin.

_____. 1994. *Oeuvres IV*. Edited by Maximilien Rubel. Paris: Éditions Gallimard.

[MECW] Marx, Karl and Frederick Engels. 1975–2004. *Collected Works*. Fifty Volumes. New York: International Publishers.

[MEW] Marx, Karl and Friedrich Engels. 1968. *Werke*. Berlin: Dietz Verlag.

Ollman, Bertell. 1993. *Dialectical Investigations*. New York: Routledge.

Plaut, Eric A. and Kevin B. Anderson. 1999. *Marx on Suicide*. Evanston: Northwestern University Press.

Pradella, Lucia. 2015. *Globalisation and the Critique of Political Economy: New Insights from Marx's Writings*. Milton Park: Routledge.

Shanin, Teodor. 1983. *Late Marx and the Russian Road*. New York: Monthly Review Press.

[Originally appeared in *Economic & Political Weekly* in 2018, under the title "Marx at 200: Beyond Capital and Class Alone." It subsequently appeared as a pamphlet in the Daraja Press & Monthly Review Essays series *Thinking Freedom* entitled *Class, Gender, Race, and Colonialism: The "Intersectionality" of Marx*. Ottawa: Daraja Press, 2020]

12

Marx at the Margins:
Ten years later

As I write these lines, the COVID-19 pandemic is ravaging a world dominated by capitalism, using the very networks that capital established for its creation of value and profit. In one sense, the virus is utterly uniform in its destructive path, traveling relentlessly across borders and oceans, and killing people wherever it finds opportunities and vulnerabilities. But in another sense, COVID-19's effects vary tremendously based upon social differences among and within nations—and even among and within political subdivisions thereof—with the biggest death toll expected in postcolonial developing nations and among oppressed racial and ethnic minorities everywhere.

This situation parallels what I encountered in writing *Marx at the Margins*. On the one hand, it is correct to say that Marx is the premier theorist of global capitalism, a system that homogenizes, forcing societies everywhere to bend to its domination and to become capitalist. On the other hand, *Marx at the Margins* attempts to show that Marx was deeply sensitive to a number of national, ethnic, racial, gender, and other differences that cut against the very homogeneity central to capital's drive for accumulation.

This kind of dialectic also appears in contemporary leftwing discourse. For several decades, many currents of leftist thought, especially in the academic world, have rejected Marxism as reductionist, Eurocentric, or patriarchal. These intellectuals put forward a radicalism of difference rooted in Nietzsche, Heidegger, or more recent thinkers like the poststructuralist Foucault. These kinds of theories gained traction among leftist intellectuals, many of whom came to view race, ethnicity, gender, and sexuality as more important than capital and class and other large, universal concepts. To some extent, these theories preserved leftwing thought in the face of neoliberal hegemony during the 1980s and 1990s, but at a steep price, as they also helped to disorient the left. By the time of the 1999 Seattle protests against globalized capitalism, and in an even more pronounced manner after the Great Recession of 2008, issues of economic inequality came to the fore once again on the left and, with them, those of capital and class. This process has deepened in the past few years, as wealth and income inequality have reached record levels even as the world economy recovered from the 2008 Recession, leaving the mass of the working people no better off than before. Rightwing populism à la Trump moved into this void with empty promises, stoking racist, misogynist, and nativist sentiment. At the same time, a new generation of leftwing intellectuals who espouse Marxism or socialism—until now more outside than inside academia—has placed capital and class once again at the center, sometimes disparaging not only those putting forward a politics of difference but even anyone who puts race or gender or sexuality at the forefront of societal analysis.

In writing *Marx at the Margins*, it was my aspiration that it would contribute to the transcendence or sublation of this kind of polarity—in both the interpretation of Marx and in today's leftwing discourse—in the true Hegelian manner of *Aufheben*: negating while also preserving at a higher level. As I write in the book's conclusion:

> Marx developed a dialectical theory of social change that was neither unilinear nor exclusively class-based. Just as his theory of social development evolved in a more multilinear direction, so his theory of revolution began over time to concentrate increasingly on the intersectionality of class with ethnicity, race, and nationalism. To be sure, Marx was not a philosopher of difference in the postmodernist sense, for the critique of a single overarching entity, capital, was at the center of his entire intellectual enterprise. But centrality did not mean univocality or exclusivity. Marx's mature

social theory revolved around a concept of totality that not only offered considerable scope for particularity and difference but also on occasion made those particulars—race, ethnicity, or nationality—determinants for the totality. (Anderson 2010:244)

I will leave it to the readers of the book and my related writings to decide whether I proved the above case.

Since its first publication a decade ago, *Marx at the Margins* has generated debates in a number of quarters. Most of the response has been quite positive, focusing particularly on the chapter on Marx's late writings, especially his still-not-fully-published notebooks of 1879–82 on non-Western and precapitalist societies and gender. Perhaps it will interest those readers to learn I am writing another book devoted solely to the Late Marx.

Marx at the Margins has generated two serious objections, however, which I address briefly below. Surprisingly few criticisms have emerged from non-Marxist critics; those oriented *toward* Marx, however, often express their differences even when they are largely in agreement. This is of course part of the Marxian dialectical tradition, and it should be welcomed.

One set of these criticisms has centered on whether Marx really changed his position in any major way on the issues discussed in chapters 1 and 2, especially his oft-criticized writings of 1848–53 on British colonialism in India and China, and on Russia. Most of these critics of *Marx at the Margins* have been Marxists opposed to the kinds of critiques made by Said and other postcolonial theorists. Here, I think the evidence is pretty clear. When Marx terms China a barbarian nation and views British attacks on that country in positive terms, when he supports British colonialism in India as a form of social progress, or when he regards Tsarist Russia as a whole (including its general population) as reactionary, I continue to find such positions untenable, even for Marx's own era. It is equally true, however, that Said and the postcolonialists usually caricature or oversimplify Marx's positions, ignoring writings even in this early period where he expresses strong opposition to important aspects of colonialism and calls for the eventual independence of India. But even if those flaws undermine the arguments of the postcolonialists as simplistic or uninformed, they do not render the overall content of Marx's writings of 1848–53 on India any easier to defend in their entirety. It is for this very reason that the change in Marx's position to one of support for the Indian and Chinese anti-imperialist resistance movements of 1856–59 and his portrayal of Russian peasant unrest in the same period as portending something akin to the French Revolution are important to consider, especially since they accompanied Marx's profound rethinking of capital and of Asian societies in the *Grundrisse*. As the young Hegel intones, in order to get a clear view of the world that will help us achieve true freedom, we need to face reality, to stare negativity in its face. Only if one grasps both the insufficiency of Marx's 1848–53 writings and the changes thereafter, I still believe, can one fully appreciate Marx's originality in his later years. And here, it must be said, the postcolonialist criticism has forced a sharpening of the interpretation and concretization of Marx's thought for today.

A second and related criticism, again from Marxists, centers on the differences I have often pointed out between Marx and Engels, seldom to Engels's credit. This group of critics has tended to defend Engels and to regard such criticisms as either incorrect or exaggerated and unfair. In this regard, I would like first to mention that I believe Engels makes highly significant contributions in two of the key areas covered in *Marx at the Margins*, the national liberation movements of Poland and Ireland, arguing effectively in his revolutionary journalism and in his organizational work that socialists needed to support them. He also writes with acuity in some of his journalism on India and China. Important also to my discussion on Ireland is Engels's greatest book, *The Condition of the Working Class in England* (1844), where he paints a searing portrait of the Irish subproletariat in Manchester, which lived in situations far worse than even the protagonists of the acclaimed Korean film "Parasite." On the fight to recover the national independence of Ireland and Poland, two of the leading political issues of the day, there is no fundamental difference with Marx.

As for Engels's shortcomings, although I generally agree with the philosophical critique of his tendency toward positivism by Lukács, my criticisms of Engels in *Marx at the Margins* center on three other issues: his reductionist writings on gender even after studying Marx's far subtler treatment in the 1879–82 notebooks (a critique begun by Dunayevskaya [1982]), his disparagement and misreading of the strength of the Union side in the U.S. Civil War, and his editing of *Capital*, Vol. I. The first of these, on gender, is fairly clear once one studies Marx's 1879–82 note-books, and this is a topic well covered for decades by Marxist feminists like Dunayevskaya (1982) and Brown (2012). In his celebrated book, *Origin of the Family, Private Property, and the State*, first published in 1884, Engels tends to reduce gender oppression to an epiphenomenon of class and property relations, something accentuated by his equally simplistic view—not borne out by Marx's Notebooks—to the effect that women suffered a world-historic defeat about 10,000 years ago that only a socialist revolution could repair. The uncritical use of such abstract universals undercuts the need for a struggle for specific gains for women under capitalism, like rights to abortion, divorce, and equal pay, even as one opposes the overall capitalist system.

On the U.S. Civil War, Engels, despite his military expertise, grossly underestimates the resilience and the progressive character of the Union side, tending at times toward the view of the contemporary Western European left to the effect that both sides were reactionary in a country so deeply capitalist that little in the way of a socialist movement was possible. While off the mark, in the sense he actually doubts the possibility of a Union victory, Engels's positions remain significant because they anticipate those of the European (and even much of the global) left today, one that too often portrays the U.S.—in undialectical fashion—as a deeply reactionary country with a culture that is irredeemably capitalist to the core.

Finally, as to *Capital*, the failure of Marx translators and even Marx scholars to take seriously the French edition of volume one suggests a privileging of Marx's writings in German over those in English or French. This attitude seems to have originated with Engels. Even Marxian scholars sometimes forget that Marx was trilingual and that some of his major writings—*The Civil War in France* (English), the drafts of his letter to Vera Zasulich (French), and *The Poverty of Philosophy* (French)—were not written in German. So, too, with *Capital*, Vol. I, at least insofar as the final version Marx himself saw through to publication: the French edition of 1872–75, an edition that contains several formulations suggesting a more multilinear pathway to revolution for societies outside Western Europe. For his part, Engels disparages the French edition in correspondence with Marx and then fails to incorporate all its textual variants, even ones Marx specifically requested, into the supposedly definitive edition Engels creates in

1890 and that remains the basis for most international editions of *Capital*. In contrast, Marx at several junctures seems to refer to the French edition as the standard version, even quoting at times—as in his correspondence with Russian revolutionaries—one of the very passages left off by Engels from his 1890 edition of the work.

To be sure, I do not think we should reject Engels as Sartre did (when Sartre wrote that it was all downhill for Marx after he and Engels joined together in 1844), but we should look at Engels's contribution critically, just as we need to do with other great Marxist thinkers like Lenin, Luxemburg, or Trotsky, who nonetheless do not measure up to Marx. Here, my mentor Dunayevskaya's theorization of these four as post-Marx Marxists in a negative sense can be an important conceptual yardstick.

And while there are other issues raised by critics of my book, these to my mind are the most significant ones meriting continued debate and discussion.

As I look back on *Marx at the Margins*—and forward to what we face in today's crisis-ridden world—three sets of issues the book raises still speak to us today. One of these is the relationship of less developed societies to the core capitalist nations, differences in social structures between these two types of societies, and how this affects the prospects for revolution, in Marx's time and ours. In this context, Marx sees Ireland's radical peasant-based nationalist movement and the struggle of Russia's communal villages in the face of capitalist encroachments as allies of the socialist working-class movements that are growing in Western Europe. He also comes around to supporting anti-colonial movements in India, writing in their favor in 1857–59 and researching their social basis in the 1879–82 notebooks. Not only are those struggling at these points of resistance potential allies of the Western industrial proletariat but they can also serve as sparks for broader action by that proletariat. These sorts of issues are behind Marx's voluminous research in his last years on societies like India, Algeria, Latin America, and Russia, where he examines in great detail precapitalist communal forms of social organization and land tenure, in some cases going all the way back to ancient Greece and Rome. In Rome and among Native Americans, Marx perceives elements of gender equality and women's social power far beyond the limited women's rights of his time.

How relevant is all of this today? At one level, it seems not very relevant except for methodological reasons, as these communal forms of society are today for the most part thoroughly penetrated by the homogenizing power of capital. But at another level, these kinds of issues retain their vitality. As Marx writes in his 1879–82 notebooks, sometimes these communal social forms of life persist in latent form underneath the atomized capitalist exterior. We can observe this today in places like Bolivia, where Indigenous movements fuel deeper social unrest based upon capital and class. At a more general level, we can also observe that the sources of deepest unrest against the global capitalist system continue to be felt at the peripheries rather than inside the wealthiest nations, in regions such as the Middle East/North Africa or Latin America. Those countries most deeply affected by imperialism in the twentieth century (like Korea, Vietnam, Congo, and South Africa) have often experienced important forms of resistance that also opposed capitalism. Has it not been these kinds of movements—especially in the Middle East, Africa, and Latin America—that over the past decade have anticipated and inspired ones in more technologically developed lands? In this sense, what Marx is researching during his last years resonates with today's struggles for human emancipation, even more so than during his own time.

A closely related second issue is that of the state and revolution, or rather the quest to abolish both the state and the capital relation in a real communist revolution of the type Marx envisions, something he does with greater clarity and force after the Paris Commune of 1871. In his writings on the Commune, Marx indicates he has changed his position in terms of abolishing versus taking over the state, now favoring decisively the former approach. How does this relate to his 1879–82 research notebooks on the peripheries of capitalism that are discussed in chapter 6? In the case of Algeria, Marx links the peasants' defense of their communal property against French colonial dispossession to the quest of the Paris Communards to create a modern, stateless society on the road toward the abolition of capitalism. Moreover, several of the non-Western societies he researches at the end of his life are also stateless, particularly the Native American ones. He closely examines the overall social relations of the latter, with particular attention to their gender and family relations.

All of this offers rich material for the consideration of what Marx really means by communism, a topic theorists like Hudis (2012), Chattopadhyay (2016), and Jeong (2015-16) have discussed with acuity in recent years.

In the twentieth century, two statist forms of socialism—Stalinism and social democracy—predominated. The first has either collapsed or mutated beyond recognition, with isolated exceptions like the Democratic People's Republic of Korea, while the second has been incapable of defending its earlier social gains in the face of neoliberalism. In place of these two exhausted models, many who wish to challenge globalized capitalism today are going directly to Marx. Here, his late writings on precapitalist classless societies that I discuss in chapter 6 (of *Marx at the Margins*) can be a nodal point, offering theoretical grounds for alternatives to the statist, capitalist order.

A third issue running through *Marx at the Margins* is the relationship of oppressed nationalities and racial or ethnic groups to working class emancipation and to socialism, as developed in chapters 2–4. Here, Marx's writings on the U.S. Civil War evidence a concern with white racism as a barrier to working class unity and progress. Similarly, in Britain he views the working class as too often imbued with anti-Irish prejudice, something that negatively impacts the development of class consciousness. Marx is not elaborating a one-dimensional theory of ideologies of oppression, however, for his dialectical analysis also points to the possibility of Black-white or Irish-English class unity against capital, if the workers from the dominant group can overcome their racism. Material and subjective circumstances are extremely important here in the sense that Marx sees a determined revolt by the Irish to liberate their country from British colonialism, or the struggles of Blacks in the U.S. for their liberation, as sparks that can help workers from the dominant ethnic group to overcome their prejudices and to solidarize with their class brothers and sisters from the oppressed minority. Such uprisings would have as part of their agenda the transformation of economic relations as well: the overthrow of the system of plantations worked by enslaved people in the U.S. or an insurrection against the landowners of Ireland, many of the latter British colonialists. In terms of these issues, as well as Marx's staunch support—and that of Engels as well—for Polish emancipation, one can point to myriad struggles today that not only validate Marx's overall positions but also vindicate his theorization of race, ethnicity, and national liberation for the benefit of those fighting these kinds of battles in the twenty-first century. Prominent examples of such struggles include those of the Palestinians and the Kurds in the Middle East, of the immigrants from

North Africa and their descendants in France, of the Black and Latinx populations in the U.S., of the Korean minority in Japan, of the Dalits in India, and of Indigenous peoples in many countries. Marx's analysis of national and ethnic struggles distinguishes between narrow forms of group consciousness and more emancipatory ones, as in how he emphasizes that the Fenian nationalists of Ireland also had a class politics that opposed all landlords, whether British or Irish. Employing a dialectical analysis, he always points to the possibility of class unity across ethnic or national lines and not only to the obstacles to achieving that. Finally, Marx always locates his dialectical analysis in a broader context of the overall capitalist system and the capitalist state, and the social forces capable of dismantling them.

References

Anderson, Kevin B. 2010. *Marx at the Margins: On Nationalism, Ethnicity, and Non-Western Societies.* Chicago: University of Chicago Press.

Brown, Heather. 2012. *Marx on Gender and the Family: A Critical Study.* Leiden: Brill.

Chattopadhyay, Paresh. 2016. *Marx's Associated Mode of Production: A Critique of Marxism.* London: Palgrave-Macmillan.

Dunayevskaya, Raya. [1982] 1991. *Rosa Luxemburg, Women's Liberation, and Marx's Philosophy of Revolution.* Second edition with additional material by the author and a Foreword by Adrienne Rich. Urbana: University of Illinois Press.

Engels, Friedrich. [1884] 1990. *Origin of the Family, Private Property, and the State.* Pp. 129-276 in Marx and Engels, *Collected Works*, Vol. 26.

Hudis, Peter. 2012. *Marx's Concept of the Alternative to Capitalism.* Leiden: Brill.

Jeong, Seongjin. 2015-16. "Marx's Communism as Associations of Free Individuals." *Marx-Engels Jahrbuch*, pp. 115-34.

Sartre, Jean-Paul. [1949] 1962. "Materialism and Revolution." Pp. 198-256 in *Literary and Philosophical Essays.* Trans. Annette Michelson. New York: Collier.

[Originally appeared as the preface to the Korean edition of *Marx at the Margins* (Seoul: Hanul Publishing, 2020)]

Index

abolitionism, 203-04. *See also* Blacks

absolute(s), 15, 19, 31, 99, 108-9, 111-3, 161, 168, 199; break and difference, 116, 118, 172; difference, 19; freedom and terror, 24-9, 28-31, 146, 148, 191; Idea, 28, 90-2, 101, 108-9, 111-3, 161, 167-8; idealism, 52, 98, 112; knowledge, 26, 87, 116, 127, 136, 142, 147-9, 150; liberation, 15, 28; mind/spirit, 15, 112, 127, 148; movement of becoming, 192; negativity, 6, 9, 13-4, 18-9, 108, 112-3, 127, 148-9, 168, 184, 190-1; opposites, 39; possibility, 159; postulate, 31. *See also* dialectic(s); Dunayevskaya, Raya; Hegel, Georg Wilhelm Friedrich; Marx, Karl.

Adorno, Theodor, 6, 18, 95, 102, 104-6, 132-4, 163 (n16), 181, 193

Adorno, Theodor (works): *Negative Dialectics*, 6

Africa 6-7, 78, 204, 223; African liberation, 7. *See also* Algeria; Libya; North Africa; South Africa; Sudan

African Americans, 181. *See also* Blacks

Allende, Salvador, 5

Algeria, 177, 179, 213, 222-3

alienation. *see* labor; Marx, Karl

Althusser, Louis, 37, 44 (n2), 61, 94, 103, 114-5, 159, 175, 181. *See also* anti-humanism

American Sociological Review, 98

Anarchism, 180-2, 186, 207

Anderson, Kevin B., 38, 53, 180 (n2)

Anderson, Kevin B. (works): *Marx at the Margins*, 9, 186, 193 (n5), 215-25

anti-colonialism, 5, 47, 54, 64, 166, 211, 222; national independence/liberation struggles, 5, 8, 17, 38, 47, 54, 54 (n4), 62, 64, 69, 73-9, 166-7, 182, 185, 207, 220, 224; self-determination struggles, 69-70, 73, 77, 78. *See also* anti-imperialism

anti-humanism, 116, 175

anti-imperialism, 74, 77-8, 166, 180, 185, 220

anti-Semitism, 93, 138, 172

Arab Spring, 4, 179-80

Asia, 47, 50, 78, 189-90, 209, 210, 220. *See also* China; East Asia; India; Japan; production; South Asia; Vietnam

automation, 109. *See also* labor; machinery; Marx, Karl

Baillie, James Black, 24 (n3)

Bakunin, Mikhail, 186-7, 207

Baran, Paul, 163 (n16)

Basso, Luca, 214

Bataille, Georges, 117

Berkeley, George, 39

Bernstein, Eduard, 84, 95, 132

Bernstein, Richard J., 161 (n 11)

Blacks, 4-5, 7, 18, 23, 108, 157, 167, 185, 187, 203-4, 224-5; Black liberation, 7. *See also* abolitionism; Africa; African-Americans; Civil War (USA); Dunayevskaya, Raya; Fanon, Frantz; Marx, Karl; Du Bois, W.E.B.

Black Lives Matter, 4

Bloch, Ernst, 35, 37, 85

Boggs, Grace Lee, 5, 107, 163 (n16). *See also* Johnson-Forest Tendency

Bolivia, 194, 223

Bolsheviks/Bolshevism, 8, 50, 54 (n4), 65, 69, 73, 79

Bottomore, Tom, 37

Bourdieu, Pierre, 158-9, 161, 159 (n 7)

Bourdieu, Pierre (works): "For a Leftist Left", 158

Brazil, 4, 179

Britain 73-4, 180, 187-8, 190, 194, 202-3, 206, 208, 210-1, 213, 219, 224-5. *See also* colonialism; imperialism

Brown, Heather, 204, 212, 221

Bukharin, Nikolai 8, 48, 59-60, 63-71, 64 (n2), 67 (n3), 74-9

Bukharin, Nikolai (works): *Historical Materialism: A System of Sociology*, 65-9, *Imperialism and World Economy* 76, 78

bureaucracy, 6, 66, 93; state, 54, 93; Soviet, 50, 54, 66

capital/capitalism, 4-5, 9, 32, 95, 141, 146, 160, 166-7, 173-6, 187-9, 191-2, 198-202, 209, 221, 223; Central European, 167; competitive, 72, 146 ; European, 187, 208; finance, 70, 77; global/globalized, 7, 9, 187, 217-8, 223-4; industrializing, 211; merchant, 69; modern, 206; monopoly, 4-5, 7, 70, 73, 76 ; nineteenth-century, 202; peaceful, 77; peripheries of, 167, 209, 223; pre-imperialist, 72; racialized, 204; state, 7, 76; world, 69. *See also* accumulation; automation; labor; Marx, Karl; Marx, Karl (works), *Capital*; production.

Chile, 5, 179

China, 27, 47, 64, 167, 190, 191, 198, 210-1, 219-20; "Cultural Revolution," 7, 139; "Great Leap Forward", 7, 139. *See also* Maoism; Mao Zedong

Civil War (USA), 186, 204, 220-1, 224

class conflict, 93; class struggle, 15, 187, 197, 203

class consciousness, 224; working-class consciousness, 158, 187

class reductionism, 8, 200, 205, 207. *See also* Post-Marx Marxism

Clinton, Hillary, 157

Cohn-Bendit, Daniel 159-60

Colletti, Lucio, 37, 87, 103-4, 113

colonialism, 9, 18, 69, 77, 160, 167, 210, 213-4, 219; Africa, 18; British, 190, 205, 210-1, 213, 219, 224; French, 223. *See also* imperialism; post-colonialism

commodities, 129, 175, 198; *See also* fetishism of commodities; labor; Marx, Karl; production; value

communism, 49-50, 53, 65, 75, 141, 173, 191, 202, 211-2, 214, 223; communist revolution, 189, 209, 214, 223; French, 61 ; primitive, 212, 214; Russian, 161, ; Stalinist, 85, 163; statist, 22, 95, 161. *See also* Marx, Karl

Communist parties, 68, 78, 98. *See also* Russia

Comte, Auguste, 96, 102

contradiction. *See* dialectic(s)

Corbyn, Jeremy, 4

counterrevolution, 23, 30, 32, 75, 96

COVID-19, 4, 217

crisis of Marxism, 53; crisis of Marxism (1914), 36, 54

Critical Theory, 99-100, 102-7, 111, 160, 182. *See also* Frankfurt School

Cultural Revolution. *See* China

Czech Republic. *See* Czechoslovakia

Czechoslovakia, 165

Dawkins, Richard, 156-7

Dawkins, Richard (works): *God Delusion*, 156

Day, Richard, 68

deconstruction, 44 (n2), 171-4

De George, Richard, 60

Deleuze, Gilles 159-60

democracy, 4-6, 28-30, 36, 54, 93, 130, 141-3, 180, 207, 224; participatory, 28; proletarian, 62; radical, 28; anti-liberal, 30; soviet, 54 (n4); social democracy, 36, 95, 116, 158, 224

Derrida, Jacques, 8, 114-8, 159, 171-6, 177 (n8)

Derrida, Jacques (works): *L'Écriture et la différence*, 115; *De la grammatologie* 115, 117; *Marges de la philosophie* 115; *Positions* 115; *Specters of Marx* 171, 175

determinism, 8, 41, 68, 157, 211. *See also* Durkheim, Émile

Dewey, John, 161, 163

dialectic(s); consciousness, 133, 142, 147, 150, 155, 157-9, 162, 191, 193, 201, 224-5; contradiction, 4, 14-6, 26, 31, 35-6, 40-2, 49, 54, 54 (n4), 72-4, 76-7, 83, 86, 130, 138, 145-8, 159-60, 166-7, 193, 198, 201; expansion of the, 14, 108; first negation, 13, 16; freedom, of, 212; Hegelian, 5, 16-7, 19, 35-6, 46-9, 60, 63-4, 72, 108-9, 126-7, 129-30, 156; negativity, of, 3, 15, 89-90, 101, 164-5; labor, of, 142; Marxist,

38, 59, 68, 73-4, 127, 162, 167-8;
organization and philosophy, of,
31, 54 (n4); revolution/liberation,
of, 22, 32, 111; self-movement,
40-2, 49; subject-object reversal,
15-16, 199; totality, 9, 17-8, 39,
48-9, 90, 102, 108, 131-2, 136,
160-2, 165-9, 173, 183, 189, 192,
202, 219; transformation into
opposite, 7, 15, 70-2; universals,
15, 18-9, 184-6, 190, 201-2, 221;
unity of opposites, 76, 168. *See
also* absolute(s)
dialectic(s), different authors on;
    Derrida, Jacques on, 8, 15-8, 159,
    173, 175-6; Du Bois, W. E. B. on,
    18; Dunayevskaya, Raya on, 3,
    5-6, 9, 18-9, 21-3, 30-1, 36, 48, 54
    (n4), 61-2, 69-70, 107-13, 127, 133
    (n1), 138-9, 148-9, 155, 162, 166-8,
    190 ; Fanon, Frantz on, 6-7, 18;
    Foucault, Michel on, 8, 21-22,
    114, 193, 218; Hegel, Georg Wil-
    helm Friedrich on, 3, 13-4, 32,
    89-90, 101, 141, 144-5, 150, 169,
    190, 201-2; Kosík, Karel on, 6,
    106, 165-6, 201; James, C. L. R.
    on, 5, 18, 191; James, William on,
    161 ; Lenin, V.I. on, 3, 5, 8, 17, 31,
    35-8, 40-51, 53-4, 54 (n4), 59-65,
    68-74, 78-9, 95, 111, 166; Lukács,
    Georg on; 3, 5-8, 17, 53, 60, 105-6,
    126-7, 129-138, 142, 150, 168; Mar-
    cuse, Herbert on; 3, 5, 7-9, 18, 61,
    85-91, 94-5, 100-2, 104, 106-113-4,
    163-6, 163 (n16); Marx, Karl on, 5,
    9, 15-7, 27, 47, 53-4, 64, 83, 85, 90,

96, 102, 131-2, 164, 169, 193-4,
201-2, 205, 213, 218, 224-5
dialectical method, 16, 83, 91, 95, 97,
173
Diderot, Denis, 145-6
Diderot, Denis (works): *Rameau's
    Nephew*, 145-6
difference; Derrida, on, 115, 117
Dilthey, Wilhelm, 84-5, 98
Dilthey, Wilhelm (works): *Die
    Jugendgeschichte Hegels*, 84, 98
Dosse, François, 159 (n 7)
Dosse, François (works): *History of
    Structuralism*, 159 (n 7)
Du Bois, W. E. B., 18, 163 (n16)
Du Bois, W. E. B. (works): *Souls of
    Black Folk*, 18
Dunayevskaya, Raya, 3, 5-6, 22, 31,
    107, 113, 155, 162, 163 (n16), 165-7,
    175-6, 185; absolute negativity,
    18-9, 108, 113, 127, 148-9, 168, 190;
    correspondence with Marcuse,
    108-9; forces of revolution/oppo-
    sitional forces, 167, 185; founder
    of Marxist-Humanism, 9, 22;
    Hegel, on, 23, 30-1, 30 (n4), 138-9,
    148, 167-8, 190; Lenin, on, 31,
    35-7, 51, 61-2, 69-70; Lenin's
    "philosophic ambivalence", 48;
    Marcuse, on, 92, 99, 103, 107,
    109-13, 163; Marx, on, 199, 214,
    220-2; state capitalism, of, 5, 7,
    22-3; totality within dialectics,
    167-8; translation of Lenin's
    Philosophical Notebooks, 166;
    translation of Lenin's Will, 64
    (n2); Trotsky, on, 21-2, 133 (n1).

See also absolute(s); Blacks; dialectic(s); Marxist-Humanism; women; youth

Dunayevskaya, Raya (works): "Dialectics of Organization and Philosophy: The 'Party' and Forms of Organization Born from Spontaneity", 31; *Marxism and Freedom: from 1776 until Today*, 23, 108, 167; "Notes on Phenomenology", 30 ; *Philosophy and Revolution, from Hegel to Sartre and from Marx to Mao*, 6, 18-9, 23, 30-1, 109, 111, 138, 167-8, 175-6; *Power of Negativity: Selected Writings on the Dialect in Hegel and Marx*, 167-8; *Raya Dunayevskaya Collection and Supplement* (Wayne State University Archives of Labor and Urban Affairs), 110-1; *Women's Liberation and the Dialectics of Revolution"*, 167

Durkheim, Émile, 83-4, 96, 102

Durkheim, Émile (works): *Suicide*, 84

East Asia, 83

Economic crisis (1929). *See* Great Depression (1929)

Economic crisis (2007-8), 4; Great Recession, 157, 179, 218

Economic crisis (2020), 4

epistemology, 21, 27, 61, 105

Emirbayer, Mustafa, 161

empiricism, 27, 86, 97-9, 101, 104, 191

Enlightenment, 13, 23-4, 26, 31, 86-7, 114, 127-8, 134, 145-6, 150, 156, 190

Engels, Frederick, 15-7, 44 (n2), 126, 157-8, 189-91, 197-8, 202-3, 205-10, 212-3, 220-2, 224; idealism, 16-7, 39-40, ; gender, on, 143, 220-1; materialism, on, 16-7, 39, 43-4, 60, 64-5; national liberation, on, 220, 224; U.S. Civil War, on, 221

Engels, Frederick (works): *Communist Manifesto*, 15, 172-3, 189-90, 197-8, 200, 203, 207, 210, 212, 214; ; *Condition of the Working Class in England*, 202, 220; *German Ideology*, 191, 209; *Ludwig Feuerbach and the End of Classical German Philosophy*, 16, 43; *Origin of the Family, Private Property, and the State*, 205, 221

England, 16, 129, 140, 187, 193, 202-3, 208-9, 211, 224; Manchester, 220. *See also* colonialism

Eurocommunism, 59

existentialism, 99, 103, 105, 115-6, 126-7, 135, 137-9, 185. *See also* Heidegger, Martin; Merleau-Ponty, Maurice; Sartre, Jean-Paul

Fanon, Frantz, 6-7, 18

Fanon, Frantz (works): *Black Skin, White Masks*, 18; *Wretched of the Earth*, 18

Fascism, 4-5, 8, 65, 85, 89, 93, 97-100, 135, 137-9, 163 (n16), 167, 177, 181

feminism, 5-6, 108, 143-4, 159, 172, 176, 182; Marxist, 221; revolutionary, 167; socialist, 182. *See also* women

Fenian Movement, 188, 225. *See also*
    Ireland
fetishism of commodities/commod-
    ity fetishism, 16-17, 44, 44 (n2),
    174-5, 192-3, 198-9
Fetscher, Iring, 37
feudalism, 29, 145, 147, 175, 189, 192,
    200, 202, 209-10
Feuerbach, Ludwig, 39, 43, 63
Fichte, Johann Gottlieb, 26, 133-5, 137
finance capital. *See* capital/capitalism
First International, 186, 203
Ford, Henry, 162
Forest, Freddie. *See* Dunayevskaya,
    Raya
Foucault, Michel, 8-9, 21-2, 114, 160,
    179-86, 189, 193-4, 218
Foucault, Michel (works): *Discipline
    and Punish*, 186; *History of Sexual-
    ity*, 183-4
France, 84, 101, 115-6, 129, 137-8, 162,
    172, 177, 187, 206-8, 223, 225;
    French Revolution, 7, 13-5, 22-3,
    25-32, 86-7, 112, 126-7, 130, 144-7,
    150, 191, 201, 220. *See also* colo-
    nialism; existentialism; imperi-
    alism; structuralism;
    poststructuralism
Frankfurt School, 18, 60, 95-6, 99, 104,
    106, 163 (n16), 182. *See also*
    Adorno, Theodor; Fromm,
    Erich; Horkheimer, Max; Mar-
    cuse, Herbert; Neumann, Franz;
    Pollock, Friedrich
Franzen, Erich, 98
freedom, 15, 23-9, 31, 86-7, 91, 96,
    100-2, 148, 158-9, 176, 201, 220;

movements, 9; political and
    intellectual, 125. *See also*
    absolute(s); Hegel, Georg Wil-
    helm Friedrich; labor, freely
    associated; new society
Fries, J. F., 93
Fromm, Erich, 163 (n16)

gay and lesbian movements, 168
Gentile, Giovanni, 139
Ghosh, Arvind, 193
Goldmann, Lucien, 18, 61-2, 83, 116,
    132, 139-40, 155-6
Gramsci, Antonio, 62, 66-7, 67 (n3),
    84, 132
Gramsci, Antonio (works): *Prison
    Notebooks*, 66-7
Grant, Oscar, 181
Great Depression (1929), 4
"Great Leap Forward." *See* China
Great Refusal. *See* Marcuse, Herbert
Grenada, 27

Habermas, Jürgen, 107, 114, 162, 176
Habitus; Bourdieu, on, 159, 161
Harris, H. S., 128, 134
Hegel, Georg Wilhelm Friedrich, 19;
    Ancient Greece, on, 126-30, 142;
    alienated labor, on, 141; Aufhe-
    bung/sublation/transcendence,
    24 (n3), 72, 96, 100, 131-2, 140,
    168, 172, 181, 194-5, 218; Being,
    Doctrine of, 90; contradiction,
    14-6, 31, 35-6, 40-2, 49, 83, 130,
    138, 147-8, 160, 167, 201; Econom-
    ics, on, 140-2, 150; Essence, Doc-
    trine of, 90; freedom, on, 86-7,

91, 101-2, 201, 220; French Revolution, 7-8, 22, 26-32, 130, 144-7, 150; gender, on, 143-4; intuitionism, on 126, 133-5, 137-9; irrationalism, on 8, 126, 135; Kant, critique of, 131-4; mediation, 39, 52, 90, 99-100, 136, 164-5; negativity/negative, 3, 6, 9, 13-5, 24-5, 30, 32, 41, 191, 220; Notion, Doctrine of the, 42-3, 90-1; Objective spirit; Practical Idea/Theoretical Idea, 31-2, 51-2, 167-8; relationship between theory and practice, 51; Romanticism/Romantics, on, 8, 126, 133-5, 139; Rousseau's general will, on, 23-6, 29, 31-2; Schelling, relation to, 135-7, 139; self-consciousness, 14-5, 24-6, 52, 142; self-determination, 88; slavery, on, 129, 142; theology, on, 91-2, 127-30, 150; totality, on, 29, 49, 102, 108, 136, 160; tragedy, theory of, 142-5, 149-50, universal/particular, 190-1, 202. *See also* absolute(s); dialectic(s); idealism; Master-Slave Dialectic/Lordship and Bondage; Nature; negativity/negation of the negation; Reason

Hegel, Georg Wilhelm Friedrich (works): *Encyclopedia*, 92, 112, 137; *Phenomenology of Mind/Spirit*, 6, 8, 14, 22-3, 27-31, 85-7, 89-91, 112-3, 116, 125, 127, 135-7, 139, 142-7, 150, 163-4, 163 (n16), 173, 190-1, 201 ; *Philosophy of History*, 26, 85, 94, 190; *Philosophy of Mind/Spirit*, 92, 112, 190; *Philosophy of Right*, 15, 27, 85-6, 93-4, 97-8, 104-5, 131, 190; *Science of Logic*, 28, 30-31, 36-7, 39-40, 42-5, 50-1, 62, 85, 87-8, 90-3, 109, 111-3, 131, 133, 137, 140, 148, 150-1, 163, 165-7, 190; *Shorter or Encyclopedia Logic*, 92, 137

Heidegger, Martin, 89, 99, 103, 105, 127, 135, 137-8, 161-2, 171-2, 218

Heine, Heinrich, 149

Hilferding, Rudolf, 36, 69

Hitler, Adolf, 97, 127, 138-9, 164

Hitler-Stalin Pact (1939), 133 (n1)

Holloway, John, 183, 185-6, 193-4

Holocaust, 18

Hook, Sidney, 97-8, 103-4, 163 (n16)

Hudis, Peter, 7, 191-4, 223

humanism, 32, 46, 107, 116, 118, 158, 173, 175, 214; dialectical, 7-8; radical, 115-6; revolutionary 111. *See also* anti-humanism; Marxist-Humanism

Hungary, 179. *See also* revolution

Husserl, Edmund, 98

Hyppolite, Jean, 29-30, 112, 116, 125-7, 130, 137, 139, 145-6

idealism, 38-40, 46, 52, 61, 63, 91-2, 114, 133, 158-9, 201; absolute, 52, 98, 112; abstract, 17; dialectical, 45, 68, 100; German, 86, 137, 156; Hegelian/in Hegel, 15, 27, 40, 60-1, 68, 87, 109, 111-3, 125; intelligent, 45-6; mystical, 87; objective, 40, 133-4, 136; ontological,

113; subjective, 137; unity of idealism and materialism, 45-6, 48, 60, 63

imperialism, 5-6, 8, 17, 32, 38, 47, 53-4, 59-60, 62, 69, 71-9, 176, 182, 207, 211, 223; American/U.S., 180; Precapitalist, 69; Japanese, 167; Western, 182. *See also* anti-colonialism; anti-imperialism; colonialism; Bukharin, Nikolai; Lenin. V. I.; Luxemburg, Rosa

India, 5, 47, 64, 167, 179, 190, 209-13, 219-20, 222, 225; Mughal India, 210; precolonial India, 210. *See also* anti-colonialism; anti-imperialism; imperialism; Sepoy Uprising

Indigenous, 225; movements, 223; opposition to capital, 194

individual, 24-5, 28, 30, 60, 86, 95, 128-9, 133, 141, 144, 156, 159-60, 185, 188, 191-2; free individual, 95; individualism, 146; individualized social relations, 189; individual will, 24-6

internationalism, 36, 77

intersectionality, 6, 214, 218

intuitionism, 126, 133-5, 137-9, 150. *See also* irrationalism

Iran, 182. *See also* revolution

Ireland, 5, 74, 186-8, 202-3, 205, 207-9, 213, 220, 222, 224-5. *See also* Fenian movement; Marx, Karl; proletariat; revolution; working class

irrationalism, 6, 8, 98, 126, 135, 137-40

Italy, 103, 177

Jacobi, Friedrich, 126, 133-5, 137-9, 150; see also intuitionism

Jacobin(s), 15, 23, 139-40, 146; Jacobin Terror, 29

James, Cyril Lionel Robert (C.L.R.), 5, 18, 37, 107-8, 163 (n16), 191. *See also* Johnson-Forest Tendency

James, Cyril Lionel Robert (works): *Notes on Dialectics, 18*

Jameson, Fredric, 19

Japan, 47, 64, 225. *See also* imperialism

Johnson, J. R. *See* James, C. L. R.

Johnson-Forest Tendency, 107. *See also* Boggs, Grace Lee; Dunayevskaya, Raya; James, Cyril Lionel Robert (C. L. R.)

Joravsky, David, 61

Kant, Immanuel, 26, 62, 86, 126, 131-7, 150, 156, 184-5; Kantianism, 31, 40, 42-4, 46, 62-3, 126, 131, 189-90, 194; Neo-Kantianism, 36, 135

Karpushin, V. A., 90, 165

Kautsky, Karl, 36, 69, 84, 132-3

Kedrov, B. M., 45 (n3), 61

Kellner, Douglas, 103-6, 113, 183, 185 (n4)

Kojève, Alexandre, 116

Kołakowski, Leszek, 61

Korsch, Karl, 46, 60, 106, 163 (n 16)

Kosík, Karel, 6, 92, 99, 103, 106-7, 165-6, 201

Kosík, Karel (works): *Dialectics of the Concrete, 6*

Kovalevski, Maxim, 210, 212

Kovalevski, Maxim (works): *Communal Property*, 210

Kurdish Liberation, 4, 224

labor, 14-5, 87, 105, 132, 140, 142, 180, 187-8, 192, 199-200, 204; alienated, 94-5, 140-1, 198; antithesis between mental and physical, 191; aristocracy of, 73; degradation of, 141 ; labor power, 129; labor camps, 23; child, 101; freely associated/free and associated, 174-5, 193, 199, 202, 209; industrial, 201; intellectual, 186 ; mental and manual division, of, 191; movement, 108, 112, 160, 182, 189-90; necessary labor time, 188-9; praxis, as, 140; private, 192; process, 105, 109, 140-1, 199 ; rank-and-file, 185; slave, 129; source of value, as, 129; reification of, 132; wage, 198, 208-9. *See also* automation; labor time; Marx, Karl; organization; value

Lange, Oskar, 163 (n16)

Lassalle, Ferdinand, 206

Latin America, 4, 78, 156, 194, 212-4, 222-3. *See also* Bolivia, Brazil, Chile, Grenada

Lebanon, 179

Lefebvre, Henri, 35, 37, 61, 116

Lenin, V. I., 7-8, 54 (n4), 68, 111-2, 126, 222; dialectics, 3, 5, 59-61, 63-4; Hegel, relationship to, 17, 35-54, 44 (n2), 61-2, 72-3, 83-4, 91-2; imperialism, 54, 69-78-9; Marcuse on, 95, 166-7; national liber-

ation, 54, 79, 207; positivism, on, 132-3, Practical Idea, 31; ; reflection theory of knowledge, 39, 45, 60. *See also* materialism; Vanguard party

Lenin, V. I. (works): "Abstract of Hegel's *Science of Logic*", ; *Imperialism: The Highest Stage of Capitalism*, 54, 69, 71-2; *Karl Marx*, 63; *Materialism and Empirio-Criticism*, 35, 37-8, 43-5, 51, 60-2, 84; *Notebooks on Imperialism*, 69; *Philosophical Notebooks*, 3, 8, 37, 60-5, 68, 71-2, 74, 76-7; *State and Revolution*, 54

Levine, Donald N., 84

Lévi-Strauss, Claude, 159

Lewis, Tyson, 183

liberation theology, 157

Libya, 180

Lichtheim, George, 60, 127

Liebknecht, Karl, 36

Lipset, Seymour Martin, 65-6

Löwith, Karl, 92, 99-100, 118, 125, 141

Löwy, Michael, 61

Lukács, Georg, 3, 6-7, 37-8, 53, 60, 62, 83-5, 106, 125-150, 163 (n16), 220; Bukharin, on, 66; fascism, on, 5, 8, 135, 137-8; fetishism of commodities, 44, 44 (n2); gender, on, 40, 150, 169, 220; Hegel, on, 28-9, 88, 125-50, 165; irrationalism, on, 5, 8, 126-7, 135, 137-40; Lenin, on, 51; reification, 17; totality, on, 17, 131-2, 168; Weber, relation to, 17-8

Lukács, Georg (works): *Destruction of*

Labor", 94-5, 98-9; *Capital*, 3, 6, 16, 36, 43-4, 44 (n2), 47, 64, 129, 140, 174, 189-90, 198-9, 191-3, 202-5, 211-2, 221; *Capital*, Vol. I, 16, 83, 157, 174, 198, 201, 209, 220; *Capital*, Vol. I (French edition), 211-2, 221-2; *Capital*, Vol. II, 211; *Capital*, Vol. III, 211; *Civil War in France*, 193, 221; *Communist Manifesto* , 15, 172-3, 189-90, 197-8, 200, 203, 207, 210, 212, 214; *Critique of Hegel's Philosophy of Right*, 15, 131; *Critique of the Gotha Program*, 191, 206; "Critique of the Hegelian Dialectic", 15, 87, 89, 94, 104; *Critique of Political Economy*, 16; *Economic and Philosophical Manuscripts*, 39, 46, 85, 163; *Eighteenth Brumaire of Louis Bonaparte*, 206; *Ethnological Notebooks*, 79, 205, 212; *German Ideology*, 191, 209; *Grundrisse*, 6, 16, 79, 129, 188, 191-2, 209, 211, 220; "Peuchet on Suicide", 206; *Poverty of Philosophy*, 204, 221; *Theses on Feuerbach*, 15, 40

Marxism, 3, 8, 16-7, 19, 27, 38, 50-1, 53-4, 59-60, 68-9, 74, 83-4, 106-7, 116, 155-6, 165, 173, 185-6, 217-8; anti-Hegelian, 61, 85, 90, 95, 104-5; materialism/materialist, 50, 126; crude, 126, 132-3; emancipatory, 185-6; established, 36, 42, 46, 53, 62-3; Hegelian, 38, 50, 61-2, 97, 103-5, 109, 113-8, ; humanistic, 61; idealism in, 61; Lenin, of, 53; Marcuse, of, 105-6;

orthodox, 35, ; Post-Marx, 3, 22, 26-7, 35-6, 65, 79, 176, 222; revolutionary, 95; Russian, 43, 65; Second International, of, 41-2, 46; schematic, 35, 36.

Marxist-Humanism, 5-7, 9, 18-9, 22-3, 30-1, 60, 99, 103, 106-7, 110, 117, 127, 165, 175-6, 185

Marxism-Leninism, 54 (n4)

Master-Slave Dialectic/Lordship and Bondage, 14-5, 18, 146, 150, 191

Materialism, 7-8, 15, 17, 27, 35, 39-40, 45-8, 50, 68, 100, 111, 157 ; crude/vulgar, 8, 17, 39-43, 48-50, 62, 126, 132, 156-7, 165; dialectical, 17, 42-3, 47, 51, 60, 67, 173; historical, 44 (n2), 157; with idealism, 60, 63; mechanical, 79 ; Marxist, 40, 45, 68; militant, 46, 48, 64; philosophical, 46; scientific, 8

McGill, Vernon J., 98

Mehring, Franz, 84, 132

Merleau-Ponty, Maurice, 38, 116

Michels, Robert, 65-6

Middle East, 223-5

Miller, A.V., 24 (n3)

Miller, David, 37

Mische, Anne, 161

modernism, 36, 137

modes of production; Asiatic, 202, 209-10; Capitalist, 167, 189, 199, 200, 202, 209

Monopoly capital. *See* capital/capitalism

mysticism, 16, 38-9, 68, 87, 103, 126, 130, 148, 174

Plekhanov, Georgi, 17, 36, 39, 42-4, 46, 49-50, 62-3, 65, 84, 132-3
political economy, 15-6, 105, 191-2; British, 105; English, 129, 140
Poland, 73, 186, 207, 220
Popkin, Richard, 116-7
positivism, 8, 36, 38, 61-2, 66-7, 84-7, 96-9, 101-4, 106, 109, 126, 132-3, 135, 156, 158, 163, 166, 220; scientific, 19
postcolonialism, 8, 217, 219-20
postmodernism, 107, 114, 160, 162, 169, 171, 176, 183, 189, 218
poststructuralism, 8, 19, 22, 53, 114, 158-9, 160-2, 165-6, 181, 218
populism; rightwing, 4, 157, 179, 218; leftwing, 211
Practical Idea. *See* Hegel, Georg Wilhelm Friedrich
pragmatism, 8, 53, 96-7, 161-6, 169; American, 161
Prague Spring (1968), 6
Pravda, 65
praxis, 15, 17, 92, 107, 140, 166; philosophy of, 66
precapitalist societies, 69, 77, 174-5, 209, 219, 222, 224
primitive communism. *See* communism
production, 132, 174, 175, 187-8, 200, 205, 198-9, 192-3, 198-200, 202; commodity, 86, 175, 198, 209; machine, 141; material, 15-6, 91, 109, 113; mental, 67 ; productive forces, 15, 66, 88, 188-90, 192,

198-9; relations/relationships, 16, 189. *See also* modes of production
proletariat, 5, 74-6, 105, 131-2, 167, 197, 202-3, 222; Irish sub-proletariat, 220; proletarian, 36, 62, 70, 131, 166, 187, 197, 203, 209, 212; Western, 73, 214, 222. *See also* working class
property; communal/collective, 189, 209, 213, 223; landed, 197, 208; statified, 21; private, 16, 93, 95; property relations/relationship, 95, 221
Proudhon, Pierre-Joseph, 204
pseudoconcrete; in; Kosík, 165-6, 169, 201-2

race, 6, 9, 18, 180, 186, 194, 200, 214, 218-9, 224; racial division, 203; racial minorities, 217, 184-5; racism, 4-5, 9, 32, 116, 156, 168-9, 174, 176, 187, 207, 218, 224
Radek, Karl, 74, 74 (n4)
reason, 8, 105, 131; commonsense, 18; critical, 93; dialectical, 4, 8-9, 18, 86-7, 95, 100-2, 107, 109-10, 163, 174-5; Dunayevskaya, Raya on, 214; Enlightenment, 86-7, 114, 190; Hegel on, 87, 96; instrumental, 102, 105-6; Marcuse on, 96, 99-102, 110; Marx on, 96, 141; thinking, 42; Western, 102; Shklar, Judith on, 143
reification, 17, 87, 131-2, 175-6
reproduction, 66, 91, 159, 192
resistance, 9, 160, 167, 179-82, 184, 194;

Fanon on, 18; Foucault on, 181-5, 189, 193-4; Marx on, 193-4. *See also* Great Refusal

revolution/uprising; American (1776), ; French (1790), 7, 13, 15, 22-3, 25-32, 86-7, 112, 126-7, 130, 144-7, 150, 191, 201, 220; Hungarian (1956), 149; Iranian (1979), 182; Iranian (2009), 180; Irish (1916 Uprising), 74; Russian (1917), 23, 32, 35, 50, 54, 54 (n4), 95; Serbian, 180; Sudanese, 179; Syrian 180

revolutionary subject. *See* subject

Rickert, Heinrich, 135

Ritter, Joachim, 27

Romanticism, 107, 126, 133-5, 137-9

Rorty, Richard, 161-2, 176

Rose, Gillian, 117

Rousseau, Jean-Jacques, 23, 29, 31

Ruben, David-Hillel, 61

Russia, 6-7, 27, 29, 75, 78-9, 95, 125, 161-2, 165, 189-91, 207, 211-4, 219-20, 222; Russian Communist Party, 75; Soviet, 48, 65-6. *See also* revolution, Russian (1917)

Sabine, George, 98

Said, Edward, 8, 210-1, 219

Sanders, Bernie, 4

Sartre, Jean-Paul, 88, 103, 116, 126-7, 137-8, 158-9, 186, 222

Sartre, Jean-Paul (works): *Being and Nothingness*, 88, 158, 158 (n5)

Schelling, Friedrich, 108, 126, 133-9, 150

Schmitt, Carl, 97

Science & Society, 98

Seattle WTO Protests (1999), 218

Second International, 7, 36, 39, 41-2, 46, 62, 67

self-determination struggles. *See* anti-colonialism

Sepoy Uprising, 211, 213

Serbia, 180

serfdom, 209-10

Shanin, Teodor, 211

Sheehan, Helena, 61, 67 (n3)

Sheehan, Thomas, 171-2

Simmel, Georg, 98, 138

slavery, 14-5, 18, 101, 128-9, 142, 146, 187, 204, 209-10, 224. *See also* abolitionism

Smith, Adam, 150

social democracy. *See* democracy

socialism, 6, 21, 67, 77, 97, 107, 165, 190-1, 209, 218, 220-2, 224; French, 105; utopian, 129

socialism or barbarism, 4

Sophocles, 143

Sophocles (works): *Antigone*, 143-5

Sorokin, Pitirim, 65

South Africa, 7, 23, 79, 223

South Asia, 212-4

soviets, 54

Spain, 180

Spivak, Gayatri, 172

Stalin, Joseph, 54 (n4), 63, 65, 78, 126, 133; Stalinism, 6-7, 28, 35, 37, 53, 85, 126-7, 132-3, 133 (n1), 138-40, 149, 163, 163 (n16), 165-6, 210

state, 64, 68, 77, 93-4, 141-5, 180-3, 194, 200, 210, 223; and revolution, 17, 62, 223; Bukharin on, 59, 62; capitalist, 54, 76, 225; Hegel on, 27-8, 93; imperialist, 76; Lenin on, 38, 54, 62; nation state, 71, 73, 76; Prussian, 93, 105; single party, 3; Soviet, 50, 100; state capitalist imperialism, 76; stateless society, 143, 223; state ownership of the economy, 95; Trotsky on, 62; welfare, 5; workers', 50.

state capitalism. *See* capital/capitalism

Stoicism, 14, 28, 129, 142

Structuralism, 19, 114, 158-9, 159 (n7), 161-2, 175

Studies in Philosophy and Social Science, 99

subject, 15, 17, 21, 51-2, 87, 92, 133, 138, 147-8, 159; working class as, 110. *See also* Blacks; women; youth

subjectivity, 7, 8, 14, 17-8, 24, 30-1, 42, 45, 52, 64, 87, 148, 176

subjectivism, Maoist. *See* Mao Zedong

Sudan, 179

Summers, Lawrence, 157

surplus labor time, 188

Sweezy, Paul, 163 (n16)

Syria, 180

Taylor, Charles, 27-8

theory, 21, 39, 67, 85, 92, 94, 96; dialectical, 13, 61, 101-2, 218-9; imperialism, of, 59, 62; matriarchy, of, 145, 147; relation between theory and practice, 5, 51, 85, 167; Sociology, 83-4, 98; surplus value, 199-200

Third World, 54, 79, 172, 185

Tillich, Paul, 92, 99

totalitarianism, 28, 30, 54 (n4), 97, 100, 148-9, 191

totality. *See* dialectic(s)

Trade Union Debate (1920), 50, 64

Trotsky, Leon, 21-2, 36, 63-4, 64 (n2), 74, 74 (n4), 79, 133, 133 (n1), 167, 222; Trotskyism, 21, 107

Trump, Donald, 4, 157, 162, 218

Ukraine, 73, 180

Under the Banner of Marxism, 46, 64-5

United States, 4-7, 85, 98, 115-7, 139, 156-7, 162, 163 (n16), 167, 177, 179-82, 186-7, 203-4, 224-5. *See also* abolitionism; African Americans; Blacks; Civil War (USA); pragmatism

USSR, 67, 110, 149

universality, 9, 14-6, 18-9, 24-5, 51-2, 95, 112, 141-3, 145-6, 168, 184-6, 189-92, 194, 198, 200-2, 218; abstract, 9, 15, 18, 76-7, 189-90, 194, 201-2, 221; concrete, 15, 186, 189-91, 201-2; universal freedom, 25; universally valid laws, 85, 93, 163; universal will, 23, 25

utopian socialism. *See* socialism

Valéry, Paul, 101

value, 129, 204, 217; value form, 168-9, 198, 201; production, 198. *See also* surplus value

Vanguard party. *See* organization

Vietnam, 6, 223; Vietnam War, 116

Weber, Max, 83-4, 132; rationalization, 17-8
Wilson, Edward O., 156-7
Wilson, Edward O. (works): *Consilience*, 156
World War I, 4, 36, 62, 71, 76, 83-4
World War II, 163 (n16), 181; post-World War II, 4-5, 29, 167-8
women, 9, 18-9, 108, 144, 157, 166-8, 172, 182, 204-6; women's liberation, 79, 185, 214, 221-2; *See also* Blacks; feminism; Marx, Karl
working class, 16, 66, 73, 75-6, 78, 95-6, 100, 166-7, 192-4, 197-200, 202-6, 208-9, 212, 224
workers, 76, 78, 94, 102, 141-2, 158, 165, 167-8, 174, 187-8, 197-9, 202-5, 208, 224. *See also* proletarian
workers' councils. *See* soviets
Yousafzai, Malala, 182, 182 (n3)
youth, 4, 18, 93, 108, 167, 176, 180-1, 185, 194

Zasulich, Vera, 189, 213-4, 221
Zeitschrift für Sozialforschung, 96, 99
Žižek, Slavoj, 19, 183